"Richard Cox has been pastor, psychologist, medical doctor, professor, academic administrator, lecturer and author. He is therefore uniquely qualified to offer a salutary critique of the interaction between the mental health community and the Christian church. He points out how religious faith and practice have been adversely influenced by embracing psychology uncritically and thus diluting the redemptive effectiveness of the Gospel. I hope his astringent yet caring message will be widely heeded"

—Vernon Grounds, Ph.D.
Chancellor, Denver Seminary

"Psychology and theology need each other and Richard Cox points the way to a new more productive partnership. He is convinced that by working together, psychology and theology can promote healing of our deepest hurts by claiming the power of the Spirit of God. Cox has much more to teach us as he shares the lessons he has learned in his own pilgrimage."

—Richard J. Mouw, Ph.D.
Fuller Theological Seminary

"This work catches up a great deal of our experience during the past half-century. It has a powerful, yet clever way of developing the theme that our churches along with the psychological establishment have accepted our cultural norms uncritically. His voice is clear and graphic, seeking both to conserve and to reform in a wide and relevant scope of issues. I commend him on writing a thorough and comprehensive overview of the circumstances surrounding our present spiritual crisis."

—David Steere, Ph.D.
Pastoral Counselor, Professor

"Richard Cox frontally attacks popularized 'integration' of psychology and theology. This amalgam, he argues, is neither good psychology nor good theology. The supposed integration is only a mixing of the two — producing adulterated syrup. And in its thirst to be relevant, the church has drunk deeply of this sugary elixir of 'feels good.' Psychology, Cox asserts, can rightfully bring relief and a better life. But only the church can provide redemption, through Jesus Christ. Cox's thoughtful book points to ways that the church can accomplish its core mission while satisfying modern seekers' true hunger. It is a provocative, well-researched book. God speed!"

—Russ Chandler
*Author, former religion writer for **The Los Angeles Times***

"Richards Cox's work is a brilliant integration of interdisciplinary knowledge, views, and wisdom that should bring creative reflection, constructive discussion, and definite action within the Christian community. He demonstrates his love for the Church and unswerving allegiance to Christ while revealing his deep sense of disappointment that the Gospel message has been compromised."

—Garrit tenZythoff, Ph.D.
Emeritus Professor of Religion (deceased March 29, 2001),
Southwest Missouri State University

"Cox's book is a unique and highly readable set of reflections on the nature of the church and postmodern reality. It will set the new tone of interaction among theology and the social/behavior based science for many years to come."

—H. Newton Malony, M.Div., Ph.D.
Senior Professor, Fuller Theological Seminary and
School of Professional Psychology

"In an age overly devoted to narrow specialization, it is refreshing to encounter a book that successfully synthesizes research from disparate disciplines, thereby reaching conclusions that are stunningly prescriptive and courageous. *The Sacrament of Psychology* by Richard H. Cox identifies the institutional church's weakness of following trendy psychology, rather than being true to its primary redemptive mission. At the same time, modern and postmodern psychology offers promises that it cannot fulfill, crippling a church with its denial of transcendence and its insistence on relativism. This is a call for both church leaders and psychologists to rethink their underlying premises and methods."

—**Stanley M. Burgess, Ph.D.**
Professor of Religious Studies,
Southwest Missouri State University

THE
SACRAMENT
OF
PSYCHOLOGY

*Psychology and Religion in the
Postmodern American
Church*

Published by InSync Communications LLC, InSync Press
2445 River Tree Circle
Sanford, FL 32771
http://www.insyncpress.com
407-688-1156

This book was set in Adobe Janson Text
Cover Design and Composition by Jonathan Pennell

Library of Congress Catalog Number: Cataloging information available from the Library of Congress
        Cox, Richard H.,
The Sacrament of Psychology
        ISBN: 1-929902-15-8

First InSync Press Edition
10   9   8   7   6   5   4   3   2
Printed in the United States of America

Any reference to patients/clients in this work are composites of many individuals drawn from the clinical work and life experiences of the author. Names and details have been changed to protect confidentiality, unless prior permission was granted by those named.

This publication was designed to provide information in regard to the subject matter covered. It is sold and distributed with the understanding that the publisher is not engaged in rendering legal, medical, or counseling services. If appropriate expert assistance is required, the services of a qualified and competent professional should be sought.

InSync Press books are available at special discounts when purchased in bulk for use in seminars, as premiums, or in sales promotions. Special editions or book excerpts can also be created to specifications. For details, contact InSync Communications LLC at the address above.

THE SACRAMENT OF PSYCHOLOGY

Psychology and Religion in the Postmodern American Church

Richard H. Cox

Dedication

*Theology has been so extensively psychologized
and psychology has been so extensively theologized
that both have lost much of their basic integrity
and, as a result, much of their inherent efficacy.*

THIS BOOK IS DEDICATED to all those in both theology and psychology who endeavor to bring hope to
those who flounder — all of us. It is especially dedicated to my life-long companion, Betty, and to our children, Rebecca, Joanna, and David, who in their love and kindness
force me to continue to struggle with truths which are not so self-
evident; and to my brother, Donald, who was already recognized as
being well on his way toward an integration of psychology and theology when that journey was interrupted by a life-ending brain
tumor at the age of thirty-four.

Table of Contents

About the Author

RICHARD H. COX is President Emeritus/Professor of the Forest Institute, an accredited graduate school of professional psychology, the Forest Foundation, and its related clinics and services. He is a charter member of the American Association of Pastoral Counselors (retired) and an ordained Presbyterian (U.S.A.) minister. Richard H. Cox is the author of numerous scholarly publications, is an international speaker and consultant, and holds doctorate degrees in psychology, medicine, and theology, as well as three honorary doctorates. He resides in Westminter, Colorado with his wife Betty with whom he raised three now-growm children

Foreword

OVER 25 YEARS AGO, Karl Menninger framed new questions for an entire generation of theologians and psychologists. Richard Cox is a worthy successor. This passionately argued book will leave some in another generation puzzled, perhaps angry and hurt, but certainly enriched by the experience of engaging this terribly important arena again. His thesis is a simple one: the church has allowed itself to be overwhelmed with psychology. What others have called the 'superstition of materialism' ascribes all power and glory to science and its accomplishments. And the church has capitulated and lost its own identity by allowing (and often encouraging) the norms and diagnoses of contemporary psychology to replace the gospel. Cox pulls no punches and spares few 'sacred cows' (in either psychology or theology) as he offers his own passionate argument. The book will leave few readers without passions rising in their own minds and hearts as they engage this carefully argued and vividly presented invitation. For this reason alone, it is a suburb addition to the literature of both fields … But be forewarned: this book is not for the faint-hearted pop-psychologist or armchair theologian; your mind and your passions will be exercised!"

—John Allan Loftus, S.J., Ph.D.
President, and Professor of Psychology and the Psychology of Religion,
Regis College, University of Toronto, Toronto, Canada

Preface

J UST AS IT HAS BEEN DONE AT ALL TIMES in history, the human race today is seeking answers. No doubt the birth of the technological/information age has helped make us feel minuscule. We seek and rarely find answers to the really tough questions of life and death. With the emergence of the greatest technology known in the history of humankind, there are more answers to how computers work than to how the human being works, more ways to fix technology than the human body, and the promise of more artificial intelligence than human wisdom. The technological advances of this era leave even the most learned minds spinning. Doubtless the disciple of this millennium will be a "Doubting Thomas" and all who attempt to elicit belief will have to be able to show nail prints in their hands!

Theology, as it relates to a fundamental knowledge and belief in God, has been the fundamental mainstay of society since the beginning of time. Long before humankind lived in a scientific world, belief in "a God" was elemental. The need for a "higher power" was in part due to the lack of scientific knowledge, thus the demand for belief. To the extent that belief is replaced with knowledge, to that extent need for a higher power is lost. In the *presence of proof there is the absence of faith*.

Our postmodern world tends to ascribe all power and glory to science and its accomplishments. Little credit is given to faith or belief. Yet even the most decorated of scientists in their own terminal illnesses do not look for additional scientific proof, but to the elements of faith and belief. The Church, which has been the primary tabernacle of belief, has allowed itself to be overwhelmed with psychology. Theology has been psychologized, and as a result, much of its mysticism and thus the value of that mysticism has been lost. Adding new knowledge to old is usually beneficial — and such is the case with adding our newly found knowledge from the behavioral sciences, but replacing old information with new knowledge is sometimes beneficial and at other times brings about such confusion as to make both the old and new information less than useful. The *knowledge* of psychology is helpful whenever dealing with human behavior. Confusing the *purposes* of psychology with the *purposes* of theology and confusing the *purposes* of theology with the *purposes* of psychology is detrimental to both. Their purposes are very different. Theology deals with God in and through humans. Psychology deals with the behavior of humans in and through humans. Psychology speaks to *human behavior* — theology speaks to *being human*. Theology is built upon the assumption of the *supernatural*. Psychology is built upon the assumption of only the *natural*. Theology places ultimate responsibility for this and the next life between the human and God. Psychology places ultimate responsibility for this life only with the human and there is no thought of the possibility of a future life following this one.

When the church uses the language, philosophies, and assumptions of psychology, it has forsaken the religion business and has taken up the business of religion. This is clear because psychology is based on temporal theories that may well be incorrect. Psychological theories deny the supernatural, which is the very basis of theology. To be certain, there are theologians who attempt to reconcile psychology and theology and there are psychologists who attempt to reconcile psychology and theology — and that is not all bad. However, when psychological language, methods, and philosophies replace or even greatly alter the basics of religion — the nature of the business has changed. The trading company is now a religion business — not the business of religion.

Psychological jargon has replaced theological language, psychological methodology has been introduced as being theological, and techniques borrowed from the psychotherapy room have neutered traditional theological thinking. When an interpretation of Christianity is based upon a prevalent philosophy and or psychology of the day, Christianity becomes Neo-Christianity. In many areas of life, when the knowledge of two disciplines are combined, we all benefit. This has certainly been true in many instances in the combination of psychology and theology. However, psychology, which has prided itself in being anything but theological, has increasingly utilized the concepts and bases of theology for emerging practice, and the church has increasingly grounded its teaching in the secularism of psychology.

The very concepts Freud used to separate psychoanalysis from theology are in truth thinly veiled tenets of virtually every world religion. While claiming to separate himself from religion, Freud built much of his thinking on age-old religious belief. Although he may have thought that he was differentiating them, he actually only confused them. "Good" is represented in Freud by the "Super Ego," "bad" is known as the "Id," and both fight for the attention of the "person," which is the "Ego." In many ways, Freud used religion against religion to form the very basis for psychoanalysis. His open hostility toward religion was built upon a lifetime of Judaism. He could not have developed his imaginary description of the human without the mystical, mythical, historical, and Judaic view of the human. One only needs to read *Pilgrim's Progress* to put both Freud and religion into proper perspective. Like few other books, the innate nature of the human is contrasted to the divine purposes of God. The human need and the human search remains the same. There is little surprise that the seeking human would replace one search engine for another if it offered more promise. I am keenly aware that the content of this book is controversial, however, the purpose is to provoke thought, and I hope action, which will benefit the current practices of both religion and of psychology. Putting my observations and opinions into print has been exceedingly difficult for me to do. While I am convinced that doing so may be helpful to many, I am also convinced that many others will view it as unnecessarily critical or hurtful. After having it read by many of my most respected colleagues, conservative, liberal, Protestant, and Roman Catholic, I can do nothing other than let it be published and pray that those who can will benefit from it and those who do not will understand the spirit in which it was written.

By understanding the differences and similarities of psychology and religion, and by allowing these two important disciplines, religion and psychology, to help — rather than to replace each other — humankind can find additional ways to cope with the ultimate questions of our time. While on this earth we will continue to be frustrated by the lack of satisfactory answers, but through diligent attention to the Gospel we can find the final support for all doubt and frustration and be able give a satisfactory answer to those who might chide our faith — to quote St. Peter: "Be always in readiness to make an answer to anyone who asks you a reason for the hope that is with you, yet with gentleness and reverence" (I Peter 3:15, *The Holy Bible*).

Acknowledgments

THERE ARE NUMEROUS PERSONS who have helped make this book possible by virtue of their influence on my life and thinking. Sometimes diverse in their agreements, at times strong in their disagreements, and sometimes corroborative, they have forced me into thinking critically about my journey of education, practice, thought, faith, and the expression of that faith that will continue throughout my lifetime. Family, students, patients, teachers, and friends have given me a legacy that they, nor I, will ever fully know. I owe a debt to them for sharing themselves and their spiritual and psychological enlightenment with me that can never be repaid. Among these persons are The Rev. Dr. Vernon Grounds, who, as Dean of a small institution of higher education I attended, taught me to read critically and to think critically about both religion and psychology; E. Mansell Pattison, M.D. (deceased), as close as a brother, with whom I spent countless hours debating, arguing, and sometimes never reaching consensus, but always growing; The Rev. Dr. Sherman Roddy (deceased), who first helped me to feel secure enough to doubt; Truman G. Esau, M.D., with whom I practiced for over ten years and spent countless hours attempting to wed psychology and religion, and certainly not least, my own brother, The Rev. Donald G. Cox (deceased), who left us at age thirty-four before his own emerging and already recognized integration of psychology and religion could come to fruition.

To Dennis McClellan, Publisher, whose insight caught the vision of this book; to Carolyn Lea, editor, whose life journey helped her understand and appreciate my message; and to Jonathan Pennell who designed the cover and pages — I offer my deepest gratitude.

And, of course, there are many, many more that should be acknowledged, but space does not permit! Although some of these persons would not necessarily agree with many things in this book, to these, and countless others who must go unnamed, I give them credit and thank them for the courage to think boldly and for encouraging me to do likewise.

Richard Cox
Westminster, Colorado
October 2001

Apologia

MANY WOULD CALL THIS section an introduction. That would be accurate but not altogether accurate. *Webster's Encyclopedic Unabridged Dictionary of the English Language* says that an apologia is "a work written as an explanation or justification of one's motives, convictions or acts." It is my firm conviction that is set forth in this book. I have no apology, but I have a strong apologia. From birth I have spent my life going to church regularly. I have attended, served, and worshiped in the church (small "c") and readily and proudly acknowledge my eternal membership in the Church (capital "C"). Thus, after nearly three quarters of a century of living and over fifty years of professional service, I feel compelled to speak out in an attempt to see our task as Christians more clearly. It should be noted that the Church (capital "C") and the church (small "c") are used throughout this book. Only in certain instances is the distinction made between the Church, i.e., the body of Christ that constitutes the larger body of believers, and the church, i.e., that is the worshipping body of local believers in a given denomination or congregation. To make this distinction in each instance would be most boring and of little value. This book is written in support of the Church, recognizing that many local congregations are making sincere efforts to remain true to traditional as well as emerging theology. As my friends and publisher know all too well, this manuscript went to press with much trepidation — not because I have stated anything that I do not believe or anything that I believe to be untrue, but with the deepest concern that the message of the book might be missed, or, even worse, misinterpreted, and cause unnecessary criticism, harm, or damage to clergy, mental health professionals, or parishioners.

The book began to take shape while continuing my education and simultaneously serving as pastor of a small church in Peoria, Illinois in the early 1950s. The church grew, and so did I. While pursuing graduate school study in theology, psychology, and medicine, it became increasingly obvious to me that these disciplines had many things in common, but also clashed on many essential points. The sick and dying patients whom I visited in the hospital did not always feel the faith they had verbally proclaimed in the church. The emotionally disturbed folks at the Peoria State Mental Hospital (as it was then called) did not seem to be greatly helped by either religion or psychology. Most adolescents continued to go through their tempestuous years without much regard for either psychology or religion. People going through tough times such as divorce, bankruptcy, business reversals, and poverty often did not report feeling much support from the religious folks who professed to care.

However, there were exceptions. I began to notice that in those exceptions there was a common denominator. Persons who felt the care of the Church bonded with a message that was less found in words, but more evident in relationship. Persons who were helped by psychological methods likewise did not find great help in words, but again found help in the nature of the patient/doctor relationship. Even in physical healing, it seemed that often the return of health was more a matter of the patients' trust in their physician than in the medicine they took. The medicine sometimes arrested, or at least slowed down, the degenerative and infectious conditions. Surgery sometimes corrected physical trauma, disease, and deformity. However, the "more complete" healing of the inner person remained a mystery, often seemingly the result of a trusting relationship only.

The church *taught* relationship. Psychotherapy *required* relationship. Both *talked* about relationship. However, relationship was seen differently in each. Persons who found healing relationships in both religion and psychology made changes in their thinking and behavior. Psychology, which at that time was primarily psychoanalytic, built its treatment upon "transference," a technique which encourages patients to re-experience their emotions, particularly those of their childhood and ("transfer") direct them at the therapist rather than at the person with whom they had initially had the experience. This cathartic process gives the therapist tremendous power and control over the patient's emotions, and hence over the patient's life. The patient becomes dependent, the doctor becomes the "father confessor," and only the two know the secrets. Thus the "relationship" is formed.

It seemed that the same process occurred in the church. Parishioners "confessed" their "sins" and it seemed very much like "catharsis." After reexperiencing one's childhood emotions in the presence of a "father confessor," the patients often felt relieved and were able to go on in life without the disabling anxiety and depression that had beset them. In the church, it was similar. Parishioners who confessed and repented were "forgiven" and were able to go on in life without the anxiety and depression they had been experiencing. Theologically speaking, "anxiety" looked very much like "conviction," and that which psychiatry called "depression" appeared very similar to what theologians called "guilt." Although the terms differed, the behavior looked alike and the end results of these behaviors were similar, i.e., anxiety and conviction each drove one toward change and mental and spiritual depression, with guilt, ensured lowered self-esteem.

Yet at that time, religion and psychology were not talking to each other very much. Religious leaders, while freely using the newly found knowledge of human behavior, were not in meaning-ful dialogue with psychologists and certainly psychology had little recognition of the spiritual dimensions of life. The pastoral care movement was just getting into full swing and there were profes-sionals from both disciplines (psychology and theology) who were attempting to find the commonalties of each other. Pastors were seeking more from psychology than psychologists were seeking from pastors. The infusion of psychological language and a new understanding of human behavior gave new life to a tired theology. Granger Westberg, D.D., one of the first in the field, published his book, *Minister and Doctor Meet*, and in many ways became the "father of pastoral counseling." Anton Boisen, Ph.D., a Presbyterian minister, who himself had been in and out of mental hospitals since the 1920s, had been treated with psychological methods, tried des-perately to find the common threads of the two disciplines and became known as the "father" of Clinical Pastoral Education. Hobart Mowrer, Ph.D., a nationally renown professor at the University of Illinois, who taught and worked as a psychologist in state hospitals, added considerable insight, although beset himself by cyclical depressions that more than once required hospitaliza-tion. As well as psychologists such as Dr. Mowrer, there were numerous clergy/psychology professionals such as Granger Westberg, Seward Hiltner, Paul Johnson, Carroll Wise, Wayne Oates, and others that made a profound impact on me and my per-ception of human behavior in the light of psychology and religion. Over the years many of these minister/psychologists became my personal friends. By that time my elder brother, also a clergyman and student of psychology, was deep into the mental health move-ment and serving as a chaplain in a state hospital. While he was pur-suing a Ph.D. degree at the University of Chicago, he invited me to sit in on some classes with him that were taught by many of the "fathers of the field" of pastoral care. My own experience by that time and these opportunities further influenced me to study the relationship of religion to psychology and vice versa. I had the privilege of coming under the influence of some of the greatest minds of our time in the fields of psychology and theology, such as Vincent J. Herr, S.J., Carl Rogers, Bruno Bettleheim, Ericka Fromm, Samuel Beck, George Yacorzynski, Paul Tillich, Paul Witty, Martin Marty, and far too many more to name. Chicago was a virtual Mecca of great minds in the 1950s, 1960s and 1970s. By traveling a few miles across town, one could sit under the teaching of guest lecturers such as Anna Freud and Karl Menninger, who were among hundreds of others brought to the great institutions in that city.

Several psychiatrists under whom I studied and several with whom I worked continued to help mold both my acceptance and my confusion regarding the two disciplines. I became one in their model (as did many other young students), a "minister/ psychologist," and continued to search for opportunities to wed the two disciplines even firmer. While some efforts were clearly successful and rewarding, there remained an unsolved mystery, namely, what was the difference and why couldn't these two disciplines get on well together, since they spoke essentially the same language and professed to do very similar things for their parishioners and patients?

As the decades piled up, I continued to study theology, psychology, and medicine. When it was time to decide on a postdoctoral medical specialty, I knew that it could not be a residency in psychiatry, although I had an invitation to do so at one of the most prestigious programs. To go into psychiatry would be like going through seminary all over again and repeating much of what I had studied in a doctorate in psychology, except with the addition of psychopharmacology and a different vocabulary. So I chose to complete a residency in Family Medicine at an institution which continues to this day to maintain a high priority for the Christian faith. I will always remember Walten I. Baba, M.D., Ph.D., my chief mentor at Swedish Covenant Hospital in Chicago, as a true model of faith in action. It was a wonderful place to observe the interactions as well as the confusion in the healing process of both the body and soul. I had many physician/teachers who believed in the power of God as well as in the value of medicine. In that specialty of Family Medicine, the similarities and the differences in psychology, religion, and medicine became more and more clear. Treating people's hurts, delivering beautiful babies to happy parents, standing at bedsides as patients died, and attempting to console their loved ones caused me to search even deeper for answers. Delivering a beautiful infant at one moment, watching an eight year old die before life had really begun, seeing a much needed mother bleed-out in surgery, observing a young breadwinner father collapse from a heart attack in the emergency room, and watching an octogenarian slip into the next life are enough to confuse anybody. The theology of a loving, kind God, I was certain, had to be true, but it was frequently extremely illusive in the face of human suffering and pain.

My years of study offered all kinds of "answers," but it seemed that the "answers" fit questions that were not being asked. The answers fit a world of already constructed questions that were based on the belief that life and death made sense. It only made sense to those not personally anguishing with the mental and physical gyrations of emotional and bodily suffering. My own spiritual innerperson grew, but for every question that seemed to find a partial answer, a thousand more questions arose.

My life had been one of teaching, preaching, and practicing in religion, psychology, and medicine. I had learned much about all three disciplines from teachers, colleagues, students, and patients, as well as from experience. Yet the integration of these fields of human behavior remained undone. It still does to this day. However, day by day and year upon year this book continued to emerge, in my head, in my practice, and on paper. I kept copious notes, diaries of thoughts, and actually conceptualized a cartoon-type book cover that would caricature my thinking. I actually began writing the manuscript in the late 1960s. I put the manuscript away and largely

gave up the idea of it ever becoming a book, until one day our son, a theologically minded neuropsychologist, ran across it in my study and, after reading it, insisted on its value for this particular time in our history. This book is not presented as an integration of psychology and theology. It does not solve the thinking person's confusion. In truth, I hope it adds questions that may even increase the confusion. I have always believed that the primary aim of teachers is not to necessarily undo confusion, but to encourage thinking. When listeners leave without having their thinking challenged, they have not been taught.

Methods as well as "knowledge" change as we study and live life. Yet there are enduring truths in both fields of theology and psychology. The challenge is in identifying those parts that are abiding from those that are fleeting. We continually learn "the truth" and yet what we believe to be "the truth" changes as we are tossed about by life's experiences. I have come to recognize that the only abiding "truth" is found in relationships, relationships that are not anchored in time with words, but in relationships with persons and with God. Somehow the words of Jesus, "I am the way, the *truth*, and the life," take on a more powerful meaning when seen within the context of our mental and physical need as played out on that huge multidimensional screen that we call life.

Both the church and the psychological sciences have a great deal to offer each other and therefore to their patients and parishioners. The language and practice of medicine, although influencing the church, have not had the depth of influence upon the church as has psychology. Therefore, this book deals primarily with the relationship of psychology to theology and theology to psychology. To the extent to which they are mixed, they are at the same time helpful and confusing. To the extent that they are separated, they regress to the Cartesian mind/body dichotomy. The challenge is to find the parts of each discipline that can and should be integrated and the parts that need to be discarded.

Both psychology and theology would speak to their "integration." I would insist that much of the time that which is called "integration" is not that at all, but "mixing." Integration and mixing are not the same thing. Mixing produces a common mass from two different substances. Integration introduces parts of other substances into the other, thus producing a product greater than the sum of its parts: a gestalt.

Ministers who would guide others must surely find ways to know themselves first. With some exceptions, this has not occurred. Psychologists and psychiatrists who would guide others must surely find the Spirit and Source of that energy within themselves first. As with ministers who have not pursued knowing themselves, psychologists and psychiatrists certainly have not by and large looked for the Spirit or Source of their energy. Persons who wish to help others must be able to transcend not only themselves, but also the words and actions of their disciplines. The method is not the message. Neither can the message be reduced to the method. The message is inseparably and inextricably interwoven with transcendence. Transcendence is a *spiritual* ability that is capable of pervading, translating, communicating, and exceeding all messages and all methods. Ministers, psychologists, psychiatrists, physicians of all sorts, and indeed all who are healers in any profession must allow God to bring about transcendence beyond our frail human selves so that we may rely upon a spiritual depth and energy beyond our knowledge and definition.

Today, after more than fifty years in professional life, preaching, teaching, and practicing, and equally importantly simply living, there are many things which are much more clear, many things that are still seen through "a glass darkly," and some that are not seen at all. However, as Saint Paul so aptly understood, "Now I know in part; then I shall fully understand even as I have been fully understood." I continue to believe and to search current literature, history, my experiences, and the experiences of others for answers. Hopefully this book will not be seen as a negative criticism of anything, but rather as a constructively critical discussion of issues that can make a difference in people's lives. It is offered to those who would follow in the steps of all those who continue the struggle of bringing hope and salvation to humankind.

1

The Church Has Gone Out of the Religion Business

Jesus spoke of his father's business — have we forgotten what this is?

RELIGION AS A BUSINESS IS NOT THE SAME AS THE BUSINESS OF RELIGION

THE CHURCH AMERICA has all but gone out of the *religion* business. In many instances it has gone into the *business* of religion, i.e., instead of attending to religion, it utilizes religion as a commodity to be marketed and uses the profits it gains to maintain the Church as a business. Instead of "rendering unto God those things which are God's and unto Caesar those things which are Caesar's" (Luke 20:25, *The Holy Bible*), the modern-day church is said to utilize both that which is God's and Caesar's for self-preservation. It can safely be argued that the "legal tender" of many local congregations is the language of psychology rather than the language of theology.

The seriousness of a linguistic exchange is that with a new language comes a new culture and the problems attendant thereto. Paul Tillich, the theologian, points out that "Language is a very good example of the difference between signs and symbols" (1957, p. 55). Language is made up of words that take on different meanings in each context, to each person who hears them, and to each one who reads them and the meanings are very different from one ethnic language to another. Although we translate one language into another, we never completely capture the meaning without understanding the culture from whence the language is drawn. So it is with psychology and theology. With lesser emphasis upon theological language and the prominence of psychological terms came a crisis that was not, and still is not, recognized in many churches and in Western culture. *The language of psychology, anthropology, sociology, and political correctness has been so subtly and deceptively introduced into the religious syntax that most parishioners and many clergy use the terms interchangeably.* However, by so doing, the power of theology is exchanged for the temporal, "science-based" emotional loading of the social sciences.

That crisis in Western culture and its churches today is a spiritual one. Morrie was quoted in *Tuesdays With Morrie* as having given us these words of wisdom: "The culture we have does not make people feel good about themselves. And you have to be strong enough to say if the culture doesn't work, don't buy it" (Albom, 1997). Although Morrie did not go on to discuss what does work, the rest of his deathbed conversations made it clear that there are only spiritual answers to the tough questions of life and death. For many reasons, our culture is not working. Technology, financial concerns, world power, managed healthcare, and the problems of ecology and the environment are in and of themselves just pockmarks on the face of the real problem — spiritual "dis-ease." Pastoral counselor

David Steere, in discussing Philip Reiff, rightly stated: "… it became no longer possible to organize our culture around a commonly accepted dynamic of moral demands and prerogatives of truth exercised by authoritarian institutions psychotherapy fell heir to the task" (1997, p. 25). He further stated, still reflecting on Reiff who wrote *The Triumph of the Therapeutic* (1966): "Whereas 'religious man' had been born to be saved, 'psychological man' was born to be pleased." He asserts that "when 'I believe,' the cry of the religious ascetic, lost precedence to 'I feel,'" the therapeutic won, and that "when the therapeutic wins out, surely the psychotherapeutic will become the secular spiritual guide of the future." There is little doubt that over 35 years after Reiff wrote those prophetic words that he was correct and further that the "therapeutic" has won. The latter years of the 20th century were marked with concern over "lost values," "moral issues," and spiritual concerns. Those same issues are no smaller in the 21st century.

Although religion and spirituality are not synonymous, it is important to recognize that the major public agents for spirituality have traditionally been religious organizations, most notably, the church. Religion has attempted to address the immediate nature of life, i.e., how to live today, according to the interpretation of values within the corporate church. Although each brand of religion, whether a denomination within Christianity or a separate world religion, would claim success, there is little if any evidence that the masses of humanity are any less ill-at-ease with their own brand or organized spirituality than anyone else. The practice of religion and a sense of personal empowerment emanate from deep within the person and are of necessity inextricably intertwined. Empowerment without principle and righteousness is not only tragic, but also aimless, i.e., empowerment bestowed by political, ethnic, gender, economic, or any other societal factor is pseudo-strength and does not stand the test of time. Such empowerment may make one feel stronger and even have a kind of "public strength," but we have all seen this kind of power diminish overnight in the wake of political and social pressures and changes.

The Church Bought the Promises of Psychology and Is Still Waiting for Delivery

Religion is supposed to offer meaning for what seems to be the meaningless answers of "the world" for the tough questions. The observance of religion provides symbols and rituals for the integration of thought and action in life. The current fearful, frantic pace of modern life leaves little room to doubt that the application of religion to daily life has failed miserably. In the past, possessing religious resources was essential — even when we knew that much of it was mystical — probably because we knew it was mystical. Living up to the ascribed and communally accepted answers provided an integration of life and society. All demands could be placed upon all persons universally. All persons were deemed to be more or less equal as victim and victor. Today it is difficult to know in truth who is the victor and who is the victim. Sometimes the victor is actually being victimized without knowing it, and sometimes the victim is actually the victor. Many of our social welfare programs appear to be one thing on the surface, but in truth are quite the opposite. All too often society is victimized by those who appear to be the victims.

INDIVIDUALITY DILUTES RESPONSIBILTY

The great individuality of our present age was unknown in earlier times because all persons were held to a similar boilerplate of belief and behavior. Spiritual values and the practice of life were not separated, nor was responsibility separated from communal accountability. A story in the book of Acts in the New Testament is an interesting indictment regarding our separation of human communal responsibility and accountability. The story of Annanias and

Saphira (Acts 5:1–12) demonstrates the seriousness of belief and communal behavior. They sold land, which was theirs to sell, but they connived to deceive the believers in their congregation regarding its sale price. They were perceived as having lied to not only the community, but to God. The price for that break with communal rules was the ultimate — both Annanias and Saphira dropped dead! In later times, even in this country, particularly in smaller communities and in stricter religious communities, what one believed and how one lived was (and in some places still is) considered one and the same thing. The community demanded consistency of the *walk* and the *talk*.

Today it is possible to profess a set of values while evidencing quite a different set of values in daily life. Furthermore, this is so commonplace that we have come to expect the business person to be dishonest during the work week (just doing good business); yet it is quite acceptable for that same person to profess quite the opposite in the church world.

We have accepted a different norm — the hedonistic norm of "just trying to get ahead." The consumer has become the valued part of the transaction — and that is understandable in the business world; however, religion has claimed to know without a doubt what the consumer needs and therefore has not asked for consumer input. We have become both consumers of consumerism and purveyors of consumerism. Furthermore, we believe that honesty is relative to being successful in reaching those goals. These rationalizations are so universally shared that no one dares to speak out against others who do the same thing. Those of us who live in "glass houses" certainly do not want to "throw stones," and since we all live in glass houses, none of us *can* throw stones — but we can at least admit that we live in glass houses and think about what to do with the pile of stones!

The principles of faith are tough to find in life. It is hard to reconcile what is so often seen as good entrepreneurship with an espoused Christian faith. Our greed to make money has wed capitalism, consumerism, and Western religion to such an extent that virtues are both more virtuous and irrelevant, at one and the same time, when financial gain is involved. It is virtually impossible to tell the difference between consumerism, capitalism, and religion. Capitalism and religion are basically inseparable in today's world.

Has Religion Failed?

Religion has not failed, but its institutions certainly have. The failure is in the *practice* of religion. The *Atlantic Monthly* (August 1996, p. 52) quotes a third-generation pastor as saying, "It's not that we don't trust God; it's that we don't trust the institutions. They've [churches] let us down ... they need a place where it is safe to say, 'I don't believe this whole God thing. I think it's a lot of malarkey.'" The safety of a place to blaspheme belief becomes a place to replace that belief with a more hedonistic and narcissistic theology. The next step is not only easy but obvious — to replace the theological "malarkey" with an entrepreneurial God who not only approves of what we do in our selfishness, but blesses it. The more we get, the more evidence we have of "God's blessing." Soon, we have equated personal gain with God's goodness and consider those who have less as being less blessed by God. In the Western way of life, capitalism and humanism have become Siamese twins.

In the idolatry of humanism, sociological theory, psychology, and consumerism, the church has gone out of its way not only to permit, but also to promote "malarkey belief." In the name of "intellectual freedom" the church has lost its very soul, i.e., the necessity that we believe anything specific to the faith. Believing whatever seems compatible with the individual's daily way of life subjects belief to the hedonism of the age, and although church members may strenuously object to this truth, they know in their hearts that what is being preached in the name of intellectualism is not always truth. New-world Western religion does not function as a standard-bearer today, if it ever did. Even the old Protestant ethos does not demand much, and by the same token there is unheard of confusion and disagreement at all levels of the Roman Catholic Church. Both Protestant and Roman Catholic churches are under fire for very good reasons. The corporate "absolutes," the uniformly agreed upon creeds, and the body-religious-politic of both the Protestant and Roman Catholic Church have given way to individual interpretation and application, without serious concern for what "the Church would think." The church is more earthly visible and obvious than is God, so when there is no concern for what the church and it's leaders think (which are clearly heard and visible), why would it occur to us to be concerned about what God Who is invisible might think? We are reminded of the Biblical words, "… if a man says, I love God, while hating his brother, he is a liar. If he does not love the brother who he has seen, it cannot be that he loves God who he has not seen" (I John 3:20, *New English Bible*).

Values are individualized; hence, although often shared and synchronous with others, they are also uniquely personal. Personal values are important and valuable, and to be certain it is important to measure up to one's own expectations. However, every human also wishes to be able to measure up to a standard greater than him/herself. Corporate values, like those espoused in church and repeated in religious ritual, are quite different from those of personal belief and practice. Somehow when a group is reciting the words of an affirmation, creed, or pledge, the individualized belief and resulting responsibility are lost. Frequently as individuals we retain the right to a private interpretation of those public affirmations that fit our private life and our personal benefit.

This is not to say, however, that simply because values are "personal" that they do not deeply effect others. One of the greatest debates in the history of the United States has been about the effect of President Clinton's admitted behavior on politics, the economy, his own family, and society at large. No one denies the far-reaching impact of a personal (in this case the President's) value system upon society. It was widely publicized that his behavior effected the interpretation of sexual behavior by America's adolescents. Perhaps as much as any modern leader's role model forced society to look at value systems, the Clinton administration did just that. The argument that "what is private is of no concern to the public" is not always true.

THE INDIVIDUAL CAN ONLY TRULY BE SACRED WITHIN THE COMMUNITY

The concept of individualism is valuable and should not be lost; however, neither should it be lost that individualism can only survive within the rules of a community! Individualizing values in the extreme has been mistaken for personalized character. The term "rugged individualism" has characterized an *avant garde*, pioneering kind of person and is sometimes seen as a highly admirable value in and of itself. We are reminded of Ayn Rand's famous book, *Atlas Shrugged*, in which individualism was idolized. This 20th century Western thinking somehow has also often been viewed as a Christian virtue and represents the kind of person who needs nothing or no one else for personal sustenance. This kind of thinking is straight out of humanistic psychology, not theology. This "bootstrap" philosophy makes it totally unnecessary to recognize and appreciate the contributions of others. It has led to a false sense of "individuality." *Individuality Is* **Reflective** *of The Community and* **Reflexive** *of Oneself.*

The "what's good for me" type of thinking has replaced a former interpersonal generosity. This kind of thinking has produced dysfunctional families and dysfunctional communities. In earlier times such individualism would have been called "selfishness." Among the "New Year's Resolutions" printed in a local newspaper, it was striking to notice the "rugged individualism" and hedonism in many of the resolutions. They included such statements as, "I intend this year to take care of myself first;" "This year I'm going to be me regardless of what anybody thinks;" and even "My husband and the kids had better get used to the new me, 'cause I'm going to look out for me, and if I'm not worth it, nobody is!"

Rarely, if ever, does rugged individualism produce the virtues esteemed in most civilizations and certainly not in the Church. St. Paul describes the rugged, self-centered, individualist as, "Now the works of the flesh are obvious: fornication, impurity, licentiousness, idolatry, sorcery, enmities, strife, jealousy, anger, quarrels, dissension, factions, envy, drunkenness, carousing and things like these." By contrast, the spiritual person is described as evidencing the fruit of the Spirit, which is love, joy, peace, patience, kindness, generosity, faithfulness, gentleness, and self-control" (Galatians 5:19–23, *The Holy Bible*). An interesting note is that most persons when speaking of this passage consider the *fruits* (plural) of the Spirit rather than *fruit* (singular). This is an important distinction, particularly in this discussion. The fruit of the Spirit is a wholistic, gestalt, unified display of the inner person, while individual parts of the whole are the evidences of our struggle for the whole and our ability most of the time to only achieve small parts of it.

Although these words come from the Christian Bible, most religions of the world ascribe to similar codes of behavior. Furthermore, one does not have to be a believer in any kind of religion or psychology to see that we can change our world drastically by simply emphasizing the differences in these lifestyles. It doesn't take much observation to see the positive benefits when even parts of kindness, gentleness, and self-control are manifested. It takes no complex investigation to determine that our world has been tragically changed already by persons who exhibit selfishness, hedonism, and greed.

All Religions Value the Community as a Basis for Individual Behavior

Rugged individualism and a religious value system are difficult to mix. By definition, the Christian way of life is a life of *dependency*: dependency upon God within the fellowship and communality of the church and with fellow believers. The world is changed by both individualism and by the religiously dependent, but in very different ways. Both are highly dependent systems; it is only the *focus* of the dependency that differs. The rugged individualists are falsely dependent upon themselves. The religious person is admittedly dependent upon God. The mixture of belief/nonbelief of the religious person and the pseudo-self-dependency of the individualist may in truth be very much the same thing. They are both ultimately dependent upon their unique belief system. The self-serving dependency upon such a system is a dead end street. It serves only the self and at best benefits only one person.

INDIVIDUALIZED INTERPRETATION HINDERS A UNIFIED VALUE SYSTEM

Even the church does not have a singular unified value system. One would think with the emphasis placed upon the Scriptures that such would be the case, i.e., it is surprising that with the emphasis upon a single manifesto (*The Holy Bible*) that an organization would not have a unified and relatively well-understood charter. However, where interpretation plays a role, and it always does, there are multiple interpretations that in fact become multiple value systems. One value system says that organizational and corporate values are models for society, groups, and others. However, this system is not often used for self-application. Values for personal application seem to be individual self-interest, self-aggrandizement, and personal fulfillment, and therefore constitute a second system. Both systems are practiced, but individually applied only when the *benefits* derived from them are personally *beneficial* enough. The importance of the person is idolized even at one's own personal expense!

THE "RIGHT TO BE ME" ENDANGERS COMMUNITY

The "right to be me" has in truth caused many persons to forget who they really are! It has caused an entire generation (maybe more) to be so caught up in themselves and their own hedonism that we created the "me-ness" generation. This generation is now the leadership of our communities and nation. No one can doubt the negative impact this movement has had upon the general welfare of everyone. As we will discuss in later chapters of this book, the "Right to Be Me Club" has generated millions of "victims." The "victims" leech off of the tax payer, they whine over things they should grit their teeth and do, arrogantly misuse "handicapped license plates," unnecessarily become welfare recipients, and form one of the most selfish cultures we have ever known. Its insidious complications and the aftermath problems will be with us for generations to come. These self-centered persons have now become parents who have taught by word and example these destructive lessons to their children. Furthermore, the single-parent family is largely a result of this exact philosophy, namely, "I must be me and have what is coming to me" regardless of whom it hurts and what it does to other people or the community itself. The time to "be good for goodness sake" is long since past. Since our definition of "good" is so confused, how can we determine what is for the sake of something we cannot define?

It Sounds Good, But It Is a Myth

The "right to be me" has caused many persons to lose knowledge, to know themselves only as defined by gross misperceptions, if not actual delusions, about what it means to live within a community. It is not possible to be oneself in a vacuum. In the late 1960s and early 1970s, there was a phenomenon which led to the "let it all hang out" culture. Many males wore their shirts open nearly to their waist with beads and sandals and females tossed out their bras. It reportedly made them feel "free." Society is still reaping the results of some of their "freedom." What it really meant was shirking responsibility, devaluing authority, and opposing anything seen as being part of "the establishment."

"No man is an island" and that which is assumed to be corporate and societal is in truth nothing more than the accumulation of individuals. The serious problem is that all too frequently, a few very aggressive, sociopathically inclined persons usurp the corporate value setting and by self-appointment attempt to establish the rules for everyone. They ignore and do not care that they do not represent the majority. The "majority" has probably never really been of great importance to those who rule, whether in business or government. It is now only a figment of our imagination that the "majority rules." Such a dictum at present is only a vestige of what the United States declares as its democratic philosophy, not democracy in action. In truth, in all likelihood such was never the case, but it sounded good and kept the troops from getting nervous.

RELIGION HAS AIDED ESTABLISHMENT OF TAX EXEMPT ORGANIZATIONS

Religions have given birth to far more ideologies and programs than the ones that are specifically church-related. Many "religious" ideas have found homes in not-for-profit organizations such as the Community Chest, United Way, the Red Cross, and many others. These groups, by virtue of their federal tax-exempt status, reap the benefits of separation of church and state, but are frequently only in name "not-for-profit." Frequently these groups do not seem to have much to do with the religious or educational identity that renders

them "tax exempt." Tax exempt, 501 C (3), corporations are too frequently little more than excuses for the amassing of personal gain.
Westernized religious thought that has wedded sociological, psychological, educational, and religious philosophies has made dis-
tinctions between the church and the non-church almost indeci-
pherable.

As a result, the institutions to which Western religions gave
birth are in serious trouble. The middle class, education, healthcare,
the family, the church, and our capitalistic enterprise as well suffer
due to the loss of distinction between religious fervor and capitalistic thinking. The creed became "that which is good for business
must be good for God." Organizations such as Christian Business
Men and Christian Business Women must struggle to keep from
supporting the idea that if a business is making money it must be
"pleasing to God." This concept is particularly difficult for many to
see if even a miniscule amount of that profit is contributed to philanthropic organizations. It is impossible for most people to make
this distinction, particularly if some of the money is given to the
church. Most ministers are quite willing to rely on the old adage
that "as long as the money is green it really doesn't matter where it
comes from." It reminds one of the story of the church member
who was counseled against gambling by her pastor, but when the
gambler won big-time, the pastor was very interested to see that she
tithed on the winnings! This kind of thinking misses the whole
point of personal integrity and furthers the idea that money, business, and religion are the same. Strange as it may seem, although
Christians must treat all of these things as sacred, in theory they
cannot be separated — they are not the same in practical application. Greed seems to permeate all branches of society equally. One
is reminded of the story of the aged, very wealthy woman who
requested that a televangelist be on each side of her bed as she was
dying. Eager that she would have her checkbook in hand, two tele-
vangelists happily made themselves available. One stood on either
side of her deathbed awaiting their anticipated but unspoken

legacy, only to be told that she wanted to die the way Jesus died, with a thief on each side!

As this humorous, but probably untrue story shows, the church has taken its confused ideas about money and religion to the masses via the media. In a day when television reaches millions, it is a sheer tragedy that too many, though certainly not all, religious persons use the media for personal financial gain. If there ever were a media for the dissemination of truth, television is it. The pulpit is there for the entire world to see. It does, and one can only hope that the church will have the power to change its current approach and narcissistic message. Unfortunately, with some notable exceptions, probably as much falsehood has been spread as truth. God and Mammon have been a problem since time began. They were major topics throughout both the Old and New Testaments, and certainly the problem of God and money has not become any less difficult to deal with in our time.

Capitalism and Christian Science

Capitalism can be dangerous in the hands of those who mix up the Gospel and business. The Gospel is not anti-business, and certainly business does not need to be anti-Gospel. It just seems so easy to bend the rules, even make up new rules, when dealing with money. Capitalism gets identified and therefore confused with evangelism. Thus the capitalistic way of life starts to look so "Christian." We rationalize that if we make more money, we can give more to the church. Even missionary endeavors, which in the past started out with high ideals, often mistook capitalistic thinking for evangelism. If people look better, smell better, eat better, live in better houses, and have better clothes, surely they are evidencing God's gifts! However, the problem is that kind of thinking starts on the wrong assumption — the assumption that if one has all these things, one surely will then find the Kingdom of God — wrong — it's the other way around — we must seek first the Kingdom of God, then these things are added.

Today, it is extremely difficult to distinguish the church from any other capitalistic enterprise when they are both examined utilizing the same criteria. The capitalistic world has adopted a "mission" statement and boldly announces itself as being "good" because it contributes so much to the betterment of the human race. Look at the slogans of the huge corporations in our country and see how they lure consumers by promoting their "mission:" from advertising slogans which promise "friendly skies," to companies that "bring good things to life," to tobacco companies that make addicting products look like they make for a better life, and to dozens more alluring "mission" applications. Even the alcoholic beverage industry attempts to promote their "mission" by encouraging drinkers to "know when to say no." The stated (or at least advertised) "mission" of nearly every commercial industry is to make our lives better, more meaningful, happier, and more enjoyable.

The Sacred and the Secular

Modern business and industry may very well have become today's secularized religion which incorporates both the "profit motive" and the "mission motive" — the best of both worlds. Several years ago (1963), Harvey Cox, a prominent theologian, published his famous book, *The Secular City*, in which he argued for a secular social-approach to theology. A sequel could be written today which would identify the "secular church." The difference would be that Cox argued that the church should meet society's changing demands. Today there would be little argument that the church has indeed succeeded in that task and has greatly secularized. It has been so successful that in many person's minds, the "goodness" of the church and the "goodness" of any other social institution are indistinguishable. While one could argue that "goodness" is "goodness," such an argument would be to lose sight of the *reasons* for the "goodness." Goodness without reason could conceivably exist, but how, by whom, and why?

THE REASON FOR DOING A DEED IS AS IMPORTANT AS THE DEED

When sight is lost as to *why* "goodness" is a virtue, one should not be able to suspect the church. It does matter *why* good deeds are done. It does matter *who* is performing the deed. It does matter if there is an ulterior motive. When we remember that one claims to be other than earth-bound, it makes a difference. When we remember that one has basic goodness in mind as an end product rather than a profit motive, it makes a difference. When we forget these differentiating aspects of "doing good," it permits considerable moneymaking. Business persons can feel that they are doing good while getting rich — an approach which is certainly demonstrated by many churchgoers and religious leaders. Equally, the church can employ secular methods for raising money and feel righteous about it.

A Cup Is Not Always a Cup!

It was Jesus who proclaimed that a "cup of cold water given in the name of a disciple" brings reward (Matthew 10:42) However, the importance of this statement is not only the value of the cold water given but the name invoked in so doing. The value of a service is the gift, the giver, and the meaning behind it. The receiver accepts all three in order to receive the gift. The famous Swiss psychiatrist, Paul Tournier (1962) in *The Meaning of Gifts* helped us to see that every gift carries with it a meaning and that no gift is devoid of the meaning behind it or the silent or spoken purpose of the giver.

A capitalistic mission has been substituted for Christian missions, not so subtly even, and it has hardly been noticed, if noticed at all. The way people dress, the food they eat, the houses they live in, the music they play and sing, the houses of worship in which they meet, and the purposes for which their financial offerings are spent is largely determined by capitalistic thinking called "furthering the Gospel." Even in the heyday of the foreign missionary movement, most missionaries were not aware of the insidious nature of capitalistic thinking, nor were they aware of the kind of pressure it put upon them to evangelize — i.e., to proselytize the heathen into becoming capitalistic believers. Giving up "primitive" ways meant taking on more materialistic ways of living. "Raising the standard of living" was inextricably interwoven with capitalistic methods and the profit motive. Western Christianity has long intermingled theology and capitalism to such an extent that it is no longer obvious to most Christians, even scholars of the faith.

Sometimes Good Intentions Go Wrong

The egregiousness of the missionary enterprise (both in the United States and abroad) was made possible by the convoluted "Western Christian mind" which attempted to paint "us" as "right" (therefore Godly) and "them" as "wrong" (ungodly). The inevitable end of such enterprises resulted in long-term failure. Many schools and hospitals all over the world, established with religious purpose, and even Christian compassion, are now but memories of formerly value-based organizations. Many hospitals throughout the world that were established by religious groups now barely show any affiliation with the denomination that funded them, or for that matter, any religious group at all, except for the cherished fund-raising activities. Colleges and universities likewise that were founded by the church with church funds now speak of themselves as "loosely affiliated" with denominational bodies. They tend to be a bit less "loosely affiliated" though, when they need money for buildings, scholarships, and salary increases. This sham relationship is not only hypocritical, but more importantly, it is usury — i.e., claiming identity with the church for only pecuniary purposes while ignoring most other aspects of the "relationship."

FREUD'S CRYSTAL BALL

The religious roots of Western culture grew deep into a history that is not easily shaken. The fact that these roots were able to penetrate a society that is usually so impenetrable reveals the incredible power of secularization and delivers proof that religion, at least institutional religion, has lost its foothold in the only organizer that ultimately determines society — the individual. The Jewish psychiatrist, Sigmund Freud, seemed to see into a crystal ball when he declared the coming loss of individuality and the individual's necessary compliance upon the thinking of the masses.

The formidable and correct perception of Freud was that he saw the demise of the great religious and philosophic frameworks and realized that the inexorable mindless rush of technology, based in industrial society with all its inhibitory and alienating pressures, required individual analysis and adjustment to reality. The amazing thing is that the technological age had not yet begun in the day of Freud. What he saw as neuroticisms and anxieties are today evidences of our slavery to the technological Western culture.

The post-Freudian word we use to describe these unfortunate results is "stress." While Freud was wrong about many things, very wrong, he was right about this! Although he did not coin the term "stress," he certainly described it accurately. "Stress," as we use it today, is essentially without definition. It only means that the pressures of life are in excess of our resources. Hundreds of books have been published on "stress," yet none of them are able to identify or define stress in anything more than general terms. In the philosophical sense of the word, stress is the best descriptor of this age. In psychological terms, stress is the emotional pressure of the age.

In theological terms, stress is the natural state of the human who is caught in the struggle between good and evil.

For Conditions Beyond Definition, We Invent Words

The only way we have found to define these concepts is to use the word "stress." The hope is that "stress" is interpreted by each person individually, in some way, to lead each person to methods of *coping*. Our use of the term "coping" is also an unfortunate promise of maintaining stability. Coping means exactly what it says, namely, like the wood-worker's coping saw, it finds ways to bend, move, circle, divert, avoid, and cope its way around the pattern laid out before it. It does not change the course of events, but literally "copes" its way around it. Coping in daily life is a substitute for an answer. It is often the best we can do. Coping becomes the best possible method around the obstacles of life and accepting the best possible answer. The genuinely best methods find ways *through* the problems, but much of the time we must settle for only finding ways *around* them. Therefore, coping must not be confused with solving the problem. Coping does not change the course of events — it moves around them.

Herein lies a basic difference between theology and psychology. Psychology is often effective in teaching patients to *cope* with *stress*. Behavior modification, a kind of psychotherapy, is a excellent example. We teach persons to modify their behavior in order to cope with the course of events, but often enough we do not teach them to effectively change the course of events with which they have to cope. Coping with stress becomes a continual process. Changing the events that cause stress allows more permanent answers. Psychology will likely be seen by historians of this age as being highly successful in dealing with certain kinds of human behavior modification. It will also no doubt be seen as dubiously valuable for having done much to change the way in which humans inflict stress upon themselves and their fellow humans.

Very much like today's psychology, the social and psychological revolutions which overcame the archaic demands of the Victorian age and its neurotic realignments are to be recognized as successful for what they claimed to do. It was certainly successful for those who identified with its values and "bought into" what they considered the positive benefits. It did indeed assist at least the wealthy and intellectuals to shrug off the lifestyle and impossible demands of Puritanical thinking. If that's what they were looking for, they were indeed successful. However, no one doubts that it failed to change the basic nature of human behavior. Today we are having much less success in dealing with "stress" because we have chosen to tackle something that we cannot even define. At least the Puritans were able to write their own "thou shalt" and "thou shalt not" list and by tribunal judgment held the community to the adopted model. The myriad causes of stress and the secondary and tertiary results are so immense and far reaching that we cannot even begin to identify them, let alone write a prescription or proscription to fit the dilemma.

Changing Perceptions Does Not Change Reality

Psychology's attempt to deal with the problem of stress proves that reality does not change, i.e., reality remains reality regardless of how we talk about it or what we call it. We can call certain behaviors by different names, and psychology has been successful in teaching us to call things a "re-frame" (a way of avoiding the direct statement of the truth), and we can give different labels to behavior. However, these psycholinguistic maneuvers do not change what is reality!

When the church chose to adopt a new language, it chose to talk about itself within a new cultural context, and that language indeed changed its message — but it did not change the purpose of the Church or the intended mission. The human dilemma is still one of sin and salvation.

Since all human behavior is purposeful, the purpose and the result of that behavior remain the same regardless of what we call it. The question of ultimate meaning remains the same. Since in today's world we talk in such "psycho-babble," it is easy to believe anything if it sounds psychologically plausible. The ability to rationalize, i.e., explain with words that which in truth cannot be explained, was well documented by the father of psychoanalysis, Sigmund Freud, who was also certainly the father of calling humans by psychological names, however despicable those names might be. It is easy to see why Freud is thought of so ambivalently in many circles. He invented such an incredibly safe (but often costly) way out of our misbehavior. It has always been interesting to me that so many folks are willing to wear a psychological label in order to avoid facing real life choices.

Thus the socially accepted answers for human imperfections were forever changed by psychology. Names and labels took the place of changing one's life. Freud could only have invented such a simplistic and fanciful belief system because he was unaware of the consilience of science and human behavior. "Consilience," as defined by Edward O. Wilson, in his deep and provocative book, *Consilience* (1998), is that point at which truths from different disciplines converge and cross over into each other, making a truth greater than either by itself and yet totally true for each discipline. Even though Freud was trained as a neurological physician, for the most part he kept human behavior and science divorced from each other. In many ways he must be placed among those who helped to promote the mind/body split, i.e., the Cartesian method of thinking about the human spirit and the human being. Just as many fundamentalist segments of Christianity provide simplistic and absolute answers to life's questions, so does Freudian psychoanalysis. Such systems can only be true if they categorize everyone in the same mold and apply their remedies with absolutism. Freud did it by the absolutism of knowing the unconscious, and some religions do it by absolutism of knowing the soul. However, in spite of its high cost intellectually and financially, Freud's thinking has dominated much of religion, education, and medicine for most of the past century, and religion has allowed it to happen.

PSYCHOLOGICAL LANGUAGE HAS REDEFINED THEOLOGY

Theological language has permitted new definitions of basic doctrines. For instance, "forgiveness," "repentance," "transgression," "sin," and many more words that formerly had specific theological definitions have been changed. As a result, the consequences of transgression have also been changed. Even many preachers substitute "making a mistake" for "sin," and certainly there is little attention paid to the concept of "repentance." Many churches have met the sociological and psychological challenge by accepting the humanistic definition of a "feel good" life. They have accepted the linguistics of the "re-frame." As a result, there is in actuality very little, if any, difference between the language and the practice of "life changing" in or outside of most churches. Since any thinking person knows the difference between that *which is good* and that which *only feels good*, our *progress* can only produce more stress.

The church and its leaders do little if any analysis of the real religious situation. A good bit of attention is given to an analysis of the maintenance of the organization itself. Its efforts are primarily aimed at institutional survival; hence that which gains popular support is of primary value. Frequently, overly weighted values are placed on real estate, the number of people in attendance, and on programs rather than on changing human behavior.

"Side Show" Christianity

This is hardly different from other aspects of modern culture whose expressions take place in the Super Bowl, elections, and military events. The church seems to believe in the "bigger the better," the "glitzier the better," the "louder the better," and many more the "____ the better" and "more the merrier" ideas. Commercial marketing, with all the Madison Avenue hype and Hollywood techniques, television-star personalities (whether real or caricatured), and fund-raising techniques that would make the most dishonest politician blush, is now integral to many local church activities. Some local church congregations have attempted such outrageous and spectacular things that they appear to be the proverbial three-ring circus. One such church didn't just imitate the circus — it actually featured a circus act. The story was carried in a Midwest newspaper. The church featured the famous Wallenda family performing a high-wire act at a Sunday morning service (*The Springfield Newsleader*, August 30, 1998). This was a case of the sideshow stealing the circus! Radio station KWTO, AM 560, reported (October 2, 1998) that a minister, in an attempt to illustrate his sermon, pointed a 357 Magnum pistol at his head with a blank in it. He died a few days later! Everyone would agree that this is one sermon that you don't want to try at home! Another church spent literally thousands of dollars on a Fourth of July fireworks display so they could outdo the city's display — and they did. Sensationalism, entertainment, and absurdity have replaced common sense religion.

There is no need for the Church to attempt to supercede the ordinary with the spectacular. Most of us have enough trouble applying and living by the ordinary, let alone the spectacular. Attempting to meet human need with spectacular, even outrageous, methods may attract the attention of many, while the message of the ordinary may only attract a few. However, the message heard by the few represents a far greater investment than the "flash in a pan" attraction of the many.

The real problem, of course, is that the church along with so many of its members has lost sight of the extraordinary message that it possesses. It has forgotten that it has the most remarkable story that has ever been told. There is nothing ordinary about the story of God sending His Son as the atonement for our transgressions!

Measuring Success

Within the church, "success" cannot be defined by the size of the crowd or, for that matter, even what seems to be the amount of attention paid to something. We tend to utilize incorrect methods to measure "success" in the church: counting the number of people in attendance, the size of the budget, the size of the church edifice, and other materially based substitutions for spiritual growth and truly religious meaning. Few churches spend as much time considering the needs of the hungry, the homeless, the imprisoned, the downtrodden, and the poor as they do the "success" of their in-church programs.

THE GREAT COMMISSION AND THE GREAT COMMANDMENT

One obvious virtue of the great missionary movement of the 18th century was the emphasis placed on giving to others. Many churches delayed building programs and capital expansions in order to send more money overseas for missionary causes. The sacrifices were evidences of the primary mission promoted by the Church. The reduction in the missionary movement left many denominations with nothing of that magnitude to take its place. When the Church proclaimed mission and evangelism as its *raison d'etre*, it had both a stated and an obvious purpose. With both mission and evangelism less emphasized today, there is little to take its place, thus leaving an enormous vacuum in the very purpose for its being. The Great Commission given to early Christians was to go and teach all nations. The Great Commandment was that we love one another. Both are of equal importance. In many segments of the church, loving one another "just the way we are" has replaced the need for teaching what we should become. When taken to the logical conclusion, if we are fine the way we are and need no reformative education, we need neither psychology nor theology.

Both Theology and Psychology Need Guidance

Both religion and psychology seem to have lost their way. Just as the church has dead-ended in a false cultural realignment, so has psychology. Psychology has not remained true to itself any more than religion has to itself. The eminent late psychologist, O. Hobart Mowrer, argued that true psychotherapy should be without financial cost to the counselee. He believed that as long as money was involved there would be an inevitable conflict of interest between getting the patient well and discharging that person from treatment because it would result in a reduction in the therapist's income. While his stand was certainly never heeded, and may have been economically impossible, his logic is hard to deny.

It was my privilege to know Dr. Mowrer. He saw tremendous value in both religion and psychology and attempted to use them compatibly and not to confuse or to devalue either one. He saw psychology losing its way due to its economic base, and he saw religion losing its way because of its inability to understand theology in the light of our emerging knowledge about human behavior. Today with our burgeoning knowledge of the sciences, both religion and psychology will inevitably become less and less understandable — unless we are willing to allow to speak to the other without displacing each other.

Psychology lost its way in very much the same fashion as did the church — by turning its message into a business, and letting the business become primary and the message become secondary to its own survival. It is difficult to keep service primary, whether in business, medicine, psychology, or religion, when the bottom line is money.

It is easy to recognize that the fields of both religion and psychotherapy have run afoul. Clergypersons are ill equipped for the pastoral tasks of our time. Pastors attempt to provide psychotherapy — a technique in which very few ministers have been trained. Psychologists and psychiatrists attempt to struggle with the underlying failures of most problems of emotional living, which are spiritual, while denying that they are dealing in the religion business. Ministers are introduced to the need for psychological thinking, but for the most part receive very little training in human behavior. By the same token, by and large psychologists and psychiatrists, do not deny the spiritual nature of the human, but likewise receive little if any training in spiritual thinking.

Theologians look to psychology for understanding contemporary humans. Similarly, many psychologists look to theology in an attempt to make psychology existentially worthwhile. The church looks to psychology and psychological techniques for methodology for its own survival, and psychology and psychiatry look to new medications and revised techniques of mind manipulation to deal with our innermost human terrors. When psychiatry does not find new medications and techniques to change human behavior, they simply revise their diagnostic criteria as to what constitutes mental illness. Religion, when floundering, accepts an amorphous, ever-changing social philosophy to replace their interpretation of theology that does not work.

No More Temporary Fixes for Permanent Problems

Even the most successful mind-manipulation does not last in the face of new trauma. Deep within the human there is a longing for wholeness — holiness — Godliness if you will. The emotionality of the moment may be dealt with by mental-manipulation, but the soul yearns for truth that transcends daily problems. Both psychology and theology agree that in order to effect a long-lasting result, the very basis of the person must be changed. There is, of course, among psychologically trained persons considerable disagreement as to the kinds of therapy that can produce such change. There is also disagreement as to whether anything in religion or psychology can alter the basic emotional make-up of the person. There is no disagreement that as humans we seek answers that do not have to be repeated every time something goes wrong. When utilizing humanistic methods, both religion and psychology fail to recognize that their primary tools are only pacifiers, and that unless the basic spiritual problem is dealt with, only pacification can be the end result. The cry can be subdued — but not the pain!

There are many helpful aspects of religion and psychology, and even in those parts that are erroneous, the church and the psychological sciences have much in common. Both are able to keep up return business by only partially finishing the task. If the church were able to more adequately deal with our loneliness and relieve our guilt, church attendance and involvement within the community of the believers would not need much encouragement or dramatic intervention. If psychology and psychiatry were able to more adequately solve the underlying problems of depression, loneliness, and anxiety, there would be no need for constant research to find new medications or continued psychotherapy year after year. As paradoxical as it sounds, the fact that the church does not apply more theological answers and the fact that the psychological sciences do not have adequate answers are strong reasons that these institutions stay in business functioning and malfunctioning, as they do!

JUSTIFICATION: A THEOLOGICAL *PROMISE*, NOT A PSYCHOLOGICAL *PREMISE*

Let us not be mistaken. Perfection is not attainable in this life. However, an approximation of "correctness" seems to have been found by many persons following what to them is the holy life.

There is a difference between "perfection" and "justification." Theologically, at least for Christians, justification is the result of belief in God's saving grace. Therefore, we can rejoice in "just-as-if-i-cation," as if we have always been whole. The doctrine of justification does not presume perfection. Quite the contrary. If we were indeed perfect, there would be no need for the concept of justification or, for that matter, any of the Christian gospel.

Psychology can appropriately develop methodology for coping in an age of anxiety, however, herein lies another basic difference between religion and psychology. Religion is about being *spiritual*, not only how we behave. Behavior, when viewed theologically, is the result of what we believe. Psychology is about *behavior*, not about being spiritual. While some more recent psychologists have attempted to wed the two, traditionally the psychology of human behavior has been only a short step above instinct. As such, the *habit* of behavior (that which we do) outweighed the *emotion* of behavior (that which we feel). Those who attempted to wed psychology and religion found themselves trying to justify behavior with a "feeling good" definition. However, in the final analysis, society does not care how we "feel." It is concerned with how we *behave* and whether we behave in conformity with the mores and folkways of the community.

Mind Games Do Not Change Feelings Into Fact

Some believe that if we could only somehow make both behavior and "feeling" religious, there would be less of a problem. It all becomes another mind game. Parishioners play the game and ministers believe it. Patients play the game in psychotherapy and their doctors believe them. When the game is played successfully enough, the minister is convinced that the parishioner is truly religious. When the game is played successfully enough, the doctor believes the patient is cured. To the extent that it can be played "sincerely," the patient (or parishioner) has adopted the "mission" of the parent (church or psychology) and is given its blessing. Of course, the doctor and the minister must play their expected role in these mind games as well. Unfortunately, many doctors and ministers are unaware that the game even exists.

"In The Name Of" Does Not Necessarily Bless

In a further attempt to identify themselves with an integration of Christianity and psychology (thus reap its dual blessings), some psychologists have undertaken to call themselves "Christian Psychologists." It is interesting that we hear of "Christian Psychologists," but, we do not seem to hear of Buddhist, Taoist, or for that matter Jewish psychologists! It is hard to be certain why the label "Christian" is important and if so, for what purpose? Or is it a shrewd marketing tool, or is it simply a method of proselytizing, or is it politically motivated? In any event, it seems that the attempt is clearly to state that they are in some way different from those who do not identify themselves as Christians.

There is no argument that a value-oriented therapist is desirable. However, is there a guarantee that a "Christian" barber, surgeon, bricklayer, or any other professional is necessarily better equipped to meet the needs of the customer than one who is an athiest? Some Christians who proudly display the icthus (sign of the fish) on their vehicles, clothing, and other possessions have sometimes been less than competent or for that matter honest. Someone said that the ultimate discrepancy is an automobile with the sign of the fish on it running a red light. Are these professionals willing to exchange competence for a public identification with Christianity, or do they think that surely one would not question the competence of one who so advertises? Somehow it seems that some feel that what one advertises, one is — or at least becomes. It also seems that at times professionals use religious titles to cover inadequate training and less than professional service. Doubtless the best of all worlds is to have a therapist who is well trained and possesses the highest Judeo-Christian values, but does not publicly advertise it.

In truth, sometimes it is helpful to have a therapist who disagrees with our thinking. That person can sometimes bring about an honest questioning that results in insight. However, there are dangers in being treated by a person who does not share a solid value base. For instance, when one is in a state of anxiety or depression, there is greater vulnerability. At that vulnerable period of time, the psychological system suffers from a psycho-immune deficiency and may be harmed by views that seem plausible, but are contrary to the inner person of the patient. Even though the patient is unaware of his/her deep value roots, nonetheless they are in place and should not be transgressed. The therapist who is not acquainted with the patient's value system will not be able to know that these values are being transgressed. The patient is too emotionally ill to recite them properly and the therapist by virtue of being of a different orientation does not know what they are. For that reason, it is all the more important that the therapist be careful to exhibit a nonverbal as well as a verbal professional role model. There is no argument that when values are involved, and they always are, especially in counseling, the orientation of the counselor is crucial. Excessive advertising seems a bit Shakespearean in that "me thinks thou protesteth all together too much." Truly Christian counselors, like others of solid value orientation, will allow the patient to grow by virtue of the therapist's transcendence rather than preaching.

One of the serious problems in many therapist's training is that they were taught that they should not convey their values and beliefs to a patient. It is impossible to keep the things we deeply believe secret. Patients are incredibly astute at "reading" their therapist. However, since therapists cannot share identically the values of every patient they treat, respect of the person, sanctity of the patient's belief, and the therapist's sensitivity to not being any more intrusive than necessary for effective treatment are the best safeguards. In medicine there is a concept known as the TD, or therapeutic dose, which means the minimum amount of medication to produce the maximum beneficial results with the least amount of unwanted side effects. This concept will go a long way in psychotherapy as well. Most often the best formula for psychotherapy is the one that utilizes minimum intervention and produces the least disruption of the person while resulting in maximum behavioral change and insight.

RELIGION IS ABOUT WHO WE ARE — PSYCHOLOGY IS ABOUT WHAT WE DO

The message of religion is more about who we *are* than what we *do*. Psychology is primarily about *what we do* which results in *who we are*. What we think is important, so much so that Proverbs states that as a person thinks, he/she shall inevitably become. No one denies the relationship between thinking, acting, and becoming. On this point, most psychologists and theologians agree! The message of the church is deeper, however, than even this thinking. It speaks to where humans came from, who the human *is*, as well as what the human *does*. In fact, when we take theology seriously, its doctrines are deeper and more invasive than any philosophy from the social sciences. The spiritual person will often, if not usually, be at odds with contemporary thought and "worldly ideas" because as will be discussed later, they bind one to the temporal rather than the transcendent. The spiritual person's future sights will certainly outweigh temporal moorings — that is precisely why they are called "spiritual."

O.K. by Whose Standards

Being O.K. doesn't mean that we are alright. Today's church, rather than *integrating* the insights from psychology has all too often *replaced* theology with psychology. The theology of hope has been replaced with the psychology of "O.K.-ness." If the primary task of today's church is to convince us that we are indeed O.K., it leaves little work for the religious assembly, which has traditionally been to help the "not O.K." to "become O.K." If you and I are both O.K., we probably don't need either psychology or the church! The Church has always dealt with the concept of unfinished business, thus requiring faith, and in return for that faith, it promised hope. When we take away hope and accept what we are as "O.K.," we know we are in deep trouble because our "O.K.-ness" is anything but acceptable even to ourselves! By the way, the concept of "O.K." was the result of Van Buren's run for president in 1840. He was nicknamed "Old Kinderhook"(O.K.) after his birthplace. He lost, but the term O.K. stuck (*Webster's Encyclopedic Dictionary*).

The term "O.K." in American psychology is largely attributable to a book published by Thomas Harris called, *I'm O.K., You're O.K.* (1974). The "O.K.-ness" movement was a direct attempt to make us *feel* good in spite of often *doing* bad. It is pseudopsychology based upon the burgeoning humanistic thinking of that time. At the time Harris' book was published, Western Christianity was losing members and starting to preach psychotheology, the religion of psychological humanism. Since theology asserts that God loves us in spite of our behavior, "O.K. theology" and "O.K. psychology" were both acceptable because they had become one and the same.

The church has allowed its parishioners to browse the church and theology in much the same manner as if the church were a shopping mall. Members determine what it means and what parts of it they want. Selective theology, of course, results in a highly individualized practice of religion in daily life. This would seem to be a healthy approach to religious life — but it is not. The problem is that many individuals attempt to inflict their individual interpretation on all the other parishioners. This is particularly true in smaller denominations and congregations where clergy are "called to preach" and little if any formal education or training is required.

Parishioners interpret the church's message to themselves, each other, and "the heathen" without knowing either the interpretation or what it is they are interpreting! It reminds one of a giant flea market where what you see is what you get!

Even the Church Can Be Deceptive

The church spends a great deal of time and money making their parishioners' perceptions come true, even if those perceptions are against its own doctrines and theological creeds. Think of the irony of the church — to utilize the proverbial inkblot test — as an approach to the soul. The time-honored Rorschach test, a projective technique devised by Hermann Rorschach which is designed to cause patients to reveal what they see in inkblots, is only valuable if the interpreter of those projections is trained and wise. The story has been told many times of the patient who was asked by the doctor why all of his projections were sexual in nature. The patient replied, "Why should I know, they're your pictures!" Things *are* as we interpret them. The doctor, in this instance, assumes that his/her interpretations are correct and those which differ are in some way incorrect because they do not conform to the average answer. Using a consensus of the average to determine correctness is fraught with extremely dangerous problems, (discussed later in this book). The church is caught in this dilemma also.

THE PROBLEM IS NOT THE STAIN OF THE SOUL ON SOCIETY, BUT THE STAIN OF SOCIETY ON THE SOUL

We are unable to see what *is* or what *ought to be*. As with the Rorschach test, we can only look at the strange, nondescript blots and project and, with even less assurance, guess at the reality of what we project. Our projections are not clear — we have not stained society, at least not at first, but we have allowed society to deeply implant itself within us. Therefore, we cannot blame the ills of society on anything other than a reciprocal relationship between our sin-seeking selves and that which we have wreaked upon society as a result of accepting society as the God of norms.

Psychology by definition measures the soul against society and against accepted societal norms. These norms are known in sociological theory as "mores" and "folkways," i.e., the behavior that has come to be accepted as "normal," "acceptable," and "socially responsible" by a given culture. To the extent that theological thought is bound to higher standards, i.e., more "Godly" behavior and more than "earth-bound" thinking, it may and often will diverge from "mores" and "folkways." Theology, by definition, must see the soul in contradiction to society for its own redemption. The person who is whole does not need a physician, and those already redeemed need no redemption. In order to be redemptive, theology must be in opposition to that which damns us!

It Doesn't Really Matter What You Call It

The problem is one of reality, not interpretation. That which is real is not changed by calling it something else. Furthermore, understanding the difference between reality and our interpretation of it is extremely difficult. The story is told of three baseball umpires discussing their methods for "calling a strike." The first umpire said, "As I see it, I call it;" the second umpire said, "No, you are wrong. Whatever it is, is what I call it;" the third and very well-seasoned umpire said, "You are both wrong. What I call it is what it is!" So it is with both psychology and religion — what we call it is what it becomes. We have confused labels with reality. Calling "sin," "human error" does not change it. Karl Menninger, M.D., a world famous psychiatrist, called our attention to this fact in his famous book, *Whatever Became of Sin?* (1973). We may psychologize human actions, we may make the action sound more palatable, and we may rationalize it because "everyone is doing it," but the effects are the same — emotional confusion, personal and interpersonal dysfunction, and self-delusionment which leads to even greater psychic imbalance.

Although the message of the church can accomplish much with a proper and correct understanding psychology, it also risks failure by offering artificial and superficial, even magical, answers to life's real problems. The great value of organized religion is the promise of thought, behavioral and life change. Magic supplies the illusion of change, but only reality produces real change.

It Is Not Magical — It Is Mystical

Theological thinking is not magical — it is mystical. Magical thinking and mystical thinking are not the same. A belief that a given happening transcends human understanding (mysticism) is very different from a happening produced to persuade others of one's own power over the physical universe (magic). Herein lies a huge problem between the concrete, absolute kind of thinking often found in fundamentalist theology and the sometimes altogether too abstract thinking of the extreme liberal. Magical thinking destroys omnipotence, omniscience, and omnipresence. These are attributes of our Creator, Who in any and all religions must be given knowledge, power, and a presence not attributable to humankind. Magical thinking and mystical thinking have both been misused to fool the common mind and hold parishioners in the control of certain theological (and political) regimes. Some persons choose to speak of the "supra-natural" rather than the "super-natural," indicating that God is of the epiphomenal as well as the phenomenal. True mystical thought is beyond the "supernatural" and by definition is epiphenomenal.

The critical difference between magical thinking and mystical thinking is that magical thinking allows one to believe deception, whereas mystical thinking leaves one without an answer, simply leaving one knowing that it is beyond human understanding. In the simplest form of fundamentalist theological thinking, if one attends church, tithes, or performs some other demonstrable act, then the following week (or in some acceptable period of time), a "good thing" happens. The believer is assured that the two events are cause and effect. That is *magical* thinking. If we look at life honestly, very good things happen to all of us all of the time. They certainly are not in any way linked to the "good" things we have done. We cannot explain them and, further, we do not attempt to link them together. This is *mysticism*.

THE CHURCH IS IN THE HORNS OF A DILEMNA

The church stands squarely between two positions: promising a message which will deliver the soul from human suffering and at the same time accomplishing the task of ultimate redemption. To help people feel good while living badly is not a reasonable solution. While this is very desirable, humanly speaking, the two may be mutually exclusive. It is certainly understandable why organizations would be tempted to utilize every bit of truth, trickery, and bribery to produce these unattainable results.

Psychology, while attempting to promise behavioral healing, can only bring about adaptation and coping, not redemption. Psychology and religion seem to envy each other, and rather than keeping their tasks straight, get them all mixed up. Some do their best to make the two disciplines complimentary, but often produce only competition. Cooperation seems like such a fine word, and something that surely no one could criticize. However, cooperation can readily become confusion. As we are all reminded daily, it is difficult to remember our job when wading in the swamps with the alligators!

Clergy Must Decide Who They Are and How Many Hats to Wear

The clergyperson's role, vocabulary, practical application, and self-image have become increasingly that of the psychologist. The phrases of Freud and Jung have more and more replaced the words of Luther, Calvin, St. Thomas Aquinas, St. Paul, and for that matter even Jesus. Sermons are extrapolations of daily conflict, and the pseudotheological answers are actually humanistic psychology. Christianity has taken on the definition of Neo-Christianity, namely, "any interpretation of Christianity based on the prevalent philosophy of a given period" (*Webster's New Revised Edition Encyclopedic Unabridged Dictionary*, 1996, p. 957). The church, which prides itself in being timeless in its doctrine, cannot escape looking at itself in a Neo-Christian framework, since so much of its time and energy is spent in the context of current and prevalent philosophy.

The transition into a Neo-Christian psychotheology was easy. It is not difficult to understand why the church and its leaders have constantly sought out new vocabularies and new *modus operandi*. After all, have not the mainline denominations lost more members than they have recruited? Have not more persons sought peace of mind through psychotherapy than through the sacraments? Given the need for personal survival, occupational security, and organizational procreation, what institution would not in the face of "death rattles" seek some kind of CPR (cardiopulmonary resuscitation)? "Religious CPR" has been used by both the Protestant and Roman Catholic Church in nearly a literal sense. The heartbeat (cardio) and breathing (pulmonary) of the church have faltered, plunging the church into a "code blue." Not unlike what would happen in a hospital with such a fatal-looking situation, the "doctors" of the church have rushed in with their "psycho-socio-politico-theological" crash carts and attempted to administer a combination of last rites and resuscitation using a strange mixture of secular and sacred remedies.

Psychological Language Is Frequently Not Even Good Psychology!

Much of the psychological language adopted by the church is in truth not even good psychology. The new "Sacrament of Psychology" leaves the church with artificial spirituality, an inadequate and incorrect concept of the human person, excessive emphasis upon behavior, and a psycho-babble vocabulary that would not be understood by either Freud or Jesus, let alone those who would be followers of either of them!

Popular theology turns out to be *humanistic* psychology. This is the psychology largely developed by psychologists early in the 20th century, many of whom were educated in both psychology and theology. Many were disenchanted with the teachings of Freud, but unable to accept the teachings of Jesus. Must we believe that mental health is the kingdom of God? This is not to say that the kingdom of God does not contain mental health, for it must. It is to say, however, that our temporal definition of mental health is very different and diametrically opposed to the values of God's kingdom. Few would equate physical health with heaven. Why should we do so with mental health? Yet this has clearly become a central message in many religious institutions.

This humanistic development was extremely harmful and unfortunate for Christian theology. Sigmund Koch (an honored philosopher/psychologist, now deceased) was quoted by David E. Leary in *American Psychologist* (Volume 56, Number 5, May 2001). Koch said, "... humanistic psychology embraced a conception of many which, if anything, was more reductive, demeaning, and callow than that of behaviorism ... by baring all, by making the private indisputably public, humanistic psychology reduced, even erased, the distinctiveness of individuals. At least behaviorism left the private alone!" Behaviorism has always been viewed by theologians as being grossly adversarial to the Christian doctrine of God's work in the human soul. Koch may not have realized how strongly he would speak to the church when he stated that humanistic psychology is even more damaging than behaviorism. Koch was essentially a cultural historian; therefore, his message is particularly important for the church to hear since it endures and its leaders speak to all cultures in all times. Koch (1992) made a remarkably strong statement to psychology and theology alike when he said, "... inviting a change of heart is a surer bridge to a tolerable future than any confident methodological manifesto." Although primarily speaking to a scientific, not theological audience, Koch brings devastating knowledge to theologians who would replace Christian theology with humanistic psychology!

It is not difficult to understand that the church is in trouble defending its integrity when it claims to "reconcile sinners" and at the same time teaches a solely humanistic "I'm O.K., You're O.K." — when by its own theology, neither is O.K. The church and all Christian theology strongly believes and teaches that apart from a mind and life-changing relationship with God, humanity is *absolutely not O.K.*!

Psychology Has Offered More Than It Can Deliver, Too

The mental health movement has promised more than it can deliver. As Dr. Alex Delaware, the fictional psychologist, contends, the psychologist's job is to patch up, assuage, and massage patients into feeling okay. To Dr. Delaware's creator, Jonathan Kellerman (a trained, Ph.D., psychologist), the story is fiction. But the church got it mixed up. The church bought the promise of psychology and is still waiting for the delivery! Rather than allowing psychological insights to bring greater insight into human thought and behavior, and producing a foundation for greater spiritual growth, all too often the psychology of improved human feeling and behavior has become an end in itself.

More "confessions" are given to psychotherapists than to priests. In the psychological setting, it is called "catharsis." Patients pay their hard-earned money to be granted "acceptance" by the therapist. The same thing in the church is called "forgiveness." It is interesting that patients are willing to pay money for a therapist's "acceptance" more readily than they are willing to accept God's forgiveness which is free when offered by a minister or priest. It may well be that this is further evidence that in many people's minds, psychology and religion are basically the same thing, and that in their beliefs, psychology and religion both *believe* the same thing and *provide* the same services. Is it possible that forgiveness is more credible when it costs money and is granted by a secular priest?

If only God can provide forgiveness, why do we look for it elsewhere? It is because we have imbued many other organizations within our society with the same sanctity and attributes as the church. We fail to see the critical distinction between organizations that attempt to "do good," and those that proclaim God. Society looks increasingly to the health industry for definitions of good and evil. We deny the obvious relationship between behavior and health. Alcohol and tobacco are two outstanding illustrations in our society that without argument lead to illness and death. Yet, psychology, medicine, and the church are equally grossly errant in their treatment of both. The concept of "sin" has been replaced with "sickness." Is this because sickness is more excusable than sin? Or is it because we are unwilling to accept the sameness of the two? None of our social institutions, including the church, practice as if they understand the word "holos," which is the root word for everything they say they are about, namely, health and holiness.

Ministers and priests flock to workshops on group therapy techniques, seminars on counseling methods, and encounter groups. The interesting fact is that although this describes the behavior of parish ministers and priests, academic institutions and seminaries which train ministers and priests have only slightly increased the actual course work in the psychological sciences. Do their leaders recognize something which they have not told us, namely, that while they know that psychological techniques are helpful, such techniques are just that, tools, not the message? No doubt many are of this persuasion. However, when their graduates discover that the message doesn't seem to result in their misguided ideas about success, they turn the tool into the task and the method becomes the message.

The Best Minds Have Tried to Integrate Psychology and Religion

Many leading minds have honestly tried to integrate religion and psychology. Smiley Blanton, M.D., one of the co-founders of the American Foundation of Religion and Psychiatry, stated, "My conception of psychiatry's role in this great effort is exactly what it was two decades ago. It is the removal of barriers in the unconscious mind that keep people from accepting or responding to the message of hope and joy and wholeness that religion has to offer. In no sense is psychiatry a substitute for religion. It is a partner, and a very important one" (1959, p. 216). Blanton did not see psychiatry as a replacement, but as a method for removing the hindrances in us so that we could allow the channels of our person to open up to God's love. The church must return to the concept that health and wholeness (holiness) are one and the same. In so doing, theology can be its own powerful psychotherapeutic tool and the message of God's love can be untainted by humanistic psychology's definitions.

Knowledge Is of God — Use of It Is in Human Hands

Knowledge about how the brain functions is neither good nor bad. Psychology is the study of the function, i.e., how the brain operates and how as a result that function relates to structure, i.e., the actual anatomy of the brain. Neurology is the study of the structure of the brain and how that structure functions when normal and abnormal.

These two sciences are full of methods. The methods are neither good nor bad. They are intended to enable us to learn more about how the human being functions and when it is malfunctioning, what can be done about it. Neither discipline is *moral*, per se. Both are sciences without an inherent morality or the lack thereof. Psychology determines if the person is functioning within reality and the scope of social acceptance. Medicine determines if the body organ is healthy and functioning within the laws of body biochemistry. "Scientific" generations to come will demonstrate how right or wrong our "knowledge" is just as this generation has demonstrated it to our predecessors. It continues, and always will be, the task of the scientist/practitioner to use knowledge toward Godly ministry.

THEOLOGY IS THE MESSAGE —
THE HOLY SPIRIT IS THE METHOD

Theology is something quite different. Theology is the message — not the method. As a message, it has no inherent power to manipulate or to serve as a method. Christian theology undergirds itself with the doctrine of the Holy Spirit that serves as the energizer, the messenger, the One who must become involved, as the method. *Thus, once again we see that theology is the message and the Holy Spirit is the method.*

The concerns of religion and psychotherapy are very much the same. Both are concerned with "guilt," "acceptance," "damnation," and a myriad of other issues. As has been stated many times already in this chapter, although they may call issues by different names, the internal spiritual and psychological dynamic are basically the same. The individual is only able to distinguish between them based on learned vocabulary. If a person has been raised in the church, that person will probably use theological terms, such as "guilt," "forgiveness, and "salvation/damnation." If that person was raised non-church, the vocabulary will be "acceptance," "resolution," and psychological healing. Once again we see how confusing it is when the languages of sociology, anthropology, and the social sciences are applied to theology.

Many persons in the church have attempted to share the language of psychology, however, more often than not, the sharing became a one-way street with the church in truth copying it. Both the church and psychotherapy are intrigued and confused by the other's vocabulary. In order to avoid overidentification with each other, they simply call the same problems by different names. In fact, without knowing it, the church aided and abetted, and more than significantly assisted in the birth and development of humanistic psychology. Now in today's preaching, humanistic psychology is the operative language of theology.

Both Professions Often Sincerely Want the Same Thing

The *message* they both wish to convey is essentially the same, however, the methods they use are very different. Many ministers and psychotherapists alike recognize the confusion and also know the extent to which they rely upon the other discipline. It has not been professionally acceptable to admit such in most church or psychological circles. The church doesn't want to be seen as a psychological service center, and psychotherapists seem to work very hard not to be seen as religious. Strange that each steals so much of the other's thunder, but each is afraid to be seen as doing so!

Psychological methods are worldly — not wrong! They are *methods, not messages.* Furthermore, the methods are differentiated as to who can benefit from them. These definitions vary from the amount of insight one possesses to the size of one's financial ability. Long before there was a discipline called psychology, its principles were applied in society and within the church. Psychology has helped to upgrade the educational program of the church, as it has all education. It has offered a base of understanding about how and why people behave as they do. In recent years, however, an unfortunate romance has developed around the word "psychology." Books that otherwise would not have sold have become best-sellers, and nearly every daily newspaper has its own "Dear_____". Radio and television talk shows are fraught with lay, pseudoprofessional, and real professional advisors. Programs that a few years ago would have been considered lewd, pornographic, insulting, debasing, and vulgar are now commonplace. The legal tender of these programs is to see who can reveal in public the most disgusting lifestyle. It is not possible to estimate the amount of human suffering and psychological (not to mention spiritual) damage that is done. It is absolutely scary to think that people would change their life mate, alter their job, or make truly life-changing decisions based on a thirty-second talk-show answer — but it happens every day!

Christian Commitment Does Not Replace Professional Training and Credentials

The church has become vulnerable to public display of inappropriate behavior. We now have workshops to train counselors and clinics to help lay persons solve their own problems, all with the aim of returning these people to the church to help lead others through the morass of their own lives. These self-appointed and self-annointed "psychological saviors" vicariously enjoy a false sense of accomplishment and believe that now that they have saved their own psyches, they have the right and duty to operate on the unsaved psyches of others.

However, professional psychology is not a gimmick or trick to attract crowds or to give people a false sense of personal growth. It is to help us better understand, predict, and treat human behavior. The church, therefore, must look seriously at this trend to overly psychologize and the trend to expect ministers to be psychoanalysts. Both Jesus (Matthew 7:15) and St. Paul (Philippians 3:2) exhorted their followers to beware of false teachers and evil workers. If they were teaching today, they might well exhort us to beware of the false claims made by the new breed of false prophets, the pseudopsychologists, the "psycho-theologists," and the "theo-psychologists."

This is not to say that the church should not address itself to the personal and domestic woes of our day. Nor is it to say that professionals should not participate in the life of the church or not offer their knowledge and services to help. On the contrary, ministers, priests, and rabbis who work within their parishes on a day-to-day basis attempting to understand psychological principles and properly apply them are to be applauded. However, the distance between what is truly "professional" and what is often passed off as "religious psychology" is often a chasm apart. The real problem is with the partially or ill-trained "therapist," whether that person be clergy or laity. It is easier to open emotional doors than it is to close them. One should not open doors that cannot be closed, particularly in other persons' lives. Our unconscious problems are entirely too sacred and too dangerous to be flushed out into the open unless they can be dealt with adequately, and professionally, finding resolution. It is often said, "Listening never hurt anyone." This is patently false. Silence can be the most powerful speech given. Silence can be interpreted by the listener in ways the speaker would never guess. Listening, by silent assent, often gives permission.

There have been divorces, suicides, homicides, and other heinous crimes because the counselee interpreted silence as approval. A school of psychotherapy known as Rogerian (named after its founder, Dr. Carl Rogers) has been misinterpreted by many therapists and misused, particularly by ministers and other lesser-trained psychotherapists because they see this method as being particularly compatible with theology. The Rogerian method is non-judgmental and permissive and claims to give "unconditional positive regard" to the counselee. Since its methodology is primarily listening and reflecting back what the counselee says, many have assumed it to be harmless at least if not helpful. No well-trained psychologist, including Dr. Rogers (under whom I studied and whom I knew well), would claim this to be true.

Damage is particularly likely if the counselor is trusted and believed to be "credentialed" by the counselee. Unfortunately, there are double standards concerning who can counsel within religious organizations and those who must meet rigorous licensing requirements in secular practice. If a person is labeled a "counselor" within the church, most people assume that he/she possesses the proper training and credentials. Unfortunately such is not always the case. On occasion the church may not feel the need or have the "know-how" to check out the credentials of persons they enlist for this extremely important and potentially dangerous ministry. Many congregations have been led down the path of pseudopsychology by a quack in expert's clothing.

Don't Be Distracted

All of the social sciences can have value for the church when used within the scope and purpose of the church. The problem is that church leaders can become enamored with the fad aspects of the sciences and then attempt to use the knowledge of them without sufficient training. They forget that they are only tools toward an end and that their end may be quite different from the intended end of the church's message.

We must remember that spirituality is not necessarily the same as mental health. The diagnostic definition of health is not what is meant by spirituality. Although the words health, holy, whole, holiness, and several other similar words are all derived from the same Greek word, *holos*, in a not-so-perfect world, there are many persons who suffer indescribable pain who are indeed holy. The Church cannot provide total wholeness or holiness. It attempts to provide the basis for spiritual living and hopeful dying. The message and mission of the church is spirituality for all people, even those who are emotionally blocked and/or in financial, personal, and spiritual poverty. The message is aimed at evangelizing sinners — not psychologizing the "worried well." The task of the church is not to join what appears to be the winning team in every generation, but to "stay the course." Winning, by definition, is not the mission — the mission is the journey.

2

Why America's Churches Are Failing

Offering a palliative psychotheology may be what parishioners like to feel, but it is not what they know they need deep in their hearts.

TO DEBATE WHETHER THE Christian religion in the United States is failing or not is to be patently blind. Reports are numerous showing the decline in membership, finances, and attendance in most of the mainline churches. The decline is due to many unknown factors, but there are a wide variety of quite readily identifiable reasons.

THE CONSUMER FRAME OF MIND

Consumerism is rooted in hedonism, the here and now, and in the accumulation and enjoyment of earthly things. One is reminded of the bumper sticker, "The one that dies with the most toys wins." Alexis de Tocqueville in 1831 observed that, "Americans cleave to the things of this world as if assured that they will never die, and yet are in such a rush to snatch any that come within their reach, as if expecting to stop living before they have relished them. They clutch everything but hold nothing fast, and so lose grip as they hurry after some new delight" (Mayer, 1969, p. 536). This astute observation was given by a Frenchman visiting the United States over 160 years ago! Things have not changed that much, and society, government, education, and for that matter, the church have done little to change this blatant exhibition of our greed. It could be easily argued that all of these social institutions have assisted with making the matter worse.

Youth largely enjoys the fruits of the former generation's labors, basks in a peace purchased by previous generation's ultimate sacrifices, and fails to recognize that one who dares to undertake a task without counting the cost is a fool. The church has not sufficiently countered this counterculture. As a result, the church has given way to a most insidious form of consumerism. Of all institutions, the church is particularly indictable to have done this, since it has always claimed to know what the consumer needs. For the church to give in to this kind of pressure shows an inherent weakness in its leadership. Offering a palliative psychotheology might be what parishioners like to feel, but it is not what they know they need deep in their hearts.

CONSUMERS ARE VENDORS, TOO

Consumerism in public business life is a very different thing. Customers go to a store to purchase their *perceived* needs and tell the merchant what they want to buy. In this case the merchant does not know what the customer really needs and must usually cater to their requests. In the case of the church, it is not the same. The church claims by virtue of its divine origin and knowledge to *know what we need* and with God's help to be able to deliver it! The bind of giving what the consumer wants, against what the consumer needs, has cost the church its vitality and integrity. This is much the same as educational institutions which have lost their way because students now tell the teachers what they as students should learn. It seems that we have ignored why teachers teach and why students are not the teachers. The church, however, is different than most businesses in that it not only claims to be accountable to its parishioners, but also to God. It claims to know what its members need and promises to deliver it, thus failing both God and its members.

THE CHURCH LOST ITS MISSION

The history of the New Testament church is steeped in missions and evangelism. The very first New Testament churches were deeply involved in both. Missions and evangelism were one and the same thing. They were the sole reasons for the church to exist. They were seen as God's specific directive to those who would be disciples. The church sent missionaries to the four corners of the then-known world. They traveled the roads, sailed the seas, and corresponded at great lengths in the interest of missionary evangelism. St. Paul himself had no less than three famous missionary journeys on which he established churches all across Asia Minor. From that time until the early 1970s, all churches (some more than others), regardless of denomination, were heavily invested in both mission work and evangelism. Churches rated their "success" by how much money they gave to missionary causes and how many souls were brought into the church. From the early 1900s until the mid-1970s, there were very popular and, for that matter, quite successful endeavors in both missions and evangelism. The Youth For Christ movement, which was largely responsible for the rise in popularity of persons such as The Reverend Billy Graham, the Child Evangelism movement that held after-school programs for children, the Gideons who placed Bibles in virtually every hotel in the world, the Christian Business Men's Association, the Christian Business Women's Association, the Fisherman's Club, the Promise Keepers, and many other movements unabashedly continue to attempt to convert unbelievers.

Only a few of these organizations have the vitality and popularity they enjoyed in earlier years. The Rev. Billy Graham is widely recognized as one example who continues to stand out as a faithful "voice in the wilderness." Citywide evangelistic crusades were popular in the 1950s and 1960s, with nationally recognized evangelists, huge choirs, and attendance reaching into the thousands. There is a movement toward continuing and reviving the mass-meeting approach with today's televised and charismatic evangelists.

These attempts, and many more, were and largely are conservative, even fundamentalist, in both mission and evangelism. However, the more liberal mainline denominations were also actively at work, particularly in missions. Most of the denominations which were members of the National Council of Churches cooperated in a central missionary training center, the Stony Point Missionary Orientation program, that was located in Stony Point, New York. Persons commissioned by most of the major denominations as overseas missionaries spent approximately three months at this center. If there was a spouse and children, they also attended and participated. The adults spent every day in study, worship, training, personal and family evaluation, and even psychological assessment as to the fitness for overseas religious duty. Other denominations such as the Southern Baptists, Conservative Baptists, Assemblies of God, and the Roman Catholic Church maintained their own programs for many of the same purposes.

These programs demonstrated the two main issues which dominated the Western church from its inception until the mid-1970s: namely, missionary and evangelistic emphasis. They were the *cause celeb* and tugged at church member's hearts and purse strings. Missions and evangelism gave the church cause to exist and, very importantly, purposeful daily activity. Furthermore, they hit at the heart of human need, namely, the need to care for our own and the need to care for others. The evangelistic aspect was largely focused on those on the North American continent. The aim was to evangelize and bring every possible person into the church. The missions emphasis was largely "foreign," meaning that persons were supported and sent to foreign countries to live, learn the language, translate the Bible into those languages, and to evangelize via teaching, preaching, nursing, medicine, agriculture, and much more.

These and a variety of other methods were used to improve the life, health, education, and society of those countries. Never mind that many of those attempts are now seen in retrospect as being in error and ill-guided. The intent was honorable, even if less than fully informed, as we now understand it. Nevertheless, the purpose gave the church a *raison d'etre*, and the rallies held to promote both missions and evangelism were electrifying. There was no question in the minds of any segment of the church, from the most fundamentalist in theology to the most liberal, that the essential mission of the church was the "Great Commission" given in Matthew 28:19–20, "Go therefore and make disciples of all nations, baptizing them in the name of the Father and of the Son and of the Holy Spirit, and teaching them to obey everything that I have commanded you." The basic mission of the church was clear. There was a specific job to do and an order to get it done. Furthermore, the order was urgent — "before it is too late." Although philosophies and methods for accomplishing the job may have varied, there was no disagreement as to what the job was and the urgency of getting on with it. Although the methods of the most conservative denominations differed drastically from those of the more liberal denominations, the end objective was the same — convert the heathen.

From an organizational point of view, whether one agrees with either the efforts and methods of evangelism or mission, these two factors gave the church a rallying cause and purpose. The cause was unifying. Petty issues could not be considered when souls were dying without salvation. All segments of the church saw the need to work together in the interest of reaching as many souls as possible, particularly those that emphasized the "last days" type of theology. It was important to work while one still could before the Second Coming of Christ. As a well-known hymn states, the task was urgent, "Work, for the night is coming, when man works no more." (This song is designated in many hymnals as a "work song.") The cause was immediate and demanding. One could not give in to self-ishness when such an important ministry was calling. The cause, as the lyrics of another well-known church song states, "Give of your best to the Master, Give of the strength of your youth." The cause was challenging. The job was too big to get done. There was no possibility of evangelizing the whole world before nightfall, but it was necessary to make every effort to do so. It would take all Christians everywhere to even make a dent. As a result, even though the Western church has always been fraught with divisions and dis-agreements, there was no disagreement on this issue. While they agreed on little else, there were many unified attempts between denominations to effect both missions and evangelism.

Both of these causes have largely been lost, certainly in the mainline church. Most missionary training centers no longer exist, with rare exception the huge rallies of evangelism are gone, the mis-sionary conferences with true "war stories" are seldom encountered, and that great zeal cannot be found in many places today regardless of theological position.

The term "missionary" was viewed as too "paternalistic" and "superior." It was felt that other cultures could not relate well to persons who had come from far distances to change them. The term "missionary" no longer represented the task at hand as the church saw it. Of course, by this time sociological and psychological sophis-tication had found its way into theological thinking. So if the church were to be internally consistent, it would need to stop attempting to change people. Instead, it was deemed important to allow self-hood and dignity of the individual, regardless of belief. As a result, the term missionary had become obsolete. There is no doubt that "missionaries" could be culturally insensitive and thus did considerable damage when viewed through anthropological eyes. However, with the change in nomenclature also came a change in mission and purpose. The purpose, although never couched in this phrase, was basically to westernize Third World countries. There was a firm belief that health, food, sanitation, safety, and democracy were theologically solid premises. It is quite true that "wholeness" of human living, including Christian living, incorporates many of these fineries. However, the difficulty arose not in including those aspects *into* the gospel, but in assuming that those items *were* the gospel. The direction and intent of the message was in question. Can health, sanitation, and safety lead to righteousness? Or does righteousness lead to health, sanitation, and safety? Herein lies the most fundamental of all theological debates revolving around evangelism and mission.

Missionaries were replaced with "fraternal workers" and later with "overseas personnel." Some of these changes were brought about by honest recognition of the value of other cultures and our ineptness and intrusiveness. However, the changes were also brought about by less available money for the church to finance its mission and a loss of interest in the two primary directives of the church, namely, missions and evangelism. The church also got caught up in the tremendous cultural, racial, and political conflicts at home. Its energies and funds were sorely strapped just to maintain itself at home, let alone try to evangelize the world.

This book is not the place to argue about what happened or why both missions and evangelism have suffered greatly and in some quarters have been all but lost. It is the place, however, to state that these two causes were the glue of the church and that glue is now largely gone. Of equally great concern is what will take their place. An organization cannot exist without a cause.

Many Church Members No Longer Believe or Practice What the Church Teaches

Most parishioners admit to giving lip service to the dogma set forth by their church on the philosophical aspects of belief. However, when it comes to agreeing with the church on the basic conflicts of our day, such as abortion (including partial birth abortion), right-to-life, capital punishment, homosexuality, ordaining homosexual ministers, the role of women in the church, same-sex marriages, parenthood by nonmarried (no intent to become married) persons, adoption of children by same-sex parents, doctor-assisted suicide, euthanasia, and many other issues, there is open opposition and frank disagreement. Certain elements of the "basic faith" are seen as essential, such as The Sermon on the Mount, the "Golden Rule," and the Ten Commandments. There is, however, almost no Biblical knowledge on the part of many members. In a recent Sunday School class of affluent university-trained adults, in a mainline Protestant Church, most class members could not name the books of the Bible or identify which books are in the Old Testament and which ones are in the New Testament. Although this is doubtless not true in all church groups, it is illustrative of a major loss of knowledge among some. Most did not know that the Protestant Christian Bible consists of 66 books. Many were unaware that the historical Roman Catholic Bible differs in the number of books in it, and very few knew the term Apocrypha (the name for the books between the Old and New Testaments in the Roman Catholic Bible). In spite of how little Protestants know about the Bible, it is common for Roman Catholics who transfer to Protestant congregations to remark even how much less they know by comparison. Considering that Christians believe the Bible to be their chart and compass for life, this admitted ignorance is astounding.

To most churchgoers, The Sermon on the Mount is seen as a humanistic guide to life, the "Golden Rule" is seen as helpful in human relations, and the Ten Commandments seem like good suggestions. There appears to be very little difference, if any, in the value and meaning of the Bible between regular churchgoers and nonattendees.

Church members are also frank in admitting the gross discrepancy between what their church teaches and what they actually practice in daily life. They also admit to the vast difference between those creeds to which they *ascribed* upon joining the church and what they now *actually believe*. They see what the church *claims* to espouse — against what it *actually* espouses — as an excellent goal to work toward, i.e., a kind of ethereal creed that is probably being practiced in heaven, but not to be taken seriously for working in our competitive, corrupt, troubled life on earth. We hear words such as "in a perfect world," these principles would work very well. The problem is that these principles were not given for a perfect world, but with the intent to make an imperfect world less imperfect.

What the church claims to teach and that which it actually teaches by modeling, action, and omission is quite different. People like hearing what makes them feel good; that which affirms them; and that which gives them permission to be different, yet individual and unique — even if that individualism runs squarely in the face of the stated beliefs of the church. We like differentiating the sin from the sinner because, as a result, we do not have to identify with our own indiscretions.

The "I'm O.K., You're O.K." approach of modern ecclesiology makes folks feel good and pretend that nobody is not O.K. It is a nice but nevertheless dwindling "O.K. Corral"!

Members Do Not Support the Church With Their Dollars

The rise in social agencies and community organizations which now tap into the pockets of church and synagogue members is huge and growing. Members no longer trust religious institutions to properly invest their money. Dollars that a few years ago went into the weekly collection plate are now given to the Red Cross, the United Way, local homeless support groups, shelters for victims of violence, community foundations, and other philanthropic agencies.

These, and many other fine organizations, are more and more becoming identified as *part* of the church. Recently, while stranded in a snowstorm in an airport, I asked several likewise stranded travelers, "What is the best thing churches do?" The answers were astounding. Several said, "Give money to the poor," but they were quick to add that they didn't think many churches do much of that. Others listed other social agency functions, which are not done by the institutionalized church either.

It is true that social agencies do good, and doing good is certainly a function of the Christian and the church, but, their basic *purpose* for doing good is fundamentally different. Social agencies try to assist humankind with a better life here and now. The church claims to utilize a better life here and now in preparation for a "soul purpose," i.e., salvation. Social agencies are concerned only about the here and now. The church by absolute creed claims to be concerned with entrance into the next life, and, in the meantime, the care of brothers and sisters everywhere.

Confusion about the purpose and function of the church is shared both by Western Protestantism and Roman Catholicism alike. The Roman Catholic Church, which in some parts of the world has done a better job in retaining its constituency (largely in the Latin Third World countries), in the United States is struggling with the same decline in attendance as are mainline Protestant churches. This difficulty is evidenced by the necessity of having to sell church buildings and make major cutbacks in outreach due to financial shortfalls. There is a critical shortage of candidates for the priesthood and sisterhood, as well as a current shortage of priests and nuns in the Roman Catholic Church. A recent convention of bishops in the Vatican was assembled specifically to address the serious loss of members from the Roman Catholic Church. The Reformation of Martin Luther, of course, began the historical exodus. However, the Roman Catholic Church was in serious decay long before the Reformation. Unfortunately, the Reformation dealt primarily with theology and didn't do much to change the actual day-to-day functioning of either the church or its leaders. It would take pages upon pages to thoroughly document this statement; however, it is evident in the writings of the post-Reformation leaders that such is the case.

People give money to that in which they believe. Political campaigns certainly prove that point! People do not necessarily give to that which they think is "right," or even "good," but to that which they think will win for them. If they think that their gift will make life better for them individually, they will give until it hurts and keep on giving. This can be seen even more dramatically in Third World countries, where poverty-stricken believers crawl on painful, bleeding knees across rough cobblestones to give their last peso to the church, while there is no food on the table! If the soul can be persuaded, the most dire poverty in the world does not stop people from giving to that in which they believe.

Some church members do not have the money to contribute. *USA Today* (Tuesday, February 13, 2001) as a front-page story reported that "Debt smothers young Americans." The story continued, "For many living in a world of easy credit, digging out of debt can become a way of life: 18 to 35-year-olds, often live paycheck to paycheck, using credit for restaurant meals and high-tech toys. A new study says the average undergraduate student owes $2,747 on credit cards." These young persons are reported to believe that they must take care of themselves and do not believe that Social Security will be available to them. Their generation's net worth fell from $12,700 to $9,000 between 1995 to 1998 in spite of the fact that the net worth of all other age groups rose. Youth are less prone to invest in home ownership, willing to pay exorbitantly high interest rates on credit card debts, and are more willing to live with excessive debt as a comfortable way of life.

There are always persons regardless of their debt-to-living ratio that can be convinced that giving is a good thing — but can the church be that convincing? Will it too take credit cards for the Sunday offering? And if so, is it willing to be part of the financial doomsday for that generation? Nickel and dime offerings will not pay for the high-tech, huge building programs that some churches are undertaking.

Ambassador magazine (January 1997) reported that contributions from the middle class dropped a staggering 20% from the years of 1990 to 1992 alone. There are 32% more nonprofit organizations than there were 7 years ago. These revealing statistics are given in an article espousing that in the face of diminishing support, nonprofit organizations might consider going into for-profit business to support themselves. The public is becoming rapidly disenchanted with many community and philanthropic agencies because of their excesses and questionable stewardship. Many church members feel the same way about their own local congregations to which they would prefer to feel more faithful.

If churchgoers truly believed in their local church — and their denomination — they would donate. Herein lies another serious problem, i.e., the local church vs. its denomination. For too many years, small-town, hard-working, tithing church members have given their funds only to see them squandered by denominational leaders on administrative top-heavy management and social and political causes with which they disagreed or, at best, knew very little about. Certainly there was not enough information to warrant their personal generosity. Even when there have been egregious financial irregularities, most local churches and parishioners have been reluctant to take legal action for two reasons: one, they believe that New Testament teaching discourages going to court against one's believer colleague. And two, they eschew the publicity and negative fallout for the church. These two reasons have given too many denominational leaders immunity and *carte blanche* to misuse church funds and to expand their personal coffers, build their own empires, and feed their insatiable egos.

Although there are many illustrations of improper stewardship by the church, a true incident occurred in a mainline Protestant denomination which promised the elderly in a Mid-Western community a retirement complex. After accepting significant amounts of money in contributions from trusting senior folks, the denominational leaders squandered the money, essentially confiscated the land, voluntarily surrendered a difficult to obtain "Certificate of Need" (which in some states is needed to build such a complex), and left the donors high and dry. Even that denomination's regional and national headquarters did not come to the aid of the duped seniors, leaving many of them with little if any faith in their church and its leaders. The denomination's actions were not simple mistakes. They had been deliberated carefully by the responsible denominational leaders. Their actions were closer to outright thievery than to anything that could be called stewardship.

Stories like this are legend within both the Protestant and Roman Catholic Church. It would be comforting to be able to think that instances such as these were isolated and a result of honest human errors. When looked at carefully, many times beneath the tragedy are individuals building their own empires, power politics, and immense personal greed. Simply because the organization is a religious one does not exempt it from all of the downfalls of human nature just like any other organization.

Not all, probably not even a small percentage of churches, intentionally misuse money. To be sure, most make every reasonable effort to be good stewards of their parishioner's contributions. This is true of most community agencies, social agencies and religious organizations. Then if that is the case, what is the problem?

One of the problems is that most local churches of America —
at least in the mainline churches (Methodist, Presbyterian, etc.) —
are local franchise holders. The customer is the parishioner and the
product is religion. When customers stop believing in the product,
the franchise is in trouble.

The church for the most part is like a franchise business. Its corporate management, administration, and rules are very much the
same as those for any fast-food chain. The parent franchise corporation (the denominational headquarters) receives a percentage of
the income from the franchisee (the local church). The reasoning
for the denominational assessment is essentially the same as it is in
the secular business world, i.e., national advertising, quality control,
and profit. The "profit" in a "not-for-profit" organization is called
a "fund balance." The only difference between "profit" and "not-
for-profit" is what is done with the money over and above expenses. In "profit" organizations, the owners reap the financial benefits.
In "not-for-profit" organizations the excess money ("fund balance")
must be reinvested and/or used for other not-for-profit purposes in
accordance with that organization's not-for-profit charter.

The money left over (profits) in a not-for-profit organization
can be used for essentially the same purposes as in for-profit organizations. Those funds can go into salaries, bonuses, buildings, adver-
tisement, and perquisites. The primary difference is the tax structure to which the organization must adhere. This tax structure
allows the not-for-profit organization to avoid paying taxes on its
"earnings," real estate, and capital holdings, as well as on purchases
it makes. Both for-profit and not-for-profit organizations are in
business, and both are in business to make money. The *purposes* for
making the money and the stewardship of that money ostensibly
differ greatly.

Many rather ingenious ways have been found to use "left-over
money" for not-for-profit purposes which have been less than righteous. The story is told of the three ministers who were discussing

their methods for collecting Sunday offerings. The first said, "I have the ushers collect the offering, place it on the altar and pray over it;" the second said, "I have the ushers collect the offering, place it on the communion table and ask God to take what he wants and the rest is used for the church;" the third said, "You just don't understand how to take up an offering. I ask the ushers to take up the collection, then they bring the offering plate to me, and, after I pray over it, I throw it up in the air and I figure what the Lord wants He'll take, and the rest is mine."

It is difficult to see the difference between greed in the name of God and greed in the name of anything else. There is actually at times more honesty in the profits of the for-profit business than in the religious one. To quote a well-known brokerage firm: "We make money the old fashion way, we earn it." The church invites, begs, sometimes cajoles through guilt, and sometimes extracts money which is hardly "freely given." There are exceptions to this, and although these may be more honorable, they usually have less money!

In order for the church to regain its good standing and thus its importance in the philanthropic minds of parishioners, it will need to do more than preach tithing and have an annual pledge drive. It will need to convince its parishioners that what they are getting is worth the money and that the church is a good steward all the way from the local pulpit to the denominational headquarters. Given the rise of nondenominational congregations, one must ask if perhaps these worshipers "have had it" with denominations and denominational leadership.

Church Members by the Droves Don't Go to Church Anymore

Although there is a minor "return to church" trend in the United States today, it remains to be seen whether it will continue. It also does not appear to be former members returning, but a younger generation, who having tried much else is giving the church one last chance. The magazine *George* reported in December 1996 that 48% in the United States attend church once or more per week, 37% attends less than once a week, and 13% attend on holidays only. In preparation for this writing, I asked laypersons and ministers of several denominations for their opinion of these figures. None of them believed that 48% attend once a week or more. Persons polled by this author included Roman Catholic priests and clergy from Methodist, Presbyterian, Baptist, Disciples of Christ, the United Church of Christ, Episcopal, and Unitarian denominations. The only persons who thought it might be true were two Mormons.

A leading publication of the Protestant church, *The Christian Century* (September 11, 1996) reported that attendance at our churches is at its lowest level since the 1970s. It reported a survey that indicated 37% of adults attended church in 1996 compared to 49% in 1991. The Barna Research group of Glendale, California reported (Web page, 2001) that "Church attendance across denomination lines has suffered a five-year decline and has sunk to its lowest level in two decades," and Bruce Hose, former director of Sunday School programs for the Alabama Baptist Convention, stated that "Not only has attendance gone down but it is a graying culture, a graying congregation." The Barna polls (Web page, 2001) indicated that churches have been losing entire segments of their membership, such as singles, men, empty-nesters, etc., even though that same research group reported that 85% of Americans claim to be Christians. Many assert that it may actually be worse than reported since people like Samford University researcher Penny Long Marler claim that actual church attendance is only about half of that which is claimed in telephone poll results. Notre Dame sociologist Mark Cheaves, as well as other researchers, also claims that respondents to telephone polls overstate church attendance by as much as 50% (*National Catholic Observer*, September 24, 1993). Other polls indicate that the statistics, by virtue of untruthful reporting, may be inflated by as much as 100%.

The Presbyterian Church (U.S.A.) will coordinate a study of about 6,500 congregations to gain a comprehensive statistical view of U.S. church life. This study will be interdenominational and include some 300,000 Christians. It will reportedly look at the strengths and weaknesses of various congregations, according to *The Orlando Sentinel* (April 24, 1998). It has not been stated when this study will be done. It is clear that many denominations are experiencing losses sufficient to present alarm. In Daytona Beach, Florida, The United Methodist Church that is 120 years old recently closed its doors because it no longer had enough money or members to keep it open. It had been in the downtown area since one year after the founding of the town.

The ministry of the downtown church is of serious concern. Since most cities have grown up in concentric circles around the "downtown," and the suburbs have flourished, many members have abandoned the center-city church. By the same token, there are unique examples of downtown churches flourishing. Certainly the downtown is in need of the church, its message, and its services, both religious and social, just as are the suburbs.

The *Wall Street Journal* (December 23, 1997) included a story titled, "As Worshipers Dwindle, A Pastor Does Double Duty," in which it stated, "Dwindling membership isn't just an aging issue. In the past, people moved into communities and the first thing they did was search out a church. That's not the case anymore." Some had attempted to say that church membership has dropped because of the "graying of America" and the move to the suburbs. If this is part of the cause, it is just a small part of it. The *Wall Street Journal* story went on to say, "An official with the Pittsburgh Presbytery is quoted as saying, '... though Americans say they believe in God, mainstream denominations are losing membership rapidly to evangelical churches ... membership in the Allegheny County Presbyterian congregations had dropped to 54,000 from 128,000 in about the last 35 years.'" *The Orlando Sentinel* (April 24, 1999) reported that "The churches of the Southern Baptist Convention, the largest U.S. Protestant denomination, are reporting a decrease in membership for the first time since 1926." According to *USA Today* (May 27, 1999), although 69% of adults consider themselves to be Christian, actual church attendance has dropped by more than 9% is since 1991. Only 43% report having attended church within the past week. It is interesting to note that the same newspaper reported that Bible reading is actually up from 38 to 45% in that same period of time. This statistic may be saying something about the difference in belief of the Scriptures and belief in the organization called the church. Similar stories are found in all mainline denominations as well as the Roman Catholic Church.

The Gallup poll reported that church attendance has been at a steady 43% for three decades, but as pointed out, with the increasing overall national population, that would mean a massive influx of people into the churches. Such has not been the case. People apparently claim to attend church when polled because it seems to be the right thing to say or it indicates their belief in what they *should* do, but in fact their answers did not match the behavior that was claimed. The Barna Research Group also reported in *USA Today* (May, 27, 1999) that "While more adults who consider themselves Christian say they are 'religious' — measures such as church attendance and Bible reading are down." Yet in the same newspaper on the same day, it was reported that Bible sales are "burgeoning." It is interesting to note that in spite of the diminutive numbers of churchgoers in the United States, "even though some Americans worship only once a year, weekly church attendance is higher in the United States than in any other nation at a comparable level of development, according to a worldwide study based at the University of Michigan" (*News Release*, University of Michigan, December 10,1997).

In various other countries, such as India, for example, huge congregations numbering in the thousands attend services multiple times each Sunday. Could it be that affluence makes it less necessary to attend church? The same report from the University of Michigan stated that "in general, the importance of religion has been declining in the developed world, says Inglehart, whereas in countries experiencing economic stagnation and political uncertainty, religion has remained strong." An interesting development is that Northern European countries are experiencing a near collapse of religion "and the Latin countries are now sending missionaries to save the souls of their former colonizers" (University of Michigan Poll, December 10, 1997).

If Inglehart's conclusions are correct, his findings have serious implications for the United States. He states, "Why America is an exception to this global trend is uncertain, although … Religion could be a legacy of America's frontier mentality, in which case a strong sense of faith was necessary in order to brave the unknown. It could also have a more contemporary cause: a social welfare system less developed than those in most Nordic and European countries" (University of Michigan, December 10, 1997). The extent to which the church supports the development of a socialized welfare approach to the problems of life may be the extent to which it votes itself out of necessity!

Thomas Reeves in *The Empty Church: Does Organized Religion Matter Anymore?* (1998, p. 64) indicates that it may be that while personal religion matters to many, organized religion does not. One must ask why this is so. Although religion is certainly a private matter, humans are still social beings and tend share with others the things that matter most. This very statement might present a dilemma in that perhaps religion does not matter at all or they would share it. And, maybe they do share it, but not in the organized assembly we know as the church. Once again we are forced to ask: have social groups, volunteer organizations, and civic clubs become the venue for this type of sharing?

There are reports of more and more Americans returning to worship services. There is a lack of adequate research; however, the *Wall Street Journal* reported (January 29, 2001) in a *Wall Street Journal/NBC News* poll that "half of Americans attend church at least twice a month." If this poll is accurate, it will serve as much-needed encouragement for the church. There are no data as to whether these attendees worship at mainline, Roman Catholic, or other churches.

An *Associated Press* (December 3, 1977) report from the Vatican City released an article stating, "Christian believers are abandoning Roman Catholicism for evangelical groups in mounting numbers, and hundreds of bishops from the Americas now gathered at the Vatican are wracking their brains over what to do about it." The problem was seen as being particularly troublesome in countries which have been predominantly Roman Catholic. Some nations report as much as one third of the population is now Protestant. Protestant groups have gained so much ground that some of the bishops declared it to be an "invasion." Most of the Protestant "invaders" are Pentecostal and charismatic in theology and practice.

It is very interesting that the minister quoted in the *Wall Street Journal* story would state that church members were leaving the "mainline" congregations to go to the "evangelical" ones. This is a tacit admission that he does not view his church as evangelical. What does he view his church as being? Is this further proof that the church (at least the mainline church) has abandoned the two primary reasons for its existence, i.e., evangelism and missions?

The church has has to contend with the fact that in the United States, over its past 200+-year history, what started out as a largely Christian religious population has changed dramatically. The population now includes over five million Moslems which "far exceed(s) the number of Jews, Episcopalians or Presbyterians" (*News-Leader*, Springfield, Missouri, July 13, 1998).

The *kind* of religion has changed as well. Most evident is the rise in the charismatic movement, that group of persons who worship in more dramatic ways such as shouting, praying with hands uplifted, and glossolalia (speaking in tongues). The charismatic movement has made more than small dents in the forms of worship even in the major denominations. The Episcopal, Presbyterian, Methodist, and other "traditional" mainline churches are including much more informality, more dramatic worship methods, and other charismatic elements into their worship services. Perhaps this is being done to recapture what is perceived as their "market share" of the church-going population.

THE PRACTICE OF CHRISTIANITY HAS CHANGED DRAMATICALLY

The increase in non-Christian religions in the United States is phenomenal and is exacting a change in many aspects of American life, not the least of which is the influence upon the practice of religion in America. Creches have come down at Christmastime, crosses are not displayed as much at Easter, Christmas carols are not sung in public schools, and prayer is a thing of the past in most public places. The change in growth in the Protestant Church has been the dramatic decrease in membership in the "mainline" churches and the incredible increase in membership in the Pentecostal groups, both as subgroups within Protestant denominations as well as huge separate denominations, such as the Assemblies of God and the Church of God in Christ. Many former Christians are embracing the faiths brought to these shores by immigrants in recent times, particularly the Islamic faiths. It was reported in the Springfield, Missouri *News-Leader* (July 13, 1999) that "Americans in the next millennium are likely to see a country with more non-Christians than those who profess to be Christian."

Not All Church Attendance Is Down

While most mainline denominations report significant losses in both membership and attendance, such is not the case universally. Individual congregations can be found that are holding their own. Some are even thriving. It would be worthwhile for these major denominations to study in depth why this is the case. There is no doubt that the more charismatic and Pentecostal churches are growing by leaps and bounds. The names of these local assemblies show overt contempt for denominational labels. Some of them are "The Church of Saving Fellowship," "The Glory to God Missionary Church," "The Light and Life Assembly," and other nondenominational, yet very descriptive names. Some more liberally minded Christians would like to say that such groups are for the more "simple-minded" folks who like to have quick, easy, and absolute answers to life's complex questions. Not so fast — while this may be true of some, one cannot paint the whole movement with this nondescript brush. The "Church fathers" need to look carefully at why these congregations and denominations are growing. The lessons might be surprising.

There Is No One Reason Why Church Attendance Is Down

There are no clear answers as to why attendance has dropped in some groups and grown in others. There are no clear answers as to why some denominations seem to succeed and others fail and die. Neither are there clear answers as to why some groups are experiencing a resurgence in attendance. While some would credit "strictness" for a return, others see "strictness" as a cause for decline. Mainline churches have believed that relaxed standards, alternate worship service times, casual dress, and a more permissive adaptation of the creeds would enhance attendance. However, it does not appear that anyone knows why anything has or has not worked when it comes to church attendance. If we knew the secret minds of church members, their reasons for attendance and nonattendance would no doubt be considerably different from that which the clergy would like to know.

Apart from its theological and ecclesiastical jargon, the church is still a social institution and must meet the standards of such. Furthermore, most people, traditionally as well as currently, have not and do not attend church primarily for easily perceived reasons. Nor do persons who attend church do so for the same reason each time they attend, just as absentees do not have the same reason each time for nonattendance. Absentees are probably more consistent in their reasons for not attending church than are those who do attend church. Many attendees give reasons that range from the falsely pious to the most flagrant nonthinking answers. Recently a group of randomly chosen persons from unidentified denominations was asked if they attended and if so why. The answers of attendees ranged from "God expects me there on Sunday morning," to "We just get up and go — it's the thing we have always done." Others said, "My folks would kill me if they thought I didn't go to church." Several said, "That's where most of my friends are." A few gave reasons that sounded more sincere and true, such as, "I need to be with people who believe like I do."

While it may be true that religion is talked about in some circles less than it was in previous times, overall, including in politics, religion continues to occupy a central place. The election 2000 was characterized by observation of the Jewish Sabbath by Joe Lieberman and Jesus Christ being named as "hero" by the now President Bush. One must inquire about how accurate and truthful are the polls. Do people give pollsters answers they think are expected or answers that are truthful? Television, radio, and newspaper media leave doubt about the reemergence of the religious mind and the impact of religion in America.

Church attendance probably has something to do with the value parishioners place upon two primary factors: one, the value placed upon corporate worship and, two, the value of social/community life. It also appears that the more fundamentalistic the denomination, the higher the percentage of church attendance tends to be. Those faiths that emphasize church attendance as a means of grace obviously obtain better conformity from members. Denominations which offer a much greater latitude of attention to attendance as well as other aspects of the faith experience no great surprise in that the members are eager to accept and practice the standard of less attendance. Not all brands of Christianity are losing members or church attendance. As has been noted, charismatic fellowships are growing by leaps and bounds, the Mormon religion is clearly growing, and there is an unprecedented establishment of independent, nondenominational fellowships. Other countries of the world where religious assemblies are growing are characterized by these same alternative approaches to mainline religion.

The Influence of Religious Thinking Has Been Lost in Society

The permeation of religion into every thought and deed as reported about the Puritan community must have been repressive. Of course, we doubt that such permeation was ever completely the case; however, history reports it that way. There is no doubt that religion was impregnated into every social institution and that, at least openly and overtly, religious thought was the basis for daily life. As a result, to this day we have the remnants of Puritan-like actions, ranging from prayer in the Senate of the United States to the "In God We Trust" motto on our money. Still, we tend to be a society of extremes. Hence, when the Puritan ethic was experienced as being too repressive, our social pendulum swung to the other extreme where we are today. We now debate whether there should be *any* involvement of the church with the state or vice versa.

The loss of the influence of religion in the state is different from the state supporting religion. It is different from the argument as to whether there should be prayer in public schools. It is different from those issues magnified by the Internal Revenue tax code. The difference lies not in official state, church, or social action. It lies in the *intentions* of individuals and groups. It is patently clear that some current political intentions are to rid all social institutions of anything religious in nature — except the church — and, since the church has adopted the norms of society in general, it remains to be seen how long the church itself will retain true religious thinking. With the prominent language of the church and many of its sermons being anthropological, sociological, and psychological, this is a legitimate concern.

CNN TV recently reported on a number of multiple family murders in which one member of the family had died and, in their grief, the parents killed the rest of the family. When interviewed, psychologists and psychiatrists attributed much of the cause to the loss of a meaningful religious community to which grief-stricken families could turn. Although the report came from The Netherlands, the situation is doubtlessly shared in the United States. The loss of religious influence is far more than persons simply not attending church. It is the loss of the fiber of thinking that links one to that which is greater than one's self. It is the loss of the innerperson's connection with a power greater than that which is human. This loss in our society is directly attributable to the church's willingness to uncritically accept existing social norms and thus give up its unique and mystical message in order to placate consumer wishes. The church can blame "the world" for intruding; however, part of the real blame belongs to church leadership for being too weak to withstand the pressure.

The essential job of the church is to be a catalyst in society. According to *Webster*, a "catalyst" is "that which causes activity between two or more persons or forces without itself being effected." The powers of society, industry, business, education, or for that matter formal religion should not be able to shake the purpose and power of the church, if it is to be a true catalyst. The Biblical citation for the power of the church states, "... I will build my church, and the forces of death shall never overpower it" (Matthew 16:18, *New English Bible*).

One must ask where this weakness of the church came from. It cannot be only the church members' fault. Church leaders, clergy, denominational administrators, and the training institutions of the church all must admit to their share of blame.

Ministers Hug the Centerline

When a person's paycheck depends upon being liked, he/she is already in trouble! One can hardly criticize the minister who knows that if she/he offends the financially righteous, there will be serious payroll consequences. Some local churches have a well-earned reputation for running ministers out of town because she/he had a mind of their own! Many ministers are literally afraid to take a position on anything of consequence, since in most congregations the faithful financial supporters are split on both sides. To take a stand is surely to offend some. A local Midwestern newspaper recently reported a fistfight that broke out in a church during choir practice. When one of the fighters pulled a knife on the other man, the two took off running down the street. The pastor was asked how he would handle it and he said, "Some sermons have to be preached, others just have to be seen ... I just told the choir to sing louder on Sunday than they ever had, and I'd preach louder." Now that's a church in action! It is also a way of remaining neutral. After all, we don't know which one of the malcontents was the bigger giver or had the most influence. As unusual as this incident is (we hope!), the lesson is very ordinary. Although most church fights do not involve fistfights and knives, the price for taking sides is just as real. The basic method of compensating clergy makes it difficult for a minister, rabbi, or priest to take a tough stand. We say, "Don't just stand there, do something." Sometimes just standing there is doing something. However, standing in an unpopular spot too often on too many issues has cost more than one clergy person their job! Since the church must speak out on all topics (or so it thinks), and since parishioners come in all political, social, educational, and personal colors and choices, many ministers have learned to dance the "chameleon charade."

It is interesting to note how many clergy always choose to be the chairperson of a committee. Since the chair cannot vote, they are safely ensconced within the role of the leader who never has to lead, but only report what the rest of the committee decides! And, of course, the religious denominational observer is well aware that even designated committees tend to make decisions only rarely. The most common decision is to refer the problem, table the problem, or otherwise figure out a way to delay action. There is a basic problem with most committees. When the task of the committee is to preserve itself and maintain anonymity, most committee work is referred for "further study" — forever — or at least until interest in the topic passes. I was once told by a patient that his family operated by the "skunk smell philosophy." Not being acquainted with that technique, I asked what it was. I was told that the "skunk smell philosophy" assumes that if you don't pay any attention to it, it will go away. Too many times such a resolution is the easy way out. However, practicing this method in the church is irresponsible at best and blatant ecclesiastical malpractice at worst.

A properly prepared sermon for the average congregation today should be inspirational, noncontroversial, and as short as possible, making only suggestions which can be safely ignored. To preach otherwise would be tantamount for the preacher to start looking for another job. Since parishioners know that most ministers do not dare to be controversial, ministers can practice what makes them look spiritual and yet be perfectly "safe" in their super-sanctimonious piety.

Most ministers have learned elementary psychology and attempt to give "unconditional positive regard" to all (in the words of Carl Rogers). That philosophy coupled with Carnegie's (1940) *How to Win Friends and Influence People* makes taking a tough stand sometimes mighty difficult. Furthermore, preaching to the center line keeps both the preacher and congregation from reaching either end of the court. Most preachers know just how far to dip into "heavy theology" before one side or the other starts to complain. The fact that no one is complaining does not mean that all is well. To be content is not necessarily to be correct or helpful.

Parishioners want and need moral, intellectual, and practical every-day life leadership. They may not know how to ask for it, but they trust and hope that their seminary-trained clergy will know their congregation's needs better than do the congregants. After all, isn't that why ministers attend graduate school — to learn what their parishioners don't know, but should be taught?

A minister friend recently told of a fellow colleague in seminary who bragged that he was able to graduate from his ministerial training without changing his mind on anything. That sort of minister could hardly be expected to lead others into new knowledge. One wonders (or does one need to spend the time wondering?) what this person saw his task as being when he became pastor of a church. When parishioners hear only that which is slightly more than a spiritual lullaby, can they be blamed for believing that they need nothing more? Although most parishioners (like any other organization) prefer to not be told what they need, nevertheless, the avowed claim is that they have hired ministers for precisely that purpose. Parishioners are therefore both relieved and disappointed when the minister joins the parishioners in a neutral stand or, even worse, a stand that is known by both the minister and the parishioner to be "waffling" or sometimes clearly against Biblical standards. Parishioners are very aware when their wants rather than their needs are the object of the minister's catering. (More will be said later about needs and wants.) Ministers who hug the 50-yard line are poor examples. We can all easily huddle on the centerline without much help.

Mainline Denominations Are Constantly on the Left of Any Position

While local ministers might be hugging the center line, their denominational leaders have for the most part been predictable in leaning to the left. Certainly this is true of the major Protestant denominations. Denominational leaders seem to think that being excessively liberal sets them apart as being especially wise and parental. Never mind, of course, that it also usually takes them out of the line of fire from would-be critics of the Church! Denominational leaders take a lofty position as if to say that if local congregations were more mature and could understand the whole picture, they would also lean to the left. Anything else is defined as local pettiness, a lack of individual and cultural differences, bigotry, and discrimination, and in short, an outright misunderstanding of the "true Gospel." Somehow denominational leaders present themselves as having a higher revelation from God, claiming to be able to extend "love" farther than others. This kind of posture is totally out of accord with the traditional role of the "priesthood of believers" in which all believers are equal, a fundamental doctrine of the Protestant church. There was no more central issue to the Reformation than Luther's insistence upon this doctrine. When Protestant church leaders assume a position of righteous hierarchy, they return to a pre-Reformation stance. These kinds of claims support a hierarchical egocentricity to say the least — and everyone knows that such claims are simply bully pulpits for the insecure. Of course, we must remember that without the dollars from the local church collection plates, these "leaders" would have no denominational benefits, including their next paycheck!

The dilemma of finding an acceptable center line is shared by all Protestant denominations and the Roman Catholic Church alike. Robert Bork (1996) in his exceedingly well-documented book, *Slouching Toward Gomorra* (p. 283), chastises the Roman Catholic Church for being so extreme on the left and indicts Protestants even more when he states: "The mainline Protestant churches are further to the left. The National Council of Churches in the United States of America (NCC), which represents most mainline Protestant denominations, has consistently taken liberal left positions on domestic issues." Bork also quotes the famous political commentator Ernest W. Lefever: "The NCC has taken the ideas of the liberal-left, clothed them in theological garments, and accorded them the status of quasi-dogma." The "on the left" position is usually assumed in the name of a more intellectual understanding of Christian doctrine and *love* toward all persons. In speaking with persons of the Roman Catholic and mainline Protestant persuasion, they all immediately stated that the church "speaks from a position of knowledge and authority, therefore they must be correct." However, these same persons were quick to state that they did not always, or for that matter usually, agree with the church when it speaks on social issues. Their opinion was that the church must maintain the "left" position to appear "in touch" and make it look like they knew what is going on in the world — the world that the pew-sitting parishioner does not know! This pseudo-intellectualism and pseudo-erudition clearly turns many church members off, both Protestant and Roman Catholic.

The word love has been grossly perverted and misused as if it is synonymous with acceptance. To the extent that the church accepts everything, to that extent it excludes nothing and to that extent it stands for nothing, stands against nothing, and represents nothing! We have been brainwashed into believing that the only Christian thing to do is to be "inclusive," i.e., to understand, accept, and approve all individual differences. Bork is absolutely correct in his observation that mainline Protestant churches have so much identified with the secular culture that church members see less reason to attend. It may well be that a number of churches no longer serve a religious purpose. Their real purpose is a social one and their administrators are merely social agency directors. Many times denominational administrators feel free to preach to others since they are safely housed in the tall buildings of the big cities. Those administrators who regularly participate in a local church congregation are less prone to "preach from on high" since they are too involved with "where the rubber hits the road." Otherwise, these administrators with all righteousness can say, "Do as I say, not as I do," for they are not in a position to *do* anything but talk. It is easy, after all, for those who are not on the firing line to give orders. The local pastor must stand the heat.

In the name of acceptance, we now virtually worship individual differences. We may not worship the difference, but we worship the right to be different. If we are not careful, what we worship will actually be the *idea* that we appreciate and accept differences. Such thinking is indeed quite self-righteous! We may actually worship acceptance itself as a virtue and elevate acceptance to a holy act without regard to what it is we are accepting. Worshipping an idea is certainly less demanding than worshipping that which requires action. Whether it is performing same-sex marriages or discussing partial birth abortion, the church holds convention after convention and can be counted on to send the matter "back to committee for further study!" Inevitably, the reason is to make certain that we do not offend any "differences." True theology clearly points out differences. Theology purposefully offends. Religious/political correctness does not except those who disagree with what is being touted.

Much has been made of celebrating diversity and unity in the church. The problem is not with recognizing and appreciating diversity. However, the etymological dissection of language becomes essential when speaking of diversity. Diversity is one thing. Divisions are another. And divisiveness is quite another. They are not the same. It is possible to have diversity without divisions and it is possible to have divisions without being divisive.

Difficulty in the church arises from basic beliefs about theology and the interpretation of the scriptures. On one hand, to be at all effective the church must have unity, uniformity, and union. On the other hand, to accomplish its mission fully, it must be diverse and have divisions and an ability to disagree agreeably. It need not have divisiveness. However, often the need for unity leads to such. At issue is the spirit of cooperation with those with whom we seriously disagree and to what extent that cooperation handicaps our methods and message.

The mantra of the age in social and educational circles is "diversity." We see workshops designed to "appreciate diversity," "increase the awareness of diversity," etc. The social science model puts this intellectual exercise high on its agenda. Few persons are addressing just how much diversity an organization can incorporate before it ceases to be the organization it claims to be. The church will have a very taut tightrope to walk in the next few years on this issue. It must take cognizance of the fact that the United States is becoming increasingly diverse ethnically, racially, and religiously. Other world religions are rapidly penetrating the Western world religion market. However, how much unity can the practice of Christian theology integrate without losing its identity as a theology that disavows much of what the other religions espouse?

The denominational level creates all sorts of dictums, affirmations, and new creeds that the local pastor and congregation repudiate. At times, in order to give the appearance of "unity," the local church does not speak out against a new affirmation — it simply ignores it. Then a stark division exists between the denominational "position" and the actual practice of the denomination's local congregations. Across America the lack of agreement between many congregations and their denominational leaders is only evident to those members who are on committees, teams, and other

denominational workforces, since few church members attend
annual meetings and conventions. The work of most committees
appointed at annual denominational conventions is to somehow
bring the local church members into agreement with the denomination leaders without losing members and/or financial support.
When this does not happen, as with other conflictual issues, the
issue is sent back to committee and stalled for at least another year,
during which time a more pressing issue may come forth. Should
that not happen, there is time for "back room" politics to work.
These politics are known, but largely of no concern to the average
church-goer.

How the local church is going to incorporate the increasing
diversity of society and remain true to its theology and mission will
take far more investment in the local congregation from denominational headquarters than is being given today. The dictums of the
Roman Catholic Church do not work when the "rubber hits the
road" for the average Catholic, and certainly most Protestants could
care less what their denominational executives have to say. Further,
and perhaps even more serious, there is the fact that the denominational and Roman Catholic hierarchy may be wrong! The local
mind is not always uneducated, unknowing, and incapable of applying theology to life. Sometimes hierarchical church leaders are so
caught up in their own image building and need to be seen as the
great "balancers of the faith" and "peacemakers" that they can't see
(or don't care to see) the forest (the local congregations) for the
trees (the large issues they deal with). Denominational leaders may
need to allow more leadership from the grass roots level in order to
get their eyes out of the upper tree limbs in the clouds!

What is the church if it is not different? What is theology if it
is not differentiating? What good is a creed that does not speak to
differences? Even a cursory glance at the New Testament reveals
that being different was what it was all about. Sometimes "being

different" was learning and living what one believed despite the differences. Usually, it was *because* of the differences.

Appearing to not accept all individual differences has become synonymous with "not believing." Of course, the difficulty is not in refusing to accept individual differences, but in refusing to accept someone else's (in this case the church's) interpretation of those differences. Beliefs are determined by various kinds of groups for all of us. In this case we are concerned with the church and its method of determining our beliefs. Since the beginning of church history, various councils have met to agree upon the creeds which "true Christians" would affirm. In a day when individualism is so accepted as it is today, such corporate agreement is difficult to come by. However, it is still important in most church circles to claim to ascribe to a common creed, even though there may be very little belief in the actual content of that creed. Local churches, like denominations, are run by committees that sometimes anoint themselves with misguided and misappropriated "divine inspiration."

Many congregations have gone so far as to assume that they can and must interpret the Scriptures for all members of their congregation and require behavioral conformity to those interpretations. Not only is this erroneous, but obviously dangerous. Such practices result in conformity and rebellion at the same time. Of course, herein is also the reason for many split congregations. When disagreements occur which are believed by some to be "biblical," the separating of the congregation from the denomination feels very righteous and the preacher is seen as a true leader opposing evil. No one has to second-guess the psychological dynamics of this kind of potentially ego-driven program.

The "committee" method of church government and denominational leadership is the foremost type of organizational management today in most churches and denominations. And, it is a very safe type. As stated earlier, the basic job of any committee is to continue itself in perpetuity. If the committee arrives at a conclusion, it may well destroy the mission of the committee, cause division, create controversy, and for that matter put committee members out of what they see as an important job! The church no longer looks to creeds, confessions, tradition, history, the forefathers, or even to *The Holy Bible* for direction — but to committees. Committees determine whether the "official" church position will include female clergy and how to treat homosexuality, abortion, and all other controversial issues. They turn their "ideas" into "beliefs" that the church will teach. They deem that it is the relevant thing to do; however, relevancy is not always Biblically right.

The local church's strength has been sapped by denominational headquarters' misuse of paternalistic leadership, the committee method of nondecision making, and intimidating the clergy from taking a formidable stand of any kind. Furthermore, most parishioners have virtually no involvement in decision making, and the management of the local church is often left up to a very few, resulting in an anemic institution.

Neutered by Relevancy

The buzzword for this age is "relevancy." The word relevancy by dictionary definition means "bearing upon or connected with the matter at hand." By attempting to become "relevant," the church has shifted its focus. It has redefined that which it is about. It has changed its message to what is perceived as the "matter at hand." It has made the matter at hand whatever is the fad or the pop issue of the day. Its time-endless purpose has been supplanted by the idiosyncrasies of an age. The message of the church must be appropriate and it must speak to the issues of the day. However, there is a difference between speaking to the issues of the day and allowing the issues of the day to transform the mission and purpose of the church. Speaking to the issues is not a green light to revise theology to accept all sides of the issue. Religion, in its purest form, speaks with clarity to principles, foundation-type thinking, and beliefs that are applicable — whatever the day and whatever the issue. True religion does not waffle!

When the church takes up the language of the day, it loses focus. When the language is not clear, it becomes impossible to know whether the church is a political, educational, social service, or religious organization. Granted, the church must impact all of these social institutions and more. However, speaking to them from the outside with a clear message is different than joining them and later trying to find a way to speak out. Attempting to "change from the inside" most often ends with being swallowed whole without even knowing it.

Great religious leaders avoided the pitfall of "relevancy" by teaching in stories and parables. Such teaching transcends the daily "pop" issue and allows for spiritual growth which is then usable whatever may be the problem. One of the great reasons for preaching and teaching in parables is that such teaching avoids the "fad of the month." The traditional church followed a calendar of Biblical readings and expositions called the lectionary. Many churches still do so. Following such an ecclesiastical calendar helps avoid undue attention to one portion of the Scriptures and overemphasis on what might be pet peeves and "hobbyhorses." Sometimes the deeper and abiding message of the church is lost in the evangelistic fervor about current political interest topics. The real problem, however, is that the basics of the faith are in jeopardy of being underemphasized and replaced by "pop" fads. No doubt, a topical ministry, based on current "hot spots" is more interesting to the average listener; however, such does not provide a continuity of religious or Biblical education. Thus the roots of the faith are at risk of being lost.

A topical ministry can be theological; however, it takes a great deal of ability and understanding to connect topics to their theological roots. Creative clergy are able to bring the current topic under a strong theological doctrinal base and thus accomplish both goals. Few are capable of this strategy. Theology has only one topic, the love of God, which provides for the faith to accept the results of all topics.

The topical approach of the church has made every issue in the community important, and every issue should be of importance. However, it is more important to apply theology to the issues than to apply the issues to theology. When theology is applied to the issues, it changes our perception and action on those items. When social issues are applied to theology, it tends to revise theology to fit the social need. Sometimes we become so contemporary that the solid, timeless base of belief is lost. Joining everything and having everything join the church is very costly. Resources are drained. There is simply not enough time, money, or energy to make the church into another all-inclusive sociopolitical agency. Furthermore, the mission of the church is to transform society, not the other way around.

The Blind Leads the Blind

Another serious problem has to do with the literacy factor. The church is probably the only teaching institution in the world that allows untrained persons to teach new converts. The majority of Sunday School teachers have no formal study in the subject matter which they are teaching, nor have they had any training in how to teach. There is no argument with the good intentions of most of these folks. It has to do with the seriousness of transmitting the faith from one generation to the next. Like ministers, some say that they have "had the call." While such may be true, "a call" does not constitute or replace an education. One is reminded of a young man who in the midst of a sweaty afternoon rested and looked up at the sky, whereupon he saw the clouds to seemingly form the letters "GPC." He was greatly inspired, believing that these letters were clearly a higher power telling him to "Go Preach Christ." When he informed his wise pastor of his revelation, the minister quickly informed him that he had misinterpreted the letters. They did not mean "Go Preach Christ," but instead meant that he should not loaf, but pay attention to his work and "Go Plow Corn!"

It seems that religious leaders would be concerned when the issue of teaching solid theology is left to untrained and often misinformed teachers. This is particularly troublesome because Sunday School teachers usually have two or three times more classroom time than does the minister for the sermon. Sunday School classes are usually given an hour, while in many churches the minister has barely 20 minutes for the sermon. It is truly strange that an organization would give nearly three times as much time to untrained personnel to lead as they do their trained staff. A further concern is that even brand new converts are frequently allowed to teach children, adolescents, and other new converts. These teachers most often have limited personal history in the church and usually have little if any training in the Bible or theology. Frequently, since they may be recent converts, they have little understanding of the church's traditions or its mission. Is not this a situation of the "blind leading the blind"?

I was recently told that a certain synagogue has so few Jews who were raised in the Jewish faith that most of their children's teachers are Gentile converts. Although there is nothing wrong with converts, they have not experienced the tradition. The same is true of many Christian assemblies. The true message of the church is found in the depth of personal experience and understanding, not in learning and being able to repeat a story. Although it is laudatory to bring in new members, it may be that simply being a member is not enough for one to be entrusted with instilling in the next generation what one has not experienced. The very idea that one is called a "teacher" implies that he/she has something to teach. Misinformation is often worse than no information at all.

The Definition of God Changes With Social Demand

Having a basic concept of God has become unnecessary in many places. In an attempt to become relevant and not offend anyone, we no longer have a functional definition of God. To call God a male is to be considered chauvinist and gender insensitive, to assume any race is to be seen as discriminatory, and to assume any anthropomorphic physiology is to be thought of as prejudiced.

"God" has become an anthropomorphic spirit — a contradiction in terms. Many persons still want a great father in heaven with a flowing white beard. Their image and belief in God is about the same as it is for Santa Claus. "He" is a person who gives us nice things when we are good and sends curses when we are bad, just like Santa Claus leaves us a piece of coal when we are bad. It is interesting that God and Santa Claus are both essentially absent except in myth, and both have a flowing white beard! The only real difference is that these kinds of "believers" want God to visit them daily but are content for Santa Claus to visit them just once a year (incidentally, on a day connected with God).

Yet, these same persons want to believe that God is spirit. Since we do not know what "spirit" is, this concept is very safe and open to great and varied interpretation. So, we have a god who is nice, gives us gifts, and at the same time is untouchable, indefinable, and an unseen spirit. There is solace for these folk in the Scriptural admonition that "God is Spirit: and they that worship him must worship him in spirit and in truth" (John 4:23–24). This passage prescribes the method by which God is to be paid attention. It also helps us to see that our anthropomorphic wishes concerning the Creator are probably very much in error.

On the other hand, to some persons, God is only a mystical character, waiting to pronounce judgment and rain down wrath and doom upon imperfect persons. This belief is as old as the universe. There is nothing unique to the Christian religion about this belief. Pagans, heathen, illiterate, and learned alike have believed in the

Sun God, the Rain God, the Harvest God, and a multitude of other gods, including a god for every season, who could bless, but was more prone to curse. The reason for worship was not so much that the gods deserved it, but that homage paid off handsomely in averting a certain god's wrath. To escape a god's vengeance was adequate blessing. Literature in early times, including the Bible, is full of stories depicting an angry God pouring down wrath upon sinful human life. God is infinitely more than can be put in a definition. This concept has troubled and baffled the wisest persons on earth since time immemorial.

The church has a Herculean job. It must interpret theology in a way that presents God in a balanced light. Presenting God in a balanced fashion, however, does not allow preachers (or anyone else) to *use* God to make people feel guilty, nor does it allow them to excuse God since we don't know exactly what "spirit" is anyway.

To be truly relevant is to stay in focus. Theology has a focus. Theology has a relevancy. The focus and relevancy of theology is in revealing God's universal truths to all persons, everywhere, in all circumstances, utilizing commonly understood languages and mindsets which helps us to believe. Although some have done so more than others, we have lost our focus and our relevancy and everything is a blur, including the concept of "God."

The Church Has Forgotten Why People Go to Church

In times past, people went to the church/synagogue for hope. They still do (those who go). Buildings, beautiful artwork, gorgeous frescoes, music, and preaching were not ends in and of themselves. For the poor peasant to enter into the beautiful sanctuary and hear music that could only be heard there, and to hear preaching which commanded respect and gave hope of answers in the present as well as in the hereafter, made it worthwhile for them to trudge long distances on foot. The small country church without the artwork, frescoes, or for that matter the "great preaching," likewise offered the worshiper distance from the daily woes of life and the promise of a better life someday. In those days there were no televisions, few radios, and most preaching was done without microphones!

However, today we have come to believe that we must be "real" — whatever that is. In earlier times "reality" was the same to the learned and unlearned alike. Reality was not manufactured or invented. It was the common bond of all who worshipped. Kings and lords and princes and paupers sat together under the same "reality" without discrimination regarding God's love and the human sinful nature. Their common goal was an application of "the faith" to daily life, with the hope of "eternal joy" at the end of this mortal journey. But now we attempt to apply life to faith rather than applying faith to life. When we apply life to faith, we can manipulate faith to fit our misinterpreted needs (wants). The "reality" of the faith of the "ancients" was extremely simple. The knowledge was that we are all sinners, but that grace and forgiveness could be found in God and in God alone. This is no different in the Christian era than in the pre-Christian era when Jews attended the synagogue (as they do today) for the same reasons — to find peace and find forgiveness for sin. People have attended places of worship and synagogues for centuries, even before the Christian era, for very simple, but intensely profound reasons. Even those considered to be "pagans" may have worshipped strange Gods, but can we doubt their reasons? Those who still go, do so for the same reasons.

Sometimes "being real" is only an illusion. Being real is offering religion for what it is, "the promise of things hoped for and the evidence of things unseen," as defined by the author of Hebrews. It is not that which necessarily makes us happy, rich, or famous. *Faith is its own reward*. To offer more is both to be grossly errant and again promise that which cannot necessarily be delivered.

In today's society there are plenty of opportunities for most people to hear great music, see great architecture, and enjoy the beauty of religious art — all through video and audio media and, more than at any time in our history, through travel. The demonstration of great preaching — that kind of oratory that stirs the soul, that kind of spellbinding information based on eternal truths which remain the same in all generations for all religions of the world, that opportunity to escape the fad concerns of the day and deal with a solid foundation of spiritual growth — is sadly lacking. When and where it does occur, there is no lack of avid listeners. The church and its leaders have simply forgotten why people go to church. People go to church for that which they cannot get any place else. When they find that the church duplicates, sometimes poorly at that, what they can and do find elsewhere, the incentive for adding yet another appointment to their already full calendar is not strong enough.

Church Members Have Forgotten the Purpose of the Church

A minister recently took a poll of his congregation in an attempt to identify what they believed the members' needs to be and to set up some kind of a program to meet them. It was astounding to find when asked "What does our church need most?" the answers included "a wastebasket at the entry so folks won't throw their worship bulletins on the floor when they leave" and "our church really needs an American flag." There is certainly nothing wrong in remembering that "cleanliness is next to Godliness," or in wanting to keep both God and country in our attention. However, there was no doubt in the pastor's mind that these were the minutia of decorum rather than items of faith. There was not a single mention of anything spiritual or religious. No one mentioned more or better music or the needs of children, the homeless, shut-ins, or other fellow parishioners in need. All of the needs mentioned were material in nature.

When faced by cavernous sanctuaries sparsely dotted by attendees, the minds of the faithful seem to use confusing logic to look for rather strange answers. We are reminded of the story of the little country church that was having a business meeting to determine whether or not they should buy a new chandelier. After much discussion and disagreement, an elderly deacon stood and pronounced, "We are not going to buy one of them there things. We can't afford it, no one knows how to spell it, and no one here knows how to play it anyway."

Ministers continue to be criticized for their preaching (sometimes rightly so, no doubt) and choirs are criticized for their poor musical quality (also doubtless correctly), but the foundation items which should be the object of constructive criticism are lost in the shuffle. Those who attend largely do so out of habit, guilt, or maybe they just forget not to go. As for preaching, the minister will be criticized regardless of what he/she does, so why not do the expedient — preach what people want to hear — don't make waves — save your job!

Members' Talents Are Often Wasted

Many particularly large mainline churches do not solicit, indeed do not utilize, their own local talent, especially when it comes to music. The reason is that performers from the congregation are not good musicians. They sing "off key" or "just can't carry a tune" or "hit too many wrong notes." (Yet, these untrained persons can teach brand new converts in Sunday Schools!) One is reminded of the woman who often sang in a small church where there was limited talent available. The deacons attempted to discourage her, but she sang solos anyway. The chairperson of the board attempted to dissuade her, but she continued to sing. Finally, when all else failed, the deacons requested that the minister have a talk with her and tell her that she just simply could no longer sing solos. He reluctantly agreed to do so. He kindly but firmly talked with her, telling her that as much as they appreciated her willingness and commitment, that she "just couldn't sing very well." Whereupon, the would-be singer said, "Oh, thanks for telling me, but don't let that bother you

— none of us think you can preach very well either, but for heaven's sake don't stop!"

In many places, churches have lost their way in regard to music. They have neither the great choirs of the cathedrals nor the participation of the congregation. Life has become entirely too busy to take sufficient time to practice. Many choirs have only a few minutes prior to the service to "run over the piece" of music. This fact may lead congregations who desire fine music to hire outside professionals who are paid to give their time to practice and performance. If this is the case, it can become a real loss, especially to young people in the churches.

Many fine professional musicians got their start singing or playing off-key an instrument in the local congregation. There are churches who pay nonmembers to provide music to the exclusion of their own members who are not so accomplished. There is a place for both. However, that doesn't do much to encourage members who are musically talented to attend church. When they attend and listen to paid outside musicians, parishioners often resent being asked to contribute for nonmembers to do with precision, but with a very different kind of commitment, what they would be willing to do for free (acceptably, though perhaps not professionally), but with sincere personal commitment. It is not difficult to see why some members have forgotten the purpose of their church. Their voice is not heard in the business dealings, their talents are not utilized, their training is not called upon, and it is often not even noted if they miss services. They recognize, however, that they will be called upon at budget time! Many local churches are often not only poor stewards of money, but also of members' talents. Fortunately, there are also those congregations that continue to struggle with stewardship of time, talent, and money. If the church has learned anything at all from psychology, it should understand that this kind of negative behavior modification produces negative relationships and ultimately hostility. Music is only one area in which the church wastes its talent, but it is so common that it clearly illustrates the point. Business acumen, decorating, landscaping, repair, and many more areas could be equally illustrated and be true of many congregations — even those that plead for money to buy the services of outsiders.

Double Standards Exist for Finances

It has been of continuing interest to persons in the business community that highly successful entrepreneurs, administrators, and leaders in the business world are so willing to tolerate such shabby business practices within the church. Frequently, however, to make matters more consternating, a successful business person is placed on a church board and immediately adopts a double standard — allowing the church to function in a way that they would not tolerate for a moment in their own business. It doubtless speaks to the belief that there is something inherently different about church finances and secular finances. The same paradox occurs in many other areas of the church such as record keeping, tax reporting of for-profit aspects of the church, and archival aspects of local church history. There appears to be an attitude that sloppiness is okay in religious affairs, particularly since it does not answer to governmental agencies. It may also be that church members are really not interested in religion, per se, but the social and personal excuses that most postmodern theology offers.

Karen Armstrong, in *A History of God* (1993, p. 91), reminded us: "Many of the people who attend religious services in our own society are not interested in theology, want nothing too exotic and dislike the idea of change. They find the established rituals provide them with a link with tradition and give them a sense of security." She also reminded us that throughout history, "When one religious idea ceases to work for them, it is simply replaced" (p. 4).

Armstrong's words offer serious thought to those contemplating the future of the church. It would seem that by now church leaders would have decided that fad theology, ignoring member's needs, and becoming a thinly veiled "not-for-profit" organization, does not endure in any age. The church might do well to choose to return to the timelessness of Biblical theology. It will need to learn to live on its own income, receiving that which its members believe it is worth. While the church expects its members to live on their own income, as well as tithe and contribute even above the tithe, when dealing with itself, the church frequently ignores budgets and other financial constraints. Then when there is a "shortfall," it is placed at the feet of members and proclaimed to be a result of those who do not have enough faith. Where is the faith of the church leaders and their ability to manage?

The Church No Longer Demands — But Suggests

This is a particularly difficult problem. With attendance declining and funds dwindling, it is ever so precarious to place unwanted demands on parishioners. However, knowledge of family systems' theory helps us with this problem. The family that can demand is able to do so because the demand is part and parcel of a successful relationship. The family that has lost relationship with each other cannot demand, for demands can only be made in love if they are to succeed. The church has lost much of the basic relationship between parishioners and itself. Without members there is no local congregation, yet, many local congregations see members existing for the benefit of the church (which is certainly correct) and fail to see that the church exists for the members. Like any other business, without customers, there is no business. However, because members feel that they are "put upon," "used," and held hostage by mis-interpreted "Biblical" demands, they feel abused. The demands are perceived as onerous, unacceptable, and out of order. And, to the extent that there is a perception of *no relationship*, that perception is truth. Of course, we know that although we say there is "no rela-tionship," there is *always* a relationship; however, it may be a very negative or counterproductive one. In the case of the church, a negative relationship places one outside the realm of the church's influence, but still very much able to have a negative influence from the outside. We are reminded that satisfied customers rarely say so — they might tell one or two others. A dissatisfied customer will tell ten or more.

Even the Ten Commandments are seen by most churchgoers as convenient suggestions. Most people, including non-churchgoers, admit that the world would probably be a better place in which to live if everyone abided by the Ten Commandments. However, only a few of the Ten Commandments are ever particularly important to them personally. Furthermore, there is no serious attempt within churches to require their members' compliance. (Not that this author would know how to go about such!) However, in the past, the church did extract a kind of conformity within the community. Once again we are reminded of the story of Ananias and Sapphira (in Acts, Chapter 5) which was the basis for financial, individual, and family honesty. The standards in that community were so strong and the enforcement of the discipline was so swift that upon being confronted, Ananias and Sapphira immediately dropped dead! The moral of this story (among others) is that this church held its members to expectations of personal behavior — in this case it was honesty and accountability. It was a very literal thing — not accountability in spirit only, but also in action.

Accountability in today's church has taken on a psychological definition which is highly humanistic and measures one against oneself. We ask, "Are you being true to yourself?" That is not the question from church history or from theology. That question is straight out of humanistic psychology. The question of the church has to do with being true to your God, your community, your church, your brothers and sisters, *and yourself*, as well as being true to eternal truth and dimensions of action that require more than your own strength. A tall demand — not a user-friendly suggestion.

Humanistic psychology went beyond the philosophical definition of "humanism." Humanistic psychology used humanism as a base for the most selfish, self-centered, hedonistic, and even narcissistic approach to human beings that ever was invented, and the church at times went just as far in the other direction into total denial of one's self. Denial became a centerpiece of the church, just as it became a centerpiece in Freudian psychology. It is obvious that throughout history, the church has had a tough time keeping itself balanced — and, of course, as long as the church deals with human beings, it will remain that way.

One could then ask, what is the problem? The problem is that true theology does not take on the image of the age or the interpretation of the moment. True theology stands for truths that are constant in all times and all places and interprets each age in the light of these accepted truths, even though we know that human nature does not support such.

Pride in Stone

The local church is the least-used amount of square footage of building space in most communities. Many congregations build huge, expensive edifices which essentially stand empty except for a few hours per week. It was recently reported that a well-known tel-evangelist plans to build the largest church auditorium in the United States. One has to question what is the need that drives such a goal. The great cathedrals were certainly monuments to ecclesiastical affluence. However, it can be said that they usually also served as rectories, abbeys, seminaries, and even living quarters and were used several times a day, every day of the week, for study and services, as well as on Sunday. The wasted space in churches is made possible by virtue of the separation of church and state and the resultant benefit of tax exemption. No for-profit corporation could or would tolerate such waste. Even tax-exempt hospitals (a dwindling number are still in truth not-for-profit) are no longer being granted the right to extensive and needless duplication of equipment.

Today there is a resurgence among many of the more evangelical churches to build lavish buildings that will seat several thousand persons. This movement seems to involve greater family participation, recreation, education, and community use. Churches who expect parishioners to give to the purchase of stone will need to make the building accessible to the community as well as its member families for meaningful life activity on a daily basis. There have been examples of multiple organizations sharing the same church building. The author knows of a building which is used on Friday evening for Jewish Sabbath services, on Saturday for a Seventh-Day Adventist Church, and on Sunday for a Bible Church! It seems that this could be a cost-effective procedure that many churches could duplicate with considerably better stewardship of space and money, to say nothing of the church's expanded community value.

The *Wall Street Journal* (December 23, 1997) noted that churches with tall spires have entered into contracts with telecommunications companies to pay handsomely for the use of their tall steeples for wireless transmitting equipment. (This is an interesting development in that one of the original reasons for a spire was to ring the bell as a communication device.) This is only one possible community use of church buildings and equipment that could be explored. More meaningful would be how unused space might assist those the church claims to be vitally interested in, i.e., the homeless, the poor, the hungry, single parents, and a variety of other needy persons. For centuries the Salvation Army has been successful in combining the Gospel with social relief, but in far more humble edifices. Many new mega-churches are performing some of the same functions in a similar but much more high-profile manner.

Anyone who has visited the great cathedrals of the world understands the spiritual impact that just walking into such a sacred place makes. However, it is not just the building. It is the remnants of holy lives that have gone before and left their indelible images in writings, music, liturgy, prayers, sermons, and, for that matter, in their crypts and burial vaults within its walls. The architecture, stained glass windows, and pipe organs are without doubt a testimony of an aesthetic God through human hands, but the emphasis upon fund raising must be for that which is done in the building — the end result in people's lives — then the stone has greater lasting value.

Another major difference between building with stone today and in the past has to do with the involvement of those who labor to build it. We now pay to have others — outsiders — build the buildings. In the past, cathedrals were built with hands that contributed more than just their physical labor. At no small price the murals were painted, the stone was cut, and the stained glass was leaded, both by paid and non-paid artists and artisans. The lack of personal physical involvement in the actual construction of church buildings makes it all the more important that contributors have personal involvement in the functions of the buildings. A small, growing congregation in a Midwest city desperately needed a new church building to take the place of the condemned old house in which they were meeting. The members of that congregation personally hammered nails, poured concrete, and put on roofing in order to make it happen. There was no doubt about the ownership of that building. This kind of personal involvement and ownership still occurs in smaller congregations, especially those without denominational ties.

The Atlantic Monthly (August 1996) devoted 16 pages to a revealing story entitled "The Next Church." It describes huge megachurches which are being built — stadiums that will seat 10,000 — coliseums for Christ, if you will. The issue is not size alone. The issues are purpose, meaning, and the end result. It boggles the psychological or sociological mind to consider how the person as an individual will fare in such cities of people. Will they not get lost in spite of the multi-minister staff and the appearance of so much individual interest? Of promise is the plan to utilize these new megachurch structures for activities all day, every day of the week — but then how to use a 10,000-seat stadium daily may pose a bit more of a problem.

The Church Has Taken on More Than Its Clergy Are Trained to Do

Clergy must be trained to do all facets of the job expected of them. They are not. For the multitude of tasks placed upon them, all clergy, regardless of denomination or religion, are woefully underprepared. Further, there is no way that clergy can be prepared for the multitude of tasks they are expected to perform in the postmodern church. They are expected to be theologians, great public speakers, social workers, mental health counselors, marriage counselors, financial wizards, building and grounds managers, and public relations experts (to name a few). On top of that, they are supposed to be community minded, good orators, and preach inspiring sermons! One study found that fewer than half of the Protestant ministers in the United States do not have a bachelor's degree from college. However, another study found that 88% of *senior* ministers in Protestant churches have a college degree. Key to this seeming discrepancy is that churches large enough to have *senior* ministers do not represent the largest number of Protestant congregations. Many ministers in a large number of churches have a 3-year (or less) Bible college education, many have a correspondence course, and many have no formal training of any kind. Often the more fundamentalist groups do not require formal education for ordination into the ministry. If a person in such a group feels the "call to preach," the elders, deacons, and fellow ministers (after examining the candidate's piety) gather for a "laying on of hands" and the aspiring preacher is ordained and thereby given all the rights and privileges available in that particular setting to even the most educated. That person may legally marry, bury, do pastoral counseling (psychotherapy), and run the business affairs of a congregation without further formal education or licensure.

Those who receive graduate seminary education (usually 3 years following a bachelor's degree), among other subjects, receive training in theology, Biblical languages, and preaching and a thorough indoctrination in the peculiarities of their particular denomination's polity. Most ministers with the title "Doctor" have been awarded an honorary Doctor of Divinity (D.D., usually bestowed by one of their own denominational institutions of higher learning) which is not given for further education, but for meritorious service. Very few ministers have an earned doctorate; however, in recent years, the Doctor of Ministry (D.Min.) degree has become popular with many in mainline denominations. While helpful in assisting the thinking pastor who has already completed at least 7 years of post-high school education to gain further expertise in a chosen area of study, such as pastoral care, history, archeology, evangelism, business, etc., the doctorate is certainly not necessary.

However, even of pastors with the earned doctor's degree, the church still asks far too much of its clergy. Why is this the case? It is because the church has taken on the roles of too many other organizations and agencies. It is attempting to be "all things to all people." It attempts to be socially correct, politically astute, financially viable, and meet far too many of its members' needs and wants. The church's true assignment is far more circumscribed, however, its leaders have adopted a function that exceeds what any one agency, social or otherwise, could possibly perform.

It's Really a Power Struggle

One of the most valuable contributions of the psychoanalytic movement is the understanding of power. Although some would argue that money is the basis of most negotiations, in truth, it is power. Money only serves as a means to the power. Negotiation likewise can serve to be a power play. In many ways, life is played out on a kind of chessboard. The skill for many is to see who they can make the pawn. In many transactions, the end conclusion may not even be desired by the winner — only winning is! One only has to attend an auction to see the frenzy that occurs and the exorbitantly high prices that can be produced, all because there are so many trying to outdo the other person. A friend of mine, who loved auctions, used to say, "I know that lamp I bought was not worth it, but once I got bidding, there's no way I was going to let that other guy have it." He would then stash it away in his barn, because he had won what he was after — power over someone else.

The church is caught in a similar dilemma. Each congregation is attempting to increase membership, improve contributions, and boast of having the most loyal members. Of course, many of those loyal members may have actually only transferred their membership from another congregation where they were equally "loyal." The church's use of power is to create more power. Power is often subtle, and so it is in the church. The power is ensconced in "what God says." It is a serious problem to assume that what the church says is the same as what God would say, as is the assumption that the preacher is right, even infallible. It is amazing how two preachers can get totally different interpretations from the same verse of Scripture. The fact that they do not agree is not the problem. In every period of time since Moses, "fathers of the faith" have gathered together to reach a consensus regarding the meaning of God's Word. The problem is that each of them assumes to have the correct meaning and preaches it as God's own interpretation and each *knows* that all other interpretations are wrong! It is difficult not to believe that the dynamics of this kind of action have more to do with personal power and glory than canonical and exegetical correctness.

The Lord's Prayer ends with "for *Thine* is the kingdom, the power, and the glory forever." This prayer is also interesting in that it is not actually the prayer of Jesus, but the prayer given to us *by*

Jesus as a *model prayer*. As a model, it speaks to what should be the Christian's stand on the ownership of the kingdom, power, and glory and certainly makes clear that we are not the owners. Most church members and preachers alike are willing to wait for the kingdom, but they are not so willing to wait for the power and the glory. It is the ownership of the kingdom — God — who in the final analysis has the power and hence, the glory. When churches, whether ministers or members, presume to promote themselves as the power, or as even having the power, they have forgotten the theological definition of omnipotence upon which is based Judeo-Christian theology: that both power and glory can never be personally owned because they both belong to God.

The Church Denies the Undeniable

Ernest Becker (1973), in his great book, *The Denial of Death*, helped us to see beyond a doubt that the great falsehood of the day is to attempt to deny the undeniable — death. *That denial is just as real in most churches as it is any place else.* Yes, funerals are held in church sanctuaries. There may even be a minor return to having funerals in churches rather than in funeral homes. However, it is only the superficiality of death that is being spoken of here. The psychological purpose of life has crowded out questions about death. To the extent that the church attempts to escape one of its primary messages, i.e., what to do about dying, to that extent the church is truly irrelevant. Meanings that are man-made are not trustworthy. Becker brilliantly elucidates how each of the great psychoanalytic thinkers came to the same bleak dead-end street and came to agree with Kierkegaard "that the only way out of human conflict is full renunciation, to give one's life as a gift to the highest powers. Absolution has to come from the absolute beyond" (p. 173). He points out that "Freud was anti-religious because he somehow could not personally give the gift of his life to a religious ideal" (1973, p. 174).

There has been a movement recently within many Protestant churches to have "memorial services" rather than funerals. Churches are to be applauded for finally seeing that the death of a righteous person is a celebration and that they no longer need to commemorate death in the traditional morbid method. Many older persons can remember when someone sat up all night in the "wake" (frequently in the deceased person's home) to keep cold cloths on the corpse (prior to modern embalming). They then sat through a 2- (or more) hour funeral (in the summertime using funeral home advertising paper fans on wood sticks) and followed the hearse to the cemetery in a long funeral procession (out of respect, drivers pulled their cars over and stopped). The mourners sang as they walked from the hearse to the grave (usually "The Last Mile of the Way"), then endured another service nearly as long as the first at the grave (giving "earth to earth, dust to dust, and ashes to ashes"), and then watched with the bereaving family as the dirt was shoveled back into the grave over the casket. The services were long and morbid by our standards. Those in attendance were exhorted in no gentle words to live righteous lives in the hope of making it to heaven to join the deceased. Believe it or not, many preachers did not hesitate to admonish those in attendance to live righteously to avoid joining the deceased! Songs such as *When the Roll Is Called Up Yonder*, *In the Sweet By and By*, *When We All Get to Heaven*, and other "heaven-type" songs were sung. Friends of the deceased would frequently stand to give "a word" of testimony about their departed loved one. There were times when the darkest of sinners were made saints right at the gravesite. Words of family and friends sometimes made the most vile person when living, look quite righteous now in death.

Those funeral services could be grim, but they made the point — the person in that casket was dead and gone. The hope was a spiritual one, and only a spiritual one. There was nothing pretty about death and dying. The seemingly hysterical activities at the funeral and gravesite were meaningful to those in attendance. Those were the last possible human efforts to reverse the ravages of this sinful life and bestow what little spirituality humans could offer. Although we sincerely believe that many of these mourners understood the grace of God, as best we can in the flesh, there was an element to those services that was not unlike the ancients pleading with the Sun God, the Harvest God, or the Moon God. Belief and unbelief are always mixed and there is no doubt that many times, out of our earthly need, we "hedge our bets" by invoking everything possible. After all, in the finest of intellectual and theological minds, the resurrection is indeed a mystery. The belief was that in the future we would be united again. They answered that age old question in the song, *Will the Circle Be Unbroken?*

The long, morbid approach to death probably had many downsides that we don't want to reinvent, but no doubt there were some positive parts to it as well. The symbols were unforgettable and the ritual was very real. Our more "modern" approach often leaves family and friends with questions. Sometimes, children and loved ones who do not "view" the body of the deceased forever wonder if that person is really dead. The brief service without prior viewing and, the even briefer internment at the graveside sometimes effects the quickness with which life for those who mourn can return to normal. Attempting to camouflage death neither allows an experience of what dying really is nor does it provide enough time for "it all to sink in" and thus permit sufficient time to grieve.

Elisabeth Kubler-Ross, M.D. (noted authority on the psychology of death) in *The Power of Healing* (1990) states, "Funerals and cremation rituals are for the living, not for the dead. People who specify in their will that they don't want a funeral service of any kind do a disservice to their survivors, because the survivors need a sense of closure in order to process the death of a loved one ... in any case, the viewing of the body is absolutely essential, especially in sudden, unexpected deaths, so survivors can verify that this person has left their lives ... without the viewing, survivors may remain in partial denial for years ... people in mourning have to come to grips with death before they can live again. Mourning can go on for years. It doesn't end after a year; that's a false fantasy. It usually ends when people realize that they can live again, that they can concentrate their energies on their lives as a whole, and not on their hurt, and guilt, and pain."

We may not wish to return to the extremely morbid approach to death. However, we have a long way to go before we integrate symbol, ritual, grief, emotion, and reality for the bereaved. We still spend an exorbitant amount on caskets and flowers making every attempt to have the corpse look "life-like." Mortuary science prides itself on advances that can produce cosmetic results that are without question more lifelike. Quite apart from the cosmetics, there are still some strange idiosyncrasies that surround a casket. The dead person is sometimes "asleep" with glasses on, and we often wonder if when fully clothed in death, do they wear shoes? It is not unusual to hear such utterances at the "wake" such as, "she looks alive enough to sit up and talk" or "he just looks asleep." Sometimes when the cause of death has been severe head trauma and the body cannot be viewed, there is unhappiness that the corpse could not be offered modern cosmetic benefits. These are but illustrations that regardless of our yeoman efforts to masquerade death, it is not possible. However, it is not a harangue about the funeral industry. It is just an attempt to help us rethink the last stage of our earthly journey, death.

This book is not the forum to discuss the Western method of observing death and dying, but it is the place to ask if churches are part of the denial of death. There is undeniably a dichotomy in the church between the admission of death and the denial of death at the same time. The current trend to replace the traditional funeral with a memorial service is testimony to that fact. There is no doubt that an emphasis on the resurrection has caused some churches to overemphasize that part of theology and underemphasize the need

for proper grief and sadness. Though it might seem an inconsisten-
cy, sadness and celebration are not incongruent and can be properly experienced simultaneously. The memorial service sometimes
assumes that one can only celebrate in the absence of grief and that
Christians who appropriately understand and practice New
Testament theology will have put their grief behind them, assuming
the hope of the resurrection.

The traditional funeral was a requiem — a high and holy sacrament. Still at this time, one of the most high and holy moments in
the more liturgical Episcopal and Roman Catholic Churches is the
funeral mass. That mass is powerful in the healing of human sorrow.
Some of most meaningful church services I have ever attended were
Episcopal funeral masses. The first was for my brother, an
Episcopal Priest, and the other was for a friend as close as a brother. More recently I attended a Roman Catholic Mass for a dear
friend. These instances, and more, have forced this writer to rethink
the value of the funeral service in contrast to the more trendy
memorial service.

The memorial service serves as an opportunity to remember
and celebrate one's life and doubtless there is a place for such.
However, maybe this is only part of what the grieving family and
friends need. Furthermore, it may well be that some persons are not
afforded sufficient opportunity to process the person's death by that
method and thereby are not adequately enabled to move through
their grief. Since often only the immediate family is invited to the
internment (which frequently precedes the memorial service), it
may be that we are assuming that the larger community of friends
needs less grief work. This is often not the case, and grief work is
not the only purpose served in the process of burying relatives and
friends. The rich rituals of the church (when employed) enable the
corporate church family to support the bereaving family.
Bereavement alone becomes introspective and the emotions
become introjected, resulting in a prolonged grief period and fre-

quently exogenous depression (external causes). When grief turns into depression and is allowed to continue as a private journey, the mind/body internalizes it, resulting in endogenous depression (internal causes), frequently requiring both psychotherapy and medication.

The "family of God" within the church is a deep source of support and becomes the voices of God on earth which invite the bereaved to continue in the normal activities of life. When these normal activities are discontinued and the bereaved withdraw into solitary states, pathology is being born. When friends and relatives are invited to participate in the entire process of death and burial, the bond is maintained and both the bereaved family and the bereaved friends of the deceased have to go only a short distance to reach each other. It can be safely argued that the extent to which friends are excluded from the "process-bonding" which occurs from the point of the death notice through the actual internment, to that extent they will not be able to fully support the mourner, share the grief, and move forward with the bereaved family in the healing process.

Many argue that the memorial service is a service of celebration. Is this to say that a sacrament (the funeral) cannot be a celebration? A funeral celebrated in the fullness of liturgy and ritual is indeed a celebration of life as well as a transition into the next life. Thus it serves as a sober reminder of our own mortality and our need for hope in the hereafter.

Funerals have been traditionally celebrated as sacraments in the church for very good reasons. Symbols and rituals are essential to thinking and to living. One of the richest contributions of the church (apart from the Gospel message) has been the adornment of the truth in beauty. Rituals and symbols have been a huge part of this adornment. Rituals consist of many symbols. Each symbol speaks to individuals in different ways. Individual symbols are not rituals, but when properly combined, they can form a gestalt of meaning which becomes a ritual. Rituals can bring a wholeness to otherwise disjointed aspects of various belief systems. Sacraments are excellent examples of rituals which are made up of many symbols.

Funerals have traditionally been given, and have therefore provided many symbols, forming common rituals. Since each symbol is interpreted privately by each individual, symbols allow individuals to identify in different ways and thus to "process" and "work through" their own grief and in truth their own dying in more individualized methods. Rituals, more than symbols, have common meaning and are largely interpreted similarly by all persons participating in them. A funeral ritual can unite all persons in a common statement, i.e., we all shall die.

The only way to deal with life is to do so within the context of death. Birth and death are only different parts of life. Life does not begin with birth and it does not end with death. Life is the essence of the spirit and it is to the spirit that the church must minister. The oddities and problems along the way are simply idiosyncrasies of existence. To get caught up in any of them is to take away from the real problem — the human predicament. If we could understand the mysteries of birth and death, we could perhaps better understand "who God is." The predicament is that we are here and now and have but finite time to prepare to go elsewhere. Clothing, food, and shelter are the concerns of most persons. There is no argument that it must be more difficult to believe without these basic needs. However, Jesus taught us not to worry about what we will eat and what will we wear (Matthew 6:31, *NRSV*). The concerns are in the journey and its destiny, but it also must be remembered that the greatest concern is in our own ultimate end. We sanctify ourselves to that end each time we contemplate death.

The Loss of Symbols and Rituals Is Critical

Worship services in the church were built upon symbols and rituals. The funeral service is only one instance in the church when symbols and rituals have been lost. Many Protestant churches pride themselves on the lack of symbolism and ritual in their services, particularly the more conservative ones. New sanctuaries are built with little attention to symbols. Some mega-churches require a careful inspection to realize that they are churches. This is unfortunate because symbols speak to the soul as words do not. Symbols allow for individual interpretation and rituals invite and enable the larger community into a common belief and celebration of that belief. Concretizing the abstract is essential to learning. Learning cannot be separated from faith. In order to learn, one must have faith in what is being taught. You can learn from a teacher you do not like, do not agree with, and do not trust, but in order to retain knowledge, you must believe that which is being taught has value. The value is always wrapped up in the meaning of the symbols or rituals of that learning. For instance, we learn certain information in college in order to pass the examination, i.e., the ritual. We learn by association, i.e., building new knowledge on old. The old knowledge can serve as symbols to which we can attach new meaning. Everything we learn is founded and expressed in symbols and those symbols can be, and usually are, tied together in rituals.

Without symbols there is a paucity of meaning, and without rituals there is a loss of community. Therefore, maintaining clear understanding of symbols and rituals is critical to teaching faith. They allow learning to occur within a framework that has been accepted and to build upon symbolic and ritualistic knowledge that has already been assimilated into our belief system. Long before we knew what we were learning, our parents, siblings, and society deeply instilled within us the symbols by which we would learn more fully all that we would ever know.

Symbols and rituals can provide a process by which one may bridge years, relationships, and multiple emotional events in one's life. They permit us to gain insight and understanding of both present and past relationships. They promote a process by which one may reconstruct and repair breaches in both present and past relationships. They provide meaning to myth, allowing one to return to and maintain a healthy, whole person within one's self, one's community, and one's family. Thus they can provide an individual process which can bring emotional healing regardless of the wishes or participation of others.

How do symbols and rituals work and why are they essential to worship? Symbols and rituals become the basis for already accepted beliefs and provide a trusted base upon which to receive new knowledge. Even new information that we doubt can be accepted if it will fit into the gestalt already in place. Symbols and rituals make adaptation, coping, and translation possible on an individual level while communicating with a larger community. They permit old information to be revisited within the context of new information and, likewise permit new information to become integrated into old information which is already in place. Symbols and rituals allow one to identify with one's value base without having to put it into new words. As a matter of fact, symbols and rituals *force* us to identify that which we *cannot* put into words. For instance, prayer is clearly a ritual that as the Scriptures state allows us to talk with God with "groanings that cannot be uttered." Symbols and ritual discourage argumentation since they are so absolutely accepted by one's self and each of us knows that everyone else has his/her own interpretation as well. They announce that the meaning of words and actions emanate from the inner person and thus are more egosyntonic, meaning that they "fit" with our innermost person. They do not readily permit technical analysis and they escape the "scientific" method. Their true meaning is entirely too personal to be analyzed by anyone else and they are not easily analyzed even by ourselves. The meaning is far more emotional than intellectual; therefore, in order to even revisit information built upon these already accepted symbols and rituals, the veil of emotion must first be penetrated. To penetrate the tough psychological membrane that sheaths our already accepted beliefs is not easy. Persons who voice little faith in the United States, for instance, can get very concerned when someone threatens to burn the American flag. Even persons who never attend church will tell you that they are comforted by the steeple with a cross on top.

Symbols have meaning — very deep meaning — the depth of which is not always known until the destruction of that symbol is threatened. Rituals likewise have deep meaning. The entire ritual is threatened when one or more symbols within that ritual are threatened. For instance, the wedding ring (symbol) does not make a wedding (ritual). However, when the wedding ring is taken off following a divorce, the entire ritual of the wedding ceremony (the ritual) becomes meaningless.

Langer points out in *Philosophy in a New Key* (1963) that we cannot live without symbols. She helped us to understand that signs and symbols are two different things: "A symbol means to each person something very unique and no one can tell another person exactly what that is. A sign, on the other hand, may be interpreted by everyone as meaning the same thing. Other signs, however, are both universally accepted and yet have highly personalized interpretations. The sign of the cross, a fish, a Star of David, a wedding band, a nation's flag, etc., while having broad general interpretation, can have highly individualized and specific meanings to each individual. However, signs (which are ritualized symbols) speak the same message to all." An illustration of such a symbol is the highway stop sign, which fortunately became a ritual and hopefully is observed by all motorists the same way!

Our own individual reality and purposes are found in our own unique symbols. We live by symbols, and it is not terribly difficult to find each individual's unique and meaningful symbols. Therapists who understand symbols and rituals have found them to be very valuable in therapeutic interventions. We find that symbols range from a keepsake, to a watch given by a relative, to a picture on the wall, or frequently to items one would never guess as even having meaning. Following the horrible September SwissAir Flight 111 airplane disaster over Halifax, Nova Scotia, CNN showed pictures of Red Cross workers collecting stones from the shoreline as mementos for the mourning relatives.

The author is reminded of a young boy, about 8 years old, who kept playing with a small, beat-up pocketknife during his therapy sessions. I noticed that he never opened it. He fondled it as if it were fragile and very valuable. His father had been crushed to death by an excavating machine only a couple of blocks from my office. I later learned that the pocketknife had belonged to his father and was in his father's pocket at the time of his death. The pocketknife became a constant reminder of his father, and it became the catalyst for serious reconstructive psychotherapy with that boy.

It is important when working with anyone in therapy to assist the person in finding the symbol, rather than the therapist finding the symbol for the patient. In families who have had a death, each member finds their own symbols, even though they may all join together in a common funeral service that becomes a ritual.

The following illustration from my own life may be helpful. As a child, I was given a medal by the Chicago Motor Club for serving as a crossing guard at an elementary school. Believing that such accomplishments were not important, and feeling like a very unimportant person, I tossed the medal on my dresser and forgot it. I do not recall whether I even showed it to my parents or not. About 50 years later my father died and my sister gave me the medal saying, "Here, this belongs to you." I asked her where she found it because I had forgotten that I ever had it. She said, "Dad had it in his pocket when he died, he always carried it with his change." Little did I know that the medal was important to my father and that it symbolized a relationship that I did not know about between my father and myself, and therefore I could not enjoy, but it was obviously very important to him. This medal continues at this time to serve as a bonding symbol for that father/son relationship. I carry it in my pocket to this day — the same as my father did for so many years.

Everyone has symbols that are personally sacred. They have established themselves out of various relationships. Many of these symbols are "unknown" until an event occurs which forces the unconscious mind to recognize truths that remained hidden sometimes for many years. Often families that cannot express love openly may well have many such symbols. Our context of symbol recognition comes out of a combination of relationships, experiences, and learning. Most meaning arises from simple learning that was taught by parents. All of us come to understand essentially the same thing from signs and rituals. The reason is found in learning. If we had been taught to go through the intersection on red lights and stop on green lights, we would perform exactly the opposite of what we now do.

This is where religion and rituals meet. We are taught what to believe. Our beliefs are all individualized and thus internalized in symbols. Corporately, that is within our particular religious preference. All members of that communion confess to similar beliefs, which they too have been taught. Those beliefs are acted out in ritual by the assembly in unison, thus making each member a part of each other, and all identify with the body to which they belong.

Many Protestant denominations build new sanctuaries devoid of traditional symbols and have all but abandoned traditional ritual. Many Roman Catholic churches have greatly reduced their rituals. They cite many modern and historical reasons for doing so. In truth, many Protestant churches initially abandoned symbols and ritual in protest of the Roman Catholic Church. That may still be the case in some instances; however, in others they simply can no longer afford the stained glass windows, elaborate chancels, sculpted saints, and tapestries. However, at the same time they have all introduced other rituals, thus replacing traditional rituals with new ones. Sometimes the new practice, which they do not call a ritual, becomes a ritual of nonritual. After all, a ritual is only the combination of many symbols. Within the church, a ritual is usually a prescribed procedure. Even if informality and spontaneity are the prescribed behaviors, they too become ritualized.

Herein lies a problem. The extent to which ritual is experienced solely as an individual symbol, to that extent its meaning is kept private and individual. To the extent that the corporate worship is thus individualized, to that extent the bonding of the fellowship cannot occur. In order for there to be a fully appreciated "fellowship of believers," it is necessary to have the symbols bound in congregational ritual. For that to happen, a prescribed set of symbols with uniformalized individual acceptance must be made available and those commonly accepted symbols must be bound together into the larger ritual that allows all to partake as one in unison.

Since symbols tend to be subject to private interpretation, although of common understanding, they must be put together in a meaningful way in order to constitute a community ritual. For instance, although the wedding band has a commonly recognized meaning, it receives individual symbolic interpretation by the recipient. It is only when the wedding band is put with the bridal gown, the wedding march, the words of the clergy, etc. that it becomes integral to the ritual. The ritual therefore includes the private and common symbols, but when combined they extend broadly enough that all persons in attendance may enter into the ritual.

The loss of symbol and ritual from corporate worship may seem like a small thing. But it is not. People cannot join together in communal activity without both symbols and rituals. We are talking about why the church is failing. If schools or other organizations chose to incorporate only highly individualized symbols into their programs, and there were no corporate rituals, those organizations would suffer the same loss of unique identity as has the church. We only need to think of organizations such as the Rotary Club, the Kiwanis Club, the Sertoma Club, the Lions Club, the YWCA, YMCA, the Boy Scouts, the Girl Scouts, and of course the United States Military to emphasize this point. Individualized symbols that are commonly accepted and incorporated into regularly observed rituals are essential for corporate life, whether it is the church or any other organization.

Not all local congregations are failing — but far too many are — both Mainline Protestant and Roman Catholic. Many of the ostensibly "successful" newer nondenominational congregations may also in truth be failing in spite of their external appearances. It depends on what one accepts as "success." The word "success" is actually alien to the Scriptures and is a commercial word. Even at that, in order to assess success, one must define it. We await definitive studies that show why some congregations not only survive but succeed and others do not. If the church were to follow the corporate business model, it would immediately undertake a massive research project. Even that might well be of little value since we have no clear definition of success in the church. The ultimate definition will, of course, not be ours but God's.

3

Created in a
New Image

To be "normal" may not be desirable.

A "NEW CREATION" IN CHRIST IS MORE
THAN A PSYCHOLOGICAL OVERHAUL

EVERY AGE PROMOTES some special image for everybody. This is the age of the "well-adjusted person" and the "worried well." Education, therapy, psychological adjustments, and other forms of behavioral science interventions are all well and good, but they are not the same as Christian conversion. Simply refurbishing, repairing, or a painstaking overhaul are not what the gospel is about. We live in a day when it is not easy to reflect the super-powerful energy of the Christ in one's daily existence. Our age has supposedly produced an educated, cultured person who by rugged individualism can fend off these troubled times — and without outside help.

To Be "Average" Is to Be Different

The well-known image of Garrison Keilor's *Lake Wobegon* is our ideal, "... where all the women are strong, the men are good looking, and all the children are above average." These magnificent-sounding ideas represent our wishful thinking. We hide behind delusional psychological imagery for this kind of thinking, and we use what we have been told are psychological norms. Actually what we call "norms" are not norms at all, but spurious statistical manipulations. However, these misguided definitions of what we call psychological norms have become the basis of wish fulfillment. After all, we are not the first generation of the human race to seek Utopia.

These norms are based on fraudulent statistics, and norms can be very dangerous, as we will discuss shortly. Furthermore, we should not accept the "normal curve" as it is called. The Gaussian curve, or normal curve, is considered to be the standard distribution of whatever is being measured, which in this case is people. This would mean that there are as many people on the low end of the curve as there are at the top end, with the majority in the middle, huddling on the 50-yard line, or the average. Society tends to accept only one end of the bell curve — the upper end — at least for ourselves, our families, and some of our friends. Keilor's imaginary community where everyone is better than the normal is the top end of that curve. This highest level of statistical significance is way out there where statisticians brag about the ".0001 level of significance." In other words, so far out that its attainment would tease the figment of one's imagination. But this is our new, grandiose self-image!

Psychological norms are established by determining the "average" — and they become the basis for expected behavior and the diagnosis of "normal." This suggests that we can know by statistical calculation how many persons (or things) will be in the middle of the curve: 45% will be very close to the center line. That leaves 55% who are to some degree not "normal." One half of that 55%

(27.5%) will be "higher" than normal and the other half also (27.5%) will be "lower" than normal. This leaves 7.4% who are split between the very top and the very bottom of the curve. The statistical method can be used for everything and everyone in the universe. This method is mathematically correct but not necessarily scientifically so. It is built on the assumption that everything follows a "normal" distribution, which is not the case. When applied to human beings and used for everything from school placement to commitment to mental institutions, it is clearly not only unscientific — but downright dangerous. But this is our new, grandiose self-image!

Statisticians take the whole, add it up, divide it by the number of entries — and there you are: forever fixed at some point from below average to superior, with your designation having been determined by whatever may be the mediocrity of the majority!

PSYCHOLOGICAL MEASUREMENTS DO NOT FIT THE HUMAN CONDITION

The tendency of our society, including the church, to accept the definitions and measurements of the social sciences, particularly psychology and psychiatry, has done everyone a serious disservice. The professions of psychology and psychiatry have attained a status in our society that has not been earned. The eagerness of humans for answers to the unanswerable has allowed an opening in all of our social systems, including religion, that may not have been available at other times in history. Furthermore, with advances in knowledge, the door to this kind of unquestioned acceptance of unproven interference to living may soon close.

"IQ" Is a Number, Not One's Intelligence

A tragic illustration of this use of the norm is found in our current use of IQ tests for children. Children are classified by their IQ, in spite of the fact that no respectable psychologist today would allow such a designation for their own child. Children are placed in "gifted programs" based on their ability to perform on "standardized intelligence tests" and can be allowed into the class or kept out based merely on one point! A case was brought to my attention: the local "gifted " program required an IQ of 135. An extremely bright and gifted child received a score of 134 on the IQ test. The school psychologist was required by the school system to classify the child as below entrance to that program! We know full well that one point in either direction does not make one student "gifted" and another one "un-gifted." Furthermore, "IQ" (which stands for "intelligence quotient") literally means the IQ number — and is not synonymous with actual intelligence. It is an arithmetic addition of several scores derived from performance on several different types of "mental processes" and "manual performance." Once again the "average" is used and each subtest is a measure of what the average child of that age would be predicted to achieve on that particular task.

Using IQ scores is the standard practice of educational systems. Such a practice provides a method for categorizing and placing students in artificial groups of "ability." This "ability" is not necessarily the performance required in that *class*, but the performance required on that particular *IQ test*. Although these two are at times argued by well-meaning educators as being similar, if not the same, they are not even close to the same. One situation calls for the youngster to complete a set of tasks in isolation, under pressure, and measured *in comparison* to his/her peers. In actual classroom learning situations, the youngster is asked to perform tasks within the context of a broad learning base and within the community of learners. Single item tasks do not measure ability. At best they measure the ability to perform that specific item, under stress, as an isolated bit of information without reference to a context. Learning does not occur out of context or in isolation. We learn by building bits of information on top of other bits of information and creating context as we go. What we know about the process of human learning should tell us that IQ tests are counterproductive in the educational process. One wonders if such educators are educated beyond their own intelligence! But this is our new, grandiose self-image.

Intelligence tests are not "culture fair" and they do not adequately account for one's earlier education. They do not account for environmental influences. Psychologists speak of "culture-free" tests. There are none which are completely free of cultural bias. There are none which take into account the cultural bias of the *examinee*. There are none which take into account the cultural (or other) bias of the *examiner*. Different types of childhood environments, genetic dispositions, and personalities influence the way we perceive, react, and interpret. Differences do not necessarily mean inferior or superior. Sometimes they only mean different. After all, the genius who can play the piano with virtuosity at age five may be an idiot savant and do nothing well but play the piano. The kid on the street may not do well in mathematics and may not be able to play the piano, but may be far better equipped to survive the streets of a ghetto than the young genius in quantum physics. Some tests unfairly discriminate those who are better in the "manual" aspects of ability from those who are better in the "thought process" parts.

IQ tests have what is called the "verbal" (thought process) portion and the "performance" (manual process) portion; then those two scores become what is called the "full scale score." The designation for special programs is mostly based on the "full scale score" which means that most programs are not really matched at all, even on IQ scores. Since most education is verbally based (thought process), some children can have a better chance in our educational system. Those who have come from homes where their parents are better educated, where the family has better environmental advantage, and where reading has been part of home life from early on have significantly better chances of higher IQ scores and as a result usually get a better shot at education and, hence, for success in life.

Diagnoses Are Often Damaging Labels

To make our world even more artificial, mental health personnel have a book called the *DSM, The Diagnostic and Statistical Manual*, published by the American Psychiatric Association. Why it is called "diagnostic" can be seriously questioned, since it is most often used to assign labels for insurance billing purposes. Why it is called "statistical" is somewhat dubious since there is absolutely no evidence that a certain percentage of persons in the various diagnostic categories will meet those criteria. Nevertheless, as anyone who has studied the *DSM IV* must admit, the diagnostic and statistical aspects of this book have had a far-flung influence in America.

These "diagnoses" are actually definitions — not diagnoses — manufactured by a small group of professionals, primarily representing only one very small segment of the mental health profession, psychiatry. The *Diagnostic and Statistical Manual* is revised and published every few years. What is termed "normal" in one version may be termed "abnormal" in the next. Although the publication is a *medical* manual, the majority of material in it is sociological, political, anthropological, and psychological. The American *Psychological* Association, whose doctors are in a much better position by education and training to describe "normal" and "abnormal" does not publish such a manual! The *DSM IV* (soon to become *DSM V*) is actually the application of a set of societal norms, bathed to be politically correct and applied to everyone regardless of race, creed ,or color by the American *Psychiatric* Association. Although many psychologists do not like the psychiatric model, insufficient ruckus has been raised to do anything about it.

It is most interesting that organizations and persons that ought to be speaking to "proper behavior," i.e., schools, churches, teachers, ministers, rabbis, priests, are set aside while a medical organization takes the lead! In medicine there is the axiom that "a correct diagnosis leads to a correct treatment." If such is true, we could face a most disastrous ending to our behavior problems in modern society. This means that behavior is diagnosed by medical minds and treated with medical methods. Certainly not even those medical minds would be willing to assume that simply because behavior has been altered by medication that the person's internal intent or thought processes have necessarily changed. True, there is no doubt that thought processes are chemical, electrical, or anatomically structural in origin. However, do we really believe that there is nothing more to human behavior? Obviously, since diagnoses are largely determined by cultural norms, both diagnoses and treatments will change as does society's expectations as interpreted by the American Psychiatric Association.

One of the most obvious illustrations of changing interpretations of behavior as seen in this manual is observed by comparing *DSM II* (1968) with *DSM IV* (1994). In 1968 the manual listed homosexuality as "302.0," Sexual Deviation, along with Fetishism 302.1, Pedophilia 302.2, Transvestitism 302.3, Exhibitionism 302.4, and other psychiatrically "diagnosable" conditions such as necrophilia (sex with dead persons) and sexual sadism (inflicting sexual pain). By 1994, the *DSM IV* had adopted the changing social "norm" for homosexual behavior as well as more socially acceptable classifications for other conditions that had been previously considered mental illnesses. The discrepancy between what is called mental health and what is called mental illness is huge and dangerous. Under one diagnostic set of guidelines, a patient could be seen as perfectly normal, but when diagnosed by a different version of the *DSM*, the same patient might be given medication or even incarcerated. At best, and at worst, a psychiatric diagnostic manual has become the accepted social conscience as to who is "normal" and who is not. But this is our new, grandiose self-image!

Although it is true that new research brings about changes in diagnostic knowledge, most changes result from social pressure, third-party financial arrangements, and that which professional leaders in society (in this case psychiatrists) consider to be "normal" at a given time in the history of the human race. That which a society thinks it can manage tends to be classified as "normal" and that which either it cannot manage and/or considers disgusting becomes classified as "abnormal."

To show how capricious this method really is, consider the "homeless." A few years ago many homeless persons would have been in mental institutions and would therefore have had a mental disorder diagnosis. As a result, such persons were taken care of by mental health organizations. Today, by a simple change in diagnosis, they are now on their own. However, not all homeless are mentally ill, but, by virtue of the facts that they "cannot be managed," do not fit societal "normalcy," and in many cases are "disgusting," all homeless, mentally ill or not, would be diagnosed as mentally ill if the *DSM IV* method of determining mental illness were used. However, it is not.

Mental illness (or health) has become one's ability to adapt to the larger societal norm. Just think of the ramifications of such a system for anyone who deviates from the social norm. For starters, think of the millions of persons who are classified as sick, and therefore are under control of the medical profession, by virtue of diagnosis, who in previous times would have simply been poor and unfortunate. The shift from *condition* to *diagnosis* changes what social institution has ultimate responsibility for these unfortunate souls. "Condition" belongs to society, but "diagnosis" belongs to the healthcare industry — a major difference.

When people are "poor" (a condition) in our society, they become recipients of "free grace," i.e., welfare, food stamps, public funding, etc. In the instance of poverty, the church and other social institutions attempt to help. When people are "sick" (a diagnosis), they must pay for that "grace" (service), i.e., hospitals, doctors, medicine, etc. It all depends upon which social institution labels the "problem." It is to the advantage of the health industry to make as many social problems as possible into medical diagnoses. The healthcare industry has much to gain.

There are traditionally five recognized "social institutions: education, politics, the family, economics, and religion. These institutions are classified as social because they reflect the primary constituents in a society and they change as society changes. There are notable exceptions such as the Amish, although even a casual observation of their communities reveals the same social tendencies. Most religious organizations have accepted social norms and have changed even their most basic doctrinal emphases to stay in accord with societal changes. Considering that the church has creeds that are assumed to contain the truth to all generations, it is remarkable that it has been so willing to change its image to meet newly accepted social norms. The new image built on psychiatry and psychology has been readily adopted by a number of denominations. Recently a friend told me of being introduced to another person and his "cohabitant." "Cohabitation" would seem to be synonymous with fornication in the Scriptural sense of the word. The purpose of this book is not to define "right" or "wrong" or to rewrite the dictionary, but to point out that the institutions in our culture (such as education and religion) which propose to differentiate "right" and "wrong" either cannot, or do not, do so, but have frequently chosen to develop new and less "judgmental" definitions.

Psychology Has Changed the Image of God

"Consider the emphasis now being placed on not referring to God in a gender mode. Speaking of God in the male gender is considered "gender insensitive" and feminine discriminatory; thus we get a hermaphroditic or possibly an asexual/genderless god. The "God-concept" is difficult enough for children (and adults) as it is. When we consider that children need ideas concretized, a gender-free God is even more incomprehensible. It must be literally impossible for them to believe in something they cannot see, that has no ethnicity, and is neither male nor female. Consider the huge debates over issues that the churches declare to be absolute in their creeds, yet at times change on the whim of social pressure.

Although a chapter on social norms cannot be found in any standard theology textbook, these norms are practiced as devotedly by most congregations as any other doctrine. Theological textbooks discuss the belief systems that the church asserts are absolute. They are the doctrines of faith, the "beliefs" we must "believe" in order to be called "believers" in that particular denomination. Since every doctrine in those textbooks is constantly changing according to social pressure and social congruence, social change itself should be considered an absolute belief. All of this is to say that the church has readily accepted social norms as being synonymous with modern theology. Again, the purpose of this discussion is not to determine that which is "right" or "wrong," but to point out the massive confusion within the ranks of those who would tell us which way to go. Churches have not only accepted, but changed the message to fit the New Image — or maybe it would sound more cultured to say Imago Nouveau! The problem is that the church continually attempts to mold its message to this new image. That alone would cause enough confusion, but in addition, the image is constantly changing.

For instance, changing diagnoses in the mental health field cause the church to constantly change its ideas, language, and hence its acceptance or rejection of "sin," and its insistence on "redemption." Consequently, a person's lifestyle is considered to be sin and in need of salvation, when all of a sudden it is deemed to be only the expression of a genetic or environmental disorder and thus no longer in need of anything but acceptance — something the church claims to do best, but has great difficulty practicing. It may even change from sin to "disability," virtually requiring by law that church architecture and practices not only accept it, but accommodate it! Jesus spoke about being "in" the world, but not "of the world." By simple observation, it would appear that the church is succeeding in being simultaneously both "in" and "of" the world by accepting both a secular definition of behavior (that of psychology and psychiatry), while claiming to adhere to a sacred one (that of the church). Of course, this position is certainly easier for rationalizing our new self-aggrandizing image!

The "Truth in Advertising" Problem in Some Churches

The real problem is that acceptance is a misnomer. In truth, we mean, the more you are like me, the more I will accept you! Acceptance is a word that sounds nice and Christian, but just stop and think about it for a moment. If one is truly so accepting that everyone is entitled to one's own opinion, there is nothing to change in anyone! Does that not mean that the church is saying, "We accept you for what you are and for what you believe, but we are going to try to change you anyway?"

The church, while speaking of "acceptance," is still the most segregated institution in our society. This fact is not only true regarding the lack of ethnic mixtures, but it is true in the heart and soul of the way most churches operate. For instance, Protestant churches lend or rent space to various ethnic groups to start and then continue church congregations within their building, but these congregations are not usually integrated into the landlord, benevolent congregation. When these ethnic churches have the funds, they build their own buildings and continue their own ethnic segregation. This is a kind of acceptance that enables both sides to continue their segregation which may or may not be good. It is not, however, the image that the church would portray or that most persons want to believe when they speak of acceptance.

The demographics of our society alone make the message and job of the church hard enough without adopting the new image as defined by non-church society. Single parents, blended families, foster children, bisexual parents, single never-intending-to marry parents, homosexual parents, and persons taking care of both their children and their parents (the sandwich generation) are only a few of the challenges facing the church, to say nothing of what the new-found biological cloning will introduce. This may suffice to identify only a few of the issues about which the church is being forced to rethink her theology. Of course these are but a few of the issues which have pressured the church to accept societal changes and adopt them as "norms."

Becoming gender-sensitive and politically correct is at this time another real problem. The image of the human being by any Judeo-Christian definition is that we are made in the image of God. This becomes next to impossible with our new elastic definition of God. It becomes even more impossible with the ethnic-less, gender-less God, Who like the three proverbial monkeys, "sees no evil, hears no evil, and speaks no evil." Attempting to teach children (and adults as well) about God is simply not feasible when there is no reality base. The concept of God becomes nothing more than a mystical fairy tale with a cast of constantly changing mythical characters playing the lead role. Some of the fathers of the American Colonies, who founded a country largely out of their religious desires, spoke of tolerance, not acceptance. There is a major difference in these concepts, both in philosophy and in practice.

A further problem of the new image is the argument that the church "accepts the sinner but not the sin." If this is true at all, it is only possible because of the church's constantly changing definition of sin. In order to continue to accept the sinner and not the sin, it is necessary to continuously accept as "normal" those elements and actions which in a former time would have been unacceptable. Of course this constant movement allows both the sin and the sinner to be "moving targets" that won't get hit by anything the church might have to say.

The new image has seriously affected the way people change their lives. This is largely because since "everyone is O.K." there is no great urgency for change. Traditionally, church-goers experienced the rituals of "confession," "forgiveness," "repentance," and "reconciliation." These rituals had many symbols attached to them. Many Protestant churches observe the "altar call" which invites penitents to confession. The Roman Catholic Church practices confession and penance; however, far fewer parishioners participate on a regular basis today than was true in years gone by.

Granted, although such practices offer a wonderful mechanism for "repeat business," they also provided not only a place to start over again, but also the knowledge of forgiveness from God and their community of believers. The ritual for repentance and reconciliation provided a "new beginning" and a definite conclusion to errant behavior. This conclusion allowed the penitent to put boundaries around certain off-limits behaviors and start a new life within other boundaries. There was (and is to those in this tradition) a literal understanding of the Pauline concept of "old things have passed away and all things have become new" (II Corinthians 5:17, *The Holy Bible*). A definite ending point and a definite beginning point separates one's "old" life from one's "new life." It is important to have that point of demarcation. In this model there was a clear distinction between "you" and your behavior — that is to say, between the sin and the sinner. In many of today's churches, we have taken acceptance to the point where such a distinction is difficult to make; therefore repentance is not seen as a need. One can now gain communal reconciliation without that ritual. The sin and the sinner have become one. The resulting problem is that if we accept the sinner without a demand for changed behavior, it is not possible to accept either the person or the person's behavior and be true to the church's verbalized theology.

It sounds so good — but is it true that we accept the sinner, but not the sin? It was certainly more distinct when specific actions had to be stopped before acceptance could be granted. There have, of course, been notable abuses of the ritual of repentance. The story is told of the faithful, church-going, self-righteous woman who constantly requested that the congregation pray for her wayward, drunken husband. At every bi-annual revival meeting, the drunken bum would "get saved" and start attending church with his wife. He would take his place in the church, thus placing his wife in a much lesser role and causing her to no longer be able to plead for his salvation. She, with her newly diminished self-worth, would immediately set out to nag, abuse, and otherwise discourage her husband until he gave up on religion and went back to drink, whereupon she could resume her righteous role, praying and soliciting for his redemption!

Likewise, there are stories (and jokes) by the thousands of the abuses of confession prior to taking the Sacrament of Holy Communion in the Roman Catholic Church. However, as we know, jokes and stories tend to crop up around the truisms of life. Without the tragic, there could be no humor. Without the value of these rituals, there would be no jokes.

Symbols and Rituals Are External Measures

Rituals and symbols can become readily confused. The story is told of the penitent who answered an "altar call" and while kneeling at the altar recalled that on one side there was a praying saint holding the penitent's hands high and loudly urging, "hang on, hang on" and on the penitent's other side there was another equally fervent praying saint pounding on the penitent's back while proclaiming, "let go, let go." The penitent did not know which action God would honor most! (The author was the penitent and experienced this first-hand!)

Remember, all action is the result of attending to our perception of symbols. All symbols unite into rituals. Rituals are made from many symbols. Without symbols and their combination into rituals, there is no basis for the establishment of meaning. Private action is the response to some symbol. Integrated symbols become ritualized. Communal action tends to be the result of a common ritual.

Of course, as we all know, personal and interpersonal behaviors in our schools, communities, and churches are accepted today which only a few years ago were *verboten*. And, while some of this may be good, how then can the Church or society promote a set of standards and an acceptable model for Christian living? Or must the church have a constantly changing definition of morals, ethics, and sin? We must be careful not to think that it is the task of society to promote Christian living. The Judeo-Christian message has always been one of reformation and redemption, in opposition to what was going on in society. It is not difficult to understand the pain of the Old Testament prophets when they were taking tough stands against the forces of the times. Being caught in the squeeze between social, political, and popular thought and God's directives has never been easy. The local church sits in this position today.

Certainly, since in order to stay in business the church must have attendance and income, the task is very tricky and really quite unique. It goes like this: Tell your customer that he/she is bad and that you are out to change him/her, but because we accept you the way you are, but not your sin, we would like for you to continue to frequent our business and to make voluntary monetary contributions to our business even though you do not as yet believe in it! And, furthermore, with our new self-aggrandizing image, who needs those services?

One of the elements not included in Keilor's folks at *Lake Wobegon* is affluence. Although there are doubtless "the haves" and "the have nots," his emphasis is on the ordinary folk who get up and go to work everyday and come home tired and hungry. Most of them do not fit the new image very well. They are in many ways still in the "old country" while living in the United States. Certainly one aspect of the "New Image" is money, not only enough money to escape poverty, but enough to live more comfortably. The Psalmist who wrote, "The Lord is my shepherd, I shall not want," was, I believe, thinking of something quite different. When modern Western religionists think of avoiding want, they think of money. Affluence is a way of life. It is a way of life that many Christians believe is their right by virtue of their faith. They are firmly convinced that God has given much to them because they are good. They believe further that God will continue to bless them if they are "faithful." The blessing of which they speak is too often interpreted in a material way. One hears church members say, "God has really blessed me, look at my new watch" (or some other material item). The argument is not that God has not blessed them; however, inevitably it is implied that such a blessing is the result of their devotion to a materialistic God as currently conceived in the Western frame of mind.

A cheapening of the church has occurred because although it preaches that parishioners should have faith for their needs, there is little evidence that the church and its leaders exemplify that faith. Church bazaars, Christmas tree sales, rummage sales, cake walks, bingo games, and a multitude of other capitalistic and entrepreneurial methods are used to raise money. In many instances, an honest day's work at an odd job, volunteering to repair the church roof, voluntary work in the church's preschool, etc. would doubtless result in greater benefit to the local congregation. Furthermore, it could more readily increase the church's coffers with work that the parishioners know how to do. Recently, I asked a friend of mine who was selling Christmas trees at a church, "How is the sale going?" His response was very interesting. He said, "Well, I'm a dentist and I could make far more money seeing a few extra patients and giving that money to the church than I can standing out here in the freezing cold trying to tell people what kind of trees these are, when I don't know one tree from the other, trying to wrap them in netting with a machine I don't know how to work, and listening to gripes that I don't have the kind or size of a tree they want anyway." He said further, "They have already told me that they want me to show my stewardship and loyalty to the church by volunteering to be a bingo caller and this I really don't understand. On Sunday they preach against sin, which includes gambling, but they want me to show my Christianity by doing it." Of course one could legitimately ask whether he would offer to work extra and contribute more! Knowing him, I know he would. Yet he performed a ritual that caused at least some of his fellow church members to hold him in esteem as a faithful, hard-working, believer. The symbol of selling Christmas trees — and the ritual of doing it year after year — how could one not admire him?

MEMBERS ARE ASKED TO SET AN EXAMPLE THE CHURCH ITSELF DOES NOT SET!

In many instances church members are asked to set an example that the church does not set for itself. The church is replete with evidence that it really does not operate completely on the faith it expects of its members. The "yearly pledge drive" is an interesting example. As parishioners, we are to trust the Lord for the needs of tomorrow, yet the local organized group that runs the church wants a guarantee for the preacher's salary and the church expenses.

Psychodynamically, asking church members to donate time to sell things is actually forcing them to admit their weekly offering is insufficient, which is doubtless true. It is often an affront to their intelligence, and disrespect for the years they have spent in training to do what they can do well, to ask them to perform other duties they cannot do well. Has anyone ever considered how it would sound if the local pastor were asked to donate a day selling used cars and the dealer would give the proceeds to the church? Volunteerism seems to go one way only, and often it is "coercerism" in the name of guilt. Parishioners do not necessarily want to volunteer. Sometimes they do not know how to do the job they volunteer for, but feel guilty if when asked they say "no."

The church, because of its capitalistic base of operation, is embroiled in this same image of affluence and as a result has the same need to raise money as any other industry. A televangelist recently proclaimed that God would honor the prayers of those who sent in money more than those who did not. Many ministers thinly veil the message (sometimes not at all) that monetary contributions make one more spiritual. (This evangelist had the tenacity to be honest as to his belief that money and God's favor are inextricably interwoven.)

How many people do you hear talking about the "successful" storefront church? In this day and age, budgets for the majority of the churches of the Western Hemisphere are not met by either the poor or even the rich. The vast amounts of money donated to churches come from middle class to lower upperclass church members. Many mainline local churches and denominations have quite healthy reserve funds and foundations that have been funded by the earlier generations who left money in their wills for specific purposes. This is an interesting phenomenon, considering that economists tell us that with rare exception "old money" is gone. They also tell us that new wealth will be a thing of the past by the end of this generation, approximately 2020. In the meantime, there will doubtless be less expendable wealth; thus the church is apt to feel the financial crunch even more. It is a well-known fact that the "yuppie generation" is having difficulty buying homes and that few have significant savings. Certainly, the ensuing generations will have less money for charitable purposes, both by actually possessing less and by a conscious choice not to give it away.

The Church Prescribes an Image for Its Members — It May Be "Smoke and Mirrors"

Image is everything and it is nothing. It is what we want it to be. It is our willingness, or lack thereof, to conform to that imaginary, media-generated, mythical caricature offered by society. But, since throughout the centuries the church has succumbed to this temptation, it must now take a serious look at what an emerging new image means. What the reduction in wealth will mean for a "new image church" and its members could be the object of much speculation. Is God changing the way people are being blessed or will people have to begin to see "blessings" in a different light? The Biblical story of the widow and her mite has little relevance for today's religious institutions. Her mite was doubtless given out of well-meaning commitment; however, with the capitalistic base of today's religious institutions, it takes far more than "mites" to support it. Church institutions need money and lots of it to maintain the physical plant, a sizable administrative staff, and programs offered. While they may preach against materialism, most religious and charitable organizations have become quite accustomed to enjoying the material benefits of an affluent society.

Churches and parishioners alike have not only become accustomed to a style of life, but have become the products of that affluent life. This economic basis will not easily change. It will be easier to declare bankruptcy and go out of business than to change. With contributions dropping steadily in the mainline churches, a certain kind of bankruptcy might already be happening. From 1997 to 1998, church budgets were down by 15%. There is evidence that the younger generation, who in some instances may be returning to church, actually cannot or does not contribute as did their predecessors. Many mainline churches are living off of dwindling endowments from past generations.

Our "new image" in this new age is not one of poverty, but of affluence. An urban city minister recently announced that folks should feel free to attend her church dressed any way they wanted, even in jeans. She further elaborated that she was also pleased to see those who attended her church "always looked nice and usually wore designer jeans!"

Although no modern day Christian would admit it, they inevitably tie prosperity to Godliness. They probably would not be willing to say that the poor are ungodly, but they certainly tend to associate their affluence as a blessing because they profess to be godly. *USA Today* printed an article by Jim Pinkerton (April 9, 1997) declaring churches as having "Devotion to the calling of making money." He cites theologians from Luther and Calvin to Michael Novak's book, *Business as a Calling*, in support of the equation of religion to business. He also returned to the work of Max Weber, a turn of the century sociologist who wrote, *The Protestant Ethic and the Spirit of Capitalism* (1964). There is no doubt that Weber saw religion as the most powerful influence on capitalism. Furthermore, he correctly pointed out that the Puritans under Cotton Mather prohibited virtually every pastime, except for making money. But, of course, that had to be an exception — for how were they to survive without money?

The modern ethic in the church allows more pastimes (in fact, are any disallowed?) than in the reported Puritanical day, plus making money. Certain pastimes were always allowed, even among the Trappists and old order Amish. They were, however, without doubt performed under considerably greater scrutiny! The combination of postmodern theology, coupled with humanistic psychology, and the permission of the church to become capitalists makes for a very attractive approach to life — particularly if one can be thought of as religious while doing so. Local congregations as "feel-good" organizations have adapted to the overall hedonistic nature of the age and rightly see that since they cannot limit the pleasure principle in their members, they might as well collect the revenue produced by those earth-centered energies. There is no doubt that the most powerful influences on the church are humanistic psychology and capitalism, a change from previous generations. Subtle but real is this new image.

Can the "New Image" Be Christian?

The new image poses serious problems for both psychology and religion. Although undiagnosed by the *DSM*, this image may very well become the description of the postmodern neurotic person *par excellence*. Certainly this sort of person has little to gain from either psychology or the church — except permission. Although there are sufficient funds to pay for psychological care, there is little recognition of need. And, by the same token, there is little need for religion. There is a tremendous push for unconditional acceptance and positive regard, accompanied by minimal responsibility and accountability — which is a contradiction in a major key. The message of the Christian Gospel is to those in need — to those who see their need — to those who somehow cannot find the "new image." The message not only provides the promises of the Christian message, but requires in return the responsibility and accountability that goes with it. This message was and still is no respecter of persons, whether commoners or kings.

The church, by and large, attempts to minister to all peoples. It, in and of itself, does not tell worshipers how to dress, or how much to put in the collection plate, or how well they should be educated. But it does — unwittingly. Walk into a sanctuary, look around, and then try to say that you don't know what kind of attire is expected in that congregation. See how many congregations actually do *not* make certain that you know how much money the "average" member gives to the church, and, listen to the sermon to see what level education it would take to understand it.

By their very sociological, geographical, economic, and psychological being, every congregation determines to whom it will minister. The problem is not in selective ministry — perhaps it is more in denying that fact. At issue here is not wealth, social status, or education by themselves, but what those items bring with them. At issue is the new image which is unique to this age and which will keep changing as society changes. And the more serious, and very great problem, is that both psychology and religion play a huge part in promising their patients and parishioners the attainment of that constantly changing image.

Is this to say that it is wrong to feel normal — to even feel good? Certainly not. Is it to say that one should be apologetic for being well educated? Of course not. Is it to say that one should dress shabbily? Again, no. What then does it say?

It says, a "new image" a new person doth not make — the "new image" is no better than the old or any other image. And, it says that "image" is a passing fancy, a fad, a feather in the wind. It says that there is nothing inherently more Godly about being poor than being rich, but it does remind us of the old fellow who said, "There is nothing wrong with being poor, but it sure is unhandy!" It says that there is nothing inherently Godly in the way we dress. It says that one is not more Godly because one is well educated and attractively attired.

We are reminded that Jesus said, "Seek ye first the kingdom of God and His righteousness, then shall all these *things* (italics added) be added unto you." The teachings of Jesus are quite clear that "things" by themselves do not represent Godliness. The image of Godliness may actually be more difficult to find in the midst of affluence. Jesus said that it is easier for a camel to go through the eye of a needle than it is for a rich man to enter the kingdom of God. Most scholars agree that this is not an indication that persons with wealth cannot get into Heaven, but that riches often get in the way of recognizing kingdom needs.

What then is the composite "new image?" It is intelligent, emotionally well adjusted, accepted without reservation, socially well connected, well dressed, without significant want (if any want at all), increasing in affluence, and above all, self-sufficient.

The "new image" is not a religious thing, even though it has been adopted by a large number of professed religious persons. It is not a psychological thing. It is the compilation of the illusions of this age acceptable to society at large. To the extent that psychology promises that "new image" and to the extent that the church promises that "new image," to that extent they will fail. The Christian promise has always been that in belief it is the *person* that becomes new — the image follows. The church has a single message and it is uniquely also the messenger. It cannot have multiple messages. Strangely enough, its message only comes in a "one-size-fits-all." Multiple, changing messages not only confuse, but are inaccurate. In the attempt to become all things to all people, the church risks becoming nothing to everyone.

4

Here and Now — There and Then

Psychology and theology are both about being — one is about human behavior and the other is about being human.

ULTIMATE MEANING GETS LOST IN ALLURING VOCABULARY

PSYCHOLOGY IS THE LANGUAGE of *human behavior*, while theology is the language of *being human*. Erik Erikson proposed that "generative man" is the ultimate and Abraham Maslow believed that the "self-actualizing" person is the final achievement of humans. Both in their brilliance are correct to a point, but they are also in error, for they both are immobilized within the temporal, here-and-now, earth-bound thinking and behavior of humankind. Certainly this kind of thinking restricts the creativity and freedom offered in the Christian message. Pascal stated that only when we transcend ourselves do we become fully human.

A person claiming the promises of Christian theology is able to take a step beyond the "self-actualizing" person of Maslow and the "generative man" of Erikson. The Christian steps into the Christlike model of transcendence and embraces a resurrection theology. To be sure, aspects of resurrection theology are by faith and beyond sight, but are nonetheless incorporated into the actual lifestyle, thought processes, and therefore the psychoneuroimmunology of the person. The mind-body connection, i.e., psychoneuroimmunology, carries belief into neurochemical and ultimately bodily function. The very neurological, psychological, and physiological innerworkings of the person are effected in every way by what we believe. All that we know and continue to learn testify to the difference between the mental and physical health of persons who espouse what I call resurrection theology, therefore, life- and eternity-based thinking! Resurrection theology is based upon the New Testament Easter story that gives Christians hope beyond the here and now. This is the only model that provides for the kind of transcendence practiced by Christians. To the extent that hope has a brain-related function — and it surely does — it is the result of what one thinks will happen in the future.

Just think how limiting it can be when the church adopts the humanistic psychological model. We settle for being "generative" or "self-actualizing" because in truth that is so much more than most of us ever achieve anyway. However, that is not the whole message of the church. The church represents what we *can hope to achieve* and therefore constantly holds out a hope beyond our reach yet within our vision.

Psychological Jargon Became Revolutionary

Psychology has become an idol of the age. Psychological terms have become common household jargon. Everything seems to be measured by the yardstick of the psychological model of development. Education, industry, politics, law enforcement, and indeed even the

church teach, follow, or at least reckon with a psychological definition of what should be the norm. The birth of psychology as a treatment modality is young by civilization's standards, barely a hundred
years, yet its influence has been tremendous. It has invaded nearly
(probably every) facet of life from Wall Street to the church. Its language is used in nearly every advertising piece, political speech, and
sermon. The "feel good" vocabulary is enticing and offers immediate gratification — something we all want and find impossible to
ignore. Psychology seems, therefore, to speak in relevant terms to
real life — the daily things we constantly need help with. To many
persons, religion no longer primarily speaks to the issues of faith
and life. This is because those who speak for theology, primarily
ministers, rabbis, and priests, have adapted to the cultural mode of
psychology. They have bought its language and hence the culture
that any language brings with it. One cannot change language without adopting the culture of that language. The language, and hence
cultural adaptation, is clearly chronicled in recent history.

The "psychological revolution" of religion was in full swing by
the late 1950s and early 1960s in the United States. Churches were
conducting group meetings (therapy), "touchy-feely" and "tell-all"
sessions, with a new kind of "group forgiveness" bestowed by the
group on the group. It became self-declared and self-accepted forgiveness. By that time, psychology and psychological language had
become so popularly associated with religious values that the two
sounded very much alike, making it quite easy to substitute one for
the other. "In recent years, a romantic haze has developed around
the word 'psychology' ... the church has become just as vulnerable
to this gimmick as any other institution" (Cox, 1966, p. 12). In a day
of waning church attendance and the "God is Dead" movement of
that time, all methods for revitalizing the church were very welcome.

Applied psychology had more than proved its value by the
1970s. Psychological knowledge and methodology had helped to

improve the educational component of the church, a seemingly sound basis for pastoral counseling had been established, hospital chaplains were commonplace, physical and mental health standards for missionary selection had been improved, and seminaries were seeing the value of looking at the overall psychological makeup of candidates for the ministry.

As often happens with new knowledge, the application of this discipline of human behavior took on a zeal and power of its own. Psychological methods and ideas became driving forces and problems of an entirely new kind arose. "Neuroses are often created which are more pathological than those with which parishioners began ..." (Cox, 1966, p. 5). The message and method of *psychology* was being mixed up and therefore was too readily mistaken for the message and method of *religion*.

The argument here is not to detract from either religion or psychology, but to state that *they are not the same and that one cannot replace the other*. Psychology is bad religion, and religion is bad psychology. Jung, probably more than any other psychological theorist, has influenced Christian theology. One of the problems with the theories of Carl Jung is that some persons have replaced psychological symbolism with true spirituality. Paul Vitz (1994, p. 4) says it very well: "Jung's discovery of the psychology of religious symbols is important, but there is with all this focusing on one's inner life a real danger of substituting the psychological experience that come through a transcendent God who acts in history. Those who make this mistake have truly treated psychology as religion." Vitz references Hostie in *Religion and the Psychology of Jung*, Sheed & Ward, 1957, who clearly shows how Jung's symbolism could easily be mistaken for religion.

Imminence And Immanence Are Big Words, But They Define Where We Live!

It is first important to clarify the difference between *imminence* and *immanence*. They are not just big words, and confusing ones at that, but they speak to a critical difference in the way we view life and react to the vicissitudes of daily human existence. They bind us to the earthly or allow us to seek the heavenly. The difference in one letter in each word, the "i" in imminent, and the "a" in immanent, makes a tremendous difference in the meaning. That which is *immanent* is earthbound, terrestrial, and indwelling in the universe. While both are of concern to the Christian, the topic of this discussion is the language of *imminence*, the language of the here and now, i.e., that which is apt to happen unpredictably at any time. "Imminence" speaks to what is likely to happen soon and it is usually used in a negative context. Although psychology is not inherently negative, it certainly emphasizes the reality of the here and now, deals with that which is apt to happen, speaks of predictable behavior, and in its most prevalent form allows little if any room for faith and hope of the religious sort. When psychology speaks of hope, it speaks of faith in *humanity*. When religion speaks of hope, it speaks of faith in the *transcendent*. Paul Tillich, a most respected Protestant theologian, stated: "We are grasped, in the experience of faith, by the unapproachably holy which is the ground of our being and breaks into our existence and which judges us and heals us" (1957, p. 78).

Transcendence is to rise above, to go beyond, to experience more than the here and now could predict or anticipate. In spite of the message, the methods and words of psychology are both imminent and immanent. Therefore, psychotherapy, which is rooted in psychology, strives to attain the transcendent, but is unable to do so. Psychotherapy deals with crises, one after another, because life is a series of immanent and imminent occurrences that daily disrupt our lives. Those unable to handle that kind of human angst frequently look to psychological methods for support. As Tillich reminds us, "The present situation is always full of 'critical' elements, of forces of disintegration and self-destruction. But it becomes 'crisis' in the religious sense, i.e., judgment, only in unity with the experience of grace. In this way historical realism becomes self-transcendent; historical and self-transcending realism are united" (p. 79).

The acceptance of psychological language ties it to the culture from which that language came, which is the culture of changing feelings, but not necessarily actions. In spite of this fact, the "worried well" along with the psychotic patients seek, and are often able to find, hope and emotional relief that far exceeds the imminence of the language and methods of psychology.

These "answers" are often temporary and need reinforcement from time to time. Patients who make only temporal adjustments in their lives without a change in basic thinking frequently suffer subsequent "breaks" and need additional treatment. The needs of the soul are much greater than methods created in the here and now can meet. They are indeed "soul" needs. Whether we view the problem as "imminent," meaning unpredictable, or "immanent," meaning indwelling, in either case, psychology is insufficient to meet those needs. *Those needs must be met by that which speaks to the soul.* Although such messages and methods do not rule out human instrumentation, they must speak of and for God.

Transcendence Is Our Father's Business

As we discussed earlier, many local congregations of the church have gone out of the religion business. They are in the psychology of religion business or even the religion of psychology business. This means they have bought earthly, immediate, anxiety-laden, short-term goals rather than heavenly, eternal long-term goals. Psychology has proved to be a most-persuasive, socially acceptable manipulation of the human mind, yet as a basis for "faith and life" it has irremediable shortcomings. The basis of both Judeo and Christian faith is God. To the Christian, that faith is rooted in the fact that God was in Christ.

Every age and every culture in history have promoted a coveted image for its people. The eminent psychoanalyst Erik Erikson (1964) helps us to understand this concept. He speaks of "generativity" and asserts that "ego-integrity versus stagnation" are the highest goals of the human. He reaches for, and embraces generativity, which is admirable. However, there is a tremendous hiatus between his concept of generativity and his belief that "hope is both the earliest and the most indispensable virtue inherent in the state of being alive" (p. 115). If we add these two tremendous concepts, we find ourselves on the next step — transcendence. The generative person is and remains locked within the human frame, the human mind, and the human predicament. That predicament finds meaning for this life and answers for the next. The transcendent person is in the process of "becoming" and "transforming," i.e., moving in a spiritual realm.

Transcendence takes into account what we were before we were born and what we will be after we have died. Our person did not start with our *birth* and it will not end with our *death*. The genetic code that produces every thought, word, and deed of which we are capable was put into place many generations before we were born, with our parents, grandparents, and great-grandparents, and many generations before that. Both physiological genetics and psychological knowledge attest to our *physiogenetic* and *psychogenetic* heritage. The DNA that makes each of us uniquely "me" has come down through many generations the same, yet changing in genetic identity with every person who is born. Recent DNA studies tell us that at birth each one us is 99% identical to every other living human being. That remaining 1%, though miniscule, represents the unique chemical and anatomical characteristics that each of us has. From that 1%, fathers are identified, prisoners are electrocuted or released, and organ donors are matched.

Likewise, we share our identity with every person with whom we have intimate contact. Body fluids become part of us, not only in disease, but in essence. They become part of us and we become part of them forever. The genetic aspects of the human will undoubtedly assume an increasingly important place in our discussion of human change in the future, whether we are speaking of psychotherapy or religion. Theology to this point has been largely able to avoid dealing with genetics as a part of religion; however, this will change — in fact, it is changing at this time, by virtue of the importance of cloning and the resultant consequences of it on theological understanding, doctrines, and the language of faith.

Probably the most verbal person regarding our psychogenetic heritage was Carl Jung, who departed from Freudian psychology and brought a mystical, spiritual sense to his theories of human behavior. The "collective unconscious," as he called it, was a way of pointing out the fact that our thoughts, words, and deeds have their roots far back in our psychological history. What we think includes a combination of all that our emotional history has had passed on to us psychologically, genetically, and environmentally, coupled with our unique personal contributions.

WHERE WE CAME FROM AND WHERE WE ARE GOING IS IMPORTANT TO ALL OF US

The importance of understanding our heritage and our future is critical in order to have proper respect and appreciation for our forebears. It is also critical in order for us to have a proper appreciation for our offspring. Everyone in existence is part of their mother and father, and every child we have will be part of us and thus of our past. The greatness of this is the privilege of carrying on the tasks that our ancestors began and in being able to have children who are an extension of us who will continue to carry on for us and our forebears.

The concept of "lineage" was so important in the Old Testament that a man whose wife could not produce offspring was permitted to take a "concubine" for the purposes of procreation, particularly to produce a son. Furthermore, much is made of Jesus' heritage, so much so that to this day his birthright is spoken of as "born of the lineage of David." That lineage gave him rights and privileges and brought to him a family majesty of royal greatness. Who our parents were and who our children will become are vital to our innermost spiritual sense of well being. The tradition of "having a son to carry on the family name" was another manifestation of the importance of what we were before we were born and what we shall be after we die. Although, fortunately, modern thinking no longer considers it absolutely essential to have a "son," there is still a vestige of that wish in every family, especially by fathers, that they will have a son "to carry on the family name." But it is more than just the name. It is the deeply rooted belief that we existed before we were born and that we shall continue to exist after we die and the not too distant belief in that somehow a son who carries the family name will extend beyond our immortality. These are irrefutable internal needs recorded from time immemorial.

No one should be serious about having been born "of nothing" and "returning to nothing" in death. We all have the need to believe that we brought something into this world and that we will leave something for others to take into their world. Illustrative of this fact is the sometimes endless journey taken by adopted children to find their "real mother" or "real father." It is easy to understand their insatiable search for "birth parents," one's biological roots, when we fully appreciate the spiritual heritage we know we have. We want to anchor to "real people" who lived in a real world in real time. Their search is not just a morbid curiosity. It is a deeply rooted spiritual need to find a certainty, a closure at both ends of life — "where did I come from and where am I going?"

The spiritual nature of being human calls for transcendence. One's life is a limited experience. Many lessons are learned and relearned in every generation. Few persons believe that all that we learn on this terrestrial globe in our short "four score and ten" will be forever lost when we leave our bodies. We believe, even though we don't know how, that we will transcend this earthly time-bound house of skin and bones that we call our "body." Virtually every religion espouses some form of resurrection theology. The power of resurrection hope is undeniable and no one more than the Christian with the celebration of Christ's resurrection is any more jubilant in this belief.

There are many ways that we accomplish transcendence. We encourage our children to carry on the values, beliefs, and sometimes even the occupations we have started. We incorporate belief systems that allow us to vicariously live on, not only through our children, but also through our friends, students, customers, patients, and extended relatives. We write letters and are flattered when we find that someone has kept them over the years. We write papers and books and leave photographs, tape recordings, videotapes, and our handiwork in sewing, woodwork, ceramics, painting, and in a myriad of other forms. We name parks, erect statues, and of course even put our names on our graves — certainly not for us to read — but to extend our existence into those who come after us. Just as hieroglyphics bear testimony to the ancient Egyptians, we have a small hope that in the future when someone finds our "mark" on something that we will not be forgotten.

Ultimate Purpose Transcends Our Daily Tasks

In order for us to give value to the menial tasks that occupy our days, transcendence is critically important. Employees who hour after hour and day after day do nothing but "piecework," custodians who endlessly mop floors, law-enforcement personnel who daily risk their lives, ditch-diggers who break their backs in the heat and cold, doctors and nurses who wish they could save the dying and heal the sick, and unappreciated school teachers all need to believe that the importance of their life is not to be found simply in the task of the day. It is the *value* of the task, however mundane it may be, that helps us to know that our life counts for more than the item at hand. It is in the knowledge that however small the task, that when all the pieces are added together, we have had some significance in a truly great accomplishment. One is reminded of the battle that was lost for "the want of a nail." We are also reminded of the worker who, when he was asked how he was doing laying bricks, responded to his questioner and said, "I am not laying bricks, I am building a cathedral."

Everything we do is far more important than the item done or the moment in which it is done. We must savor the moment for that is all we have. Yet, none of us fully believes that for a minute. The moment is important because of all of the moments that have gone before and all those that shall come afterward. Those who are always waiting for a "better time" usually never find it. The finest time is now, indeed it is the only time we have. Some religions celebrate this concept in their doctrine of reincarnation, while we as Christians proclaim that we were *in* the Spirit before birth and shall be *with* the Spirit after we die — resurrection theology.

However, we must not buy the "now," i.e., imminence and generativity, as forms of spirituality. Many religious leaders jumped on the humanistic bandwagon of imminence and generativity as being god-like. As previously stated, generativity as understood by Erikson is more than most of us achieve. However, should we be able to achieve both imminence and generativity, imminence is tied to the here and now and generativity is tied to this lifetime. Imminence is devoid of faith and generativity is landlocked both with disappointment and inevitable negativity. Most psychological methods and tools are based on the assumption that we can change human destiny. Even if we can change this life, and make everything "imminent," imminence can be the harbinger of anxiety, the very basis of our angst.

A religious view must by definition be based on faith and hope in order to achieve transcendence. The ultimate human form is therefore not the "generative" person, or even the "ego integrity" person, but the transcendent person. To transcend is to rise above and go beyond. Within the definitions of "imminence" and "transcendence," we see clearly why religion and psychology are mutual friends and mutual enemies.

The person of faith cannot be bogged down by "*imminence*" which expects early disaster. Keeping clearly in mind the difference between *imminent* and *immanent* helps us to see the task of the church and of ourselves as witnesses in today's world. Imminent speaks to that which is likely to occur at any moment, that which is near, and as a result calls us to action, now. Frequently, imminent refers to things which are not only impending but also negative. Certainly the Christian cannot look at any newspaper or news program without realizing the necessity of being a positive force in an extremely disruptive world. Immanent speaks of that which is within, that which is indwelling and inherent, for Christians — the Spirit of God. Transcendence allows us to rise above both the *imminent* and the *immanent*, that which is hanging over our heads and that which resides within ourselves — that which is about to happen and that which indwells the earth. It allows the best of that which is within to couple with faith which is beyond reason and thus to produce a far richer and more powerful person than could be developed any other way.

Jesus spoke of this virtue prior to the Ascension while teaching his disciples: "He who believes in me will also do the works that I do; and greater works than these will he do, because I go to the Father" (John 14:12). Jesus was saying that in spite of the fact that He raised the dead, healed the sick, and gave sight to the blind, that true believers would be able to do even more! This doctrine is certainly beyond our comprehension, but as Christians must be kept within out grasp! **This is doubtless the most profound statement of transcendence overcoming both *imminence* and *immanence* that can be found anywhere in literature!**

Psychology has taught us well concerning "self-fulfilling prophecy." Imminence is certainly the foundation for most self-fulfilling prophecy. To transcend is to march forward firmly on faith. When walking on well-known ground, it cannot be called transcendence, for we know where the chuckholes are and no faith is required. Faith is "the assurance of things hoped for, the conviction of things not seen" (*The Holy Bible, RSV*, Hebrews 11:1). In contrast to imminence — which is the harbinger of anxiety — transcendence is the harbinger of hope. Transcendence allows us to have that internal sense that we are not entrapped either within our degenerating minds and bodies nor are we limited by our time on this earth.

Everything Is Based on Belief

It is interesting to note that both "imminence" and "transcendence" are based on *belief*. The assumption of psychology is that its principles are based on knowledge, even scientific knowledge. There are many parts of psychology which are indeed based on laboratory findings and solid empirical research. Most psychology which deals with human behavior, however, is based on observation, phenomenological understanding, and clinical experience. As has been discussed, our "norms" are the result of acceptable statistical samples which establish that which is "normal," i.e., average. This definition can easily accept "imminence" as a base of operation, since humans certainly seem to gravitate to the norm or the mean of any statistical measure. However, "transcendence" is the ability to rise above the norm; it is the belief that humans can achieve a state of mind and a resultant lifestyle that is grounded in the extraordinary, the "yet not seen but believed."

One of the basic principles of all psychotherapy, whether spoken or not, is to give a person *hope*. The "generative" person establishes something to work toward, i.e., "actualization" (Maslow) of his/her full potential. However, the energy for that journey is left to the innate abilities and creative potential of the individual. The "transcending" person has all which is humanly available *plus* the energies of hope, faith, and a belief in powers greater than him/herself. Alcoholics Anonymous (AA) recognized many years ago that a psychology of imminence was insufficient to provide the tools to deal with addiction; therefore its founders adopted a creed based on transcendence. Step Two of their Twelve Step Program states: "Came to believe that a Power greater than ourselves could restore us to sanity" (Alcoholics Anonymous, 1952). AA recognized that when the end product is based solely in the here and now, their program would not work.

RELIGION BRINGS PURPOSE TO HUMAN BEHAVIOR

It is the value base that religion provides that makes what we do important. Otherwise, its importance is simply in human relationships. That is not to say that such relationships are unimportant. It is just to say that they are temporal at best. Few friendships last a lifetime, and none to our knowledge cross the time line into the next life. However, it is religion that brings the eternal into the temporal and offers a reason beyond this life for what we perceive as proper behavior. This is where religion enters the picture: it is where religion and psychology meet. It is where psychotherapy and religion join together to become a gestalt, a product greater than the sum of its parts. It is where psychotherapy is able to transcend human understanding and offer human growth beyond human expectation. Psychology of this sort provides a stage upon which the problems of life may be acted out. Psychotherapy by itself frequently allows patients to "act out" their feelings and to understand why they behave in a certain way, but it is not able to actually *resolve or change* anything. It is like the story about the fellow who saw his friend walking down the street and greeted him by saying, "Hi, are you on your way to the psychiatrist?" His friend responded, "Oh, no, I don't go anymore," to which the first person questioned, "Then that means you are cured and don't spit on people anymore?" The friend said, "Oh, no, I still spit on them, but now I know why!" Knowledge does not guarantee a change in behavior or understanding and it certainly does not guarantee a change of heart.

The only person who successfully "graduates" from psychotherapy is the person who by some method, Christian or otherwise, learns to evidence the "fruit of the Spirit," which is uniquely Christian. Although one usually hears this scripture as plural, i.e., "fruits" of the Spirit, it is actually singular. This is because the Christian is called upon to be a whole person who evidences the Holy Spirit in and through the total being, not in pieces at various times. No one doubts the difficulty yet the desirability of attaining this state. To have, hold, and incorporate all of them into the innermost, unconscious life style of a person is without doubt not a work of humanness, but the work of the Holy Spirit. Such an experience is truly the transcendent life. Most of us must admit to enjoying parts on a regular basis, but the entirety somehow awaits a future time!

Can anyone doubt that these attributes transcend our world of greed, hostility, violence, irritable lifestyle, and impatience? The Christian message offers the basis for a true behavior *change* — not behavior *modification*. Modified behavior is adaptation. Adaptation is unequivocally different from change wrought by the power of the

Gospel. Gospel-produced change is conversion (a change in function), transformation (change in form), and salvation (saved from destruction). These changes demonstrate a reversal of the innerperson and its conscious and unconscious actions. Christian theology offers the only hope of understanding and practicing the transcendent life.

Without an ongoing experience in the "transcendent," everything else is only "imminent" and is a dead end street. When psychology and religion unite, we have a combination of reality-based behavior and energy available for adaptation, growth, and *change* which is not rooted in the imminence of the here and now, is not grounded in negativism, and is truly beyond the capability of the human by oneself. This kind of growth not only goes beyond the "norm," but it cannot be measured and, hence, can have no norm.

There can be no doubt that the primary (maybe the only) crisis in today's world is a spiritual one. The crisis includes but is not limited to the religious. An understanding of human development, human behavior, and the knowledge of how to motivate change are valuable tools for everyone, religious or not. Although separating "religion" from "spiritual" may seem a moot point to some, it is important to keep in mind that things "religious" tend to evidence the external habits and attitudes of person, while things "spiritual" evidence the internal, though not necessarily verbalized, innerperson.

So, the question remains: is it possible to combine religious values, even spiritual growth, with psychological knowledge and psychotherapeutic intervention? The answer is absolutely "yes."

Long before there was a discipline called "psychology," its principles were employed in the church and throughout the world and that continues to be true today. Before and after Freud, his predecessors, and successors, and for many centuries before that, we labeled human behavior as "psychological." The wisdom and experience of psychological knowledge was present and used. The greater question is not the knowledge base of psychology, but the value base of a given psychological framework and the tools which develop out of such framework. Use of the psychological and religious together has been practiced in Christian (and other) religions for centuries.

Confession, a required discipline in the Roman Catholic Church, is a good example. The Protestant Church, which disavowed confession as a religious discipline, resurrected confession under the guise of "growth groups" in the late 1950s. It resurrected "forgiveness" by offering "psychological acceptance." The results of confession, a state of being that is sought by many persons, was missing in the Protestant Church. Psychology, which understands isolation, guilt, and abandonment, was instrumental in bringing back that missing element, although it was not called confession and was not offered within a theological framework. Long before psychologists recognized the need for forgiveness, the church had seen the results of forgiveness in the lives of persons who through confession found a way to "start over" and "transcend" their past.

Sometimes the tools that develop out of a psychological framework can in truth be more religious than those that develop out of church-based counterparts. The psychological sciences are not beholden to any interpretation of the Scriptures or any other "sacred" book. As a result, if they are to have meaning, they must appeal to the spirit within the individual. Every theological organization (Protestant, Roman Catholic, and all groups that may or may not be Christian) constantly struggles to keep theology based on their own denominational interpretation of the Holy Scriptures and their particular creeds. Although one cannot blame them for attempting to keep their beliefs "pure" and "true" to the Scriptures, in truth, many persons have been enslaved and their own spiritual journeys have been diminished by such. In fact, many early pioneers in psychology, who did not have contempt for religion as did Freud, saw what the church was doing as a kind of "holding hostage" of its members. They attempted to integrate creedal theology with their newly found knowledge of human behavior.

As stated earlier, many psychologists started their formal training in theology and then combined it with psychology. Such was the case with psychologists such as Carl Rogers, Rollo May, and this author. Others, such as Paul Tillich, remained in theology and brought us incredible psychological insights. These persons and many others have shown that it may not matter so much which discipline is considered primary. If those professionals can transcend their studies and themselves, they have hope of finding the true meaning of God's creation — the human being: the ultimate of all of God's creation — made in his image — with the end purpose of glorifying God and enjoying Him forever.

Human Behavior Is the Primary Focus of Both Religion and Psychology

Psychology tells us about "humans;" theology tells us about the "the human." In other words, psychology describes us and theology reveals us. Psychology uses temporal words to observe the here and now. Theology uses spiritual words to show us who we are inside. To confuse these facts is to expect things that cannot be. Psychology talks about *what we have done*. Religion talks about *what we can do*. Psychology recognizes *what we are*. Religion looks at *what we can become*.

When speaking the language of human behavior, life takes on a very mediocre hue at best. Human behavior, even our own, is not always that uplifting and worthy of reward. Theological language allows for a colorful picture with a hope to live "above the ordinary" and not settle back into the "average." However, just as psychology by itself, when speaking of human behavior, can have a hollow ring, religion likewise can and often does have a very hollow ring of a "pie in the sky" mentality.

The transcending person (since none of us reaches transcendence in this life) lives within the bounds of imminence, while actualizing his/her potential and reaching beyond the here and now with both belief and methods which are more than just earthbound. There is no necessity to become "other-worldly" and lose touch with day-to-day reality. To recognize both reality in the here and now and the realty of that which is based in belief is not an easy task. Neither psychotherapy nor religion can be effective without both. The ability to instill a faith in oneself beyond the reality of one's current behavior is an art that only skilled, personally transcending pastors and psychotherapists have. To only speak of human behavior within the context of the old cliché of "picking up yourself by your own bootstraps" is both a "put down" and an untruth.

Most persons would long ago have "picked themselves up" if they could have done so. Church members would not have tolerated the inconsistencies and problems of the church had they been able to save themselves. Millions of hurting patients would not have paid their hard-earned money to psychiatrists and psychologists if their own "bootstraps" had been sufficient. To put forth that old argument is to only further exacerbate their sense of low self-worth. Christian theology does not espouse the "boot-straps" doctrine, but by endorsing the message of psychology encourages us to believe that we can do it alone — a psychological message in opposition to Christian theology. If the church could allow the *methods* of psychology to open the doors of the mind and the *message* of theology to be the "main feature," there would be hope of getting theology and psychology back into proper perspective. Furthermore, ministers, who possess a greater understanding about how the mind works, could produce more significant results by incorporating that knowledge into their sermons (as teaching) and administrative duties than by attempting to use these methods. The same is true of psychiatry and psychology, in that psychotherapy does not need the message of theology in words, but it cannot serve the human soul without that message in the values instilled and the role model displayed by the therapist. Josiah Royce, when discussing Sigmund Freud's visit to Clark University nearly a century ago, warned against "confusing theology with therapy" (Royce, as cited in Holifield, 1983, p. 209): *Neither needs the other's methods — neither can serve well without the other's message.*

Psychology Would Be Lost Without the Language of Religion

Psychology has borrowed heavily from the language of religion. Psychologists speak of "catharsis" which is by any definition "confession." They speak of "acceptance" which is by definition "forgiveness," and they speak of "empathy" which is "love." All of these concepts are basically theological, as are many concepts in modern psychotherapy. Psychology speaks of "human potential" as if we know apart from a value base what that potential is. Some would argue that this takes us right back to a philosophical/theological debate about the depravity or divinity of the human being. Perhaps it does, but more useful is the discussion that whatever we are and do, it is possible to become something greater and to perform better. The concept of "potential" apart from a spiritual value base is meaningless. Clergy and psychotherapists instinctively and by training and experience know this to be true. As a result, both the clergy and therapist offer their assistance as agents for change.

The church struggles very hard to do everything it can to be in the here and now, i.e., imminence, while preaching transcendence. The two messages do not mix. It is like the words to the old song, "your lips tell me no, no, but you are saying yes, yes with your eyes."

It is not the *method* which allows parents to deal more effectively with their teenage youngsters; nor is it the *method* which chases away depression; nor is it the *method* which allows us to cope with the vicissitudes of life — it is *the message, a message which each of us must (and we are able) to translate into our own methods.*

5

The New Snake
and the
New Garden

Psychology is a new serpent in the garden of religion.

HUMANISTIC PSYCHOLOGY AND THE
DOCTRINE OF ORIGINAL SIN MAY BE RELATED

THE BIBLICAL STORY OF ADAM AND EVE in the Garden of Eden presents an unending stream of questions. Whether observed through theological or psychological eyes, and whatever one's belief regarding its chronological and historical authenticity may be, the account in Western religion is clearly the basis for the origin of sin. This aspect is for certain: the story introduces the human race to temptation, human choices, and the struggle between good and evil. Prior to Eve's encounter with the serpent, and Adam's encounter with Eve's new "knowledge," all was serene and there was no concept of good and evil. However, both Adam and Eve clearly had been given the *capacity* for thinking and for doing both good and evil, for when the choice was presented, they did not require lessons to perform well! It is clear that they had an innate ability to make excuses for what they had done. They also had the ability to blame someone else for their actions.

Temptation Is the Original and Enduring Sin

Human beings, following the Adam and Eve superhighway, always seem to welcome the opportunity to displace responsibility while enjoying the fruits of that for which they did not work. The introduction of pain and work, as the end result of not being able to handle temptation, may be the most important lesson to be learned by God's creatures. Although some would see the introduction of sin as the most cogent lesson, sin is in truth the result of the primary failed responsibility, i.e., dealing with temptation. The first and ultimate task is to recognize the reality of temptation and yet maintain innocence. "The Lord's Prayer" identifies the preemptor of all sin as temptation:

> *Our Father which art in heaven,*
> *Hallowed be thy name*
> *Thy Kingdom come. Thy will be done on*
>   *earth as it is in heaven.*
> *Give us this day our daily bread*
> *And forgive us our debts, as we forgive our debtors*
> *And lead us not into temptation, but deliver us from evil:*
>   *for thine is the kingdom, and the power, and the glory,*
>   *for ever. Amen.*

While mentioning no other sin, the "model" prayer states, "lead us not into temptation, but deliver us from evil ...," thereby recognizing that the origination of sin is the inability to handle temptation. Echoing similar words, Lari White, in *Lord Lead Me Not* (1993), reminds us that, seemingly, the harder we try to resist temptation, the easier it becomes to give in to it.

Much has been made in theology of the "doctrine of original sin." All of the ingredients of that sin stemmed from temptation — temptation to be as God — starting with the serpent itself who clearly wanted to replace God; then with Eve who was tempted by the serpent so she could be as all knowing as God; then with Adam who was tempted by Eve to join both her and the serpent in *their* temptation. It was a threefold temptation — Eve, the Serpent, and Adam. Unhappy with their lot in life, they entered into what psychologists call sublimation. Sublimation is the diverting of energy from its immediate goal to one perceived to be higher or better. The concept of sublimation, as introduced by Freud, utilizes the deepest biological and emotional drives of the human being. Ultimately this kind of thinking process becomes totally unrealistic. Adam and Eve succumbed to this kind of thought process and entertained the unattainable by delusional thinking — to be as God! One could almost say that the original sin was allowing one's mind to be messed with! Before the serpent began the first behavior modification session in history, there was no such thinking.

Temptation is a dangerous thing — it is a mental thing — it can only be visited with the mind. The process begins with imagination, then continues with visual imagery, next with delusional thinking, and finally with action. The process of temptation is characterized well in the Old Testament story of Achan, who "saw, coveted, and took." The Scripture states, "... when I saw among the spoil a beautiful mantle from Shinar, and two hundred shekels of silver, and a bar of gold weighing fifty shekels, then I coveted them, and took them ..." (Joshua 7:21, *RSV*). First one "sees," either in reality or figuratively, then the temptation mechanism swings into play, employing the most vivid scenery and choreographed covetousness. It then becomes an ultimate novel believed to be truth. Once a myth becomes real, action is the logical result and it is no longer a temptation, but a reasonable opportunity. Temptation tickles the mind and warms the cockles of one's heart in preparation for action.

Some of Freud's mechanisms of defense, which support and maintain the ego, come into full play — such as sublimation which was previously mentioned as the start of delusional thinking. Freud's mechanisms of defense are in truth mindgames. They are by definition unconscious, i.e, unknown to our conscious mind. They are methods, according to Freud, which protect the conscious mind from painful stimuli. One might say that they "trick" the mind into thinking and/or acting in a way other than reality. These mindgames are not in and of themselves "good" or "bad." According to Freudian thinking, if it were not for these unconscious mental mechanisms, the human mind would face so much reality that it would be overwhelmed.

There are several Freudian "mechanisms of defense." One of them at work in the account of Adam and Eve is rationalization, i.e., making up good reasons to do bad things. Then there is Freud's mechanism of displacement, i.e., putting the burden on something or somebody else — "the devil made me do it." And finally, there is denial, the mechanism recognized by psychologists as the most damaging of all — "I did not do it!" All of these mental gymnastics are seen in the account of Adam and Eve and are repeated every day in all of our lives.

Temptation and the Serpent Might Have Given Birth to Humanistic Psychology

So, the story of Adam and Eve is relived in our own lives on a daily basis. Adam said to God, "She made me do it." Eve said to God, "The serpent made me do it," and of course the serpent, succumbing to its own temptation to replace God, became the first psychologist to the human race. The serpent took it upon itself to interpret what God had said. The serpent asked the first question, already knowing the answer: "Did God say, 'You shall not eat of any tree of the garden'?" Eve replied to the serpent, "We may eat of the fruit of the trees of the garden; but God said, 'You shall not eat of the fruit of the tree which is in the middle of the garden, nor shall you touch it, or you shall die.'" But the serpent said to the woman, "You will not die; for God knows that when you eat of it your eyes will be opened, and you will be like God, knowing good and evil" (Genesis 3:4–6 *NRSV*). We can safely believe that what Eve said to the serpent was *essentially* accurate, however, perhaps not totally. Later in the narrative, God asked her, "Have you eaten from the tree of which I commanded you not to *eat*?" Nothing is said about not *touching* the tree. This may have been the first account of embellishing the truth. Embellishment is an interesting psychological mechanism by which we make things sound too ridiculous to be believed or conversely so wonderful as to be believed. In this case, it seems reasonable that since God had given Adam and Eve the garden to enjoy with only this one limitation, that to add God's prohibition against even touching something made it seem somewhat preposterous. Children (and others) employ this technique frequently. The little boy says, "He called me a name and hit me," when only half (we never know which half) is true. However, the embellishment presents a credibility problem for the little boy, if no one else. The greater the embellishment, the greater the illusion of credibility for his own unacceptable behavior.

The serpent told Eve that what she believed to be true was not. The serpent did not blame Eve. The blame was squarely put on God for having given her faulty information. The serpent started by establishing doubt regarding God's veracity: "Did God say, 'You shall not eat from any tree in the garden'?" (Genesis 3:1, *NRSV*). It was then that Eve probably embellished what was really the case. The serpent then took the opportunity to capitalize on her human weakness to temptation and tell her the "real truth." An interesting sideline is that the serpent who was created before Adam and Eve already knew what God had said. The serpent used known information to establish doubt in the mind of Eve. This portion of the account establishes credence to the concept of the ubiquitous nature of the Evil One. What the serpent thought was, "I know what you were told, and I know how to entice you to accept my temptation." Playing into what psychologists call the ego, the serpent promised Eve that she was capable of becoming all she needed in and of herself. The serpent's message was clear: "Eat of this tree and you won't need God." You need only yourself to be whole. You need no one or nothing else. Be done with reliance upon others — no more dependency and certainly no more co-dependency! Little did Adam and Eve and the serpent know, but they just invented humanistic psychology.

OUR CURRENT CONDITION
IS UNDERSTANDABLE

The process of using known expectations, such as "should," "ought," and the like, is a basic technique in humanistic psychology for establishing emotional unrest and a willingness to entertain new behaviors. Being dissatisfied with one's lot in life is a necessity for being willing to entertain new ways of living. The promise of being happy without relying on anyone or anything else is delusional, but enticing to many. The concept of "dependency" has been so maligned that the human race believes that to depend upon anything or anyone is a basic fault and leads to mental illness. This is a ridiculous untruth. We start life dependent, we live throughout life dependent, and we end life dependent. The question is not whether we are dependent — that is a given — the question is whether the relationships we build use dependency as a strength to all persons in the relationship or whether we are human leeches and emotional parasites. In one situation, relationships are "used" and hence dependency is unhealthy for both parties. In the other, each party gains from the other without transgression of the other's person, which must be recognized as the optimal functioning of any relationship.

When supervising young psychotherapists I've found that frequently their number one goal is to relieve anxiety, and when such occurs early in the therapy, it is reported as a successful intervention. Anxiety is a friend — just like pain is a friend. Without pain one could die without knowing there was an illness that might have been cured. Anxiety is a friend which reminds us that there is something wrong and that it should be corrected. To relieve anxiety too quickly renders the patient without the emotional energy to continue the therapeutic journey. Thus, sometimes relieving anxiety prematurely may look good to the patient in the short run, but in the long run it short circuits lasting benefits.

Some psychological helpers want to define anything other than total self-reliance as an unhealthy dependency. Although it is enticing to be promised true self-hood, the promise of being happy without relying on anyone else or anything else is delusional.

Blaming Our Parents

When Adam and Eve yielded to temptation, what was comfortable became uncomfortable and the natural became unnatural. They were fully clothed in natural attire until the "fall," after which they perceived themselves to be "naked." God, and for that matter even the serpent, did not see them any differently, but *they saw themselves* as being different. God asked, "Who told you that you were naked?" (Genesis 3:10, *NRSV*). So, the saga ended with the pain of self-knowledge, not with God knowledge. They attempted to correct their pain of self-knowledge by becoming the first haberdashers to humankind, by tailoring fig leaf aprons! Covering their nakedness allowed them a kind of denial. Adam, Eve, the serpent, and God all knew what was underneath the fig leaves, but that is how denial works. Denial creates a myth that we believe to be true and thus makes us act as if it were true.

We assume Adam and Eve covered their genitals because the Scriptures say that they "sewed fig leaves together" and made "loin-cloths," although some translations attribute the clothes making to God. In our Western acculturated minds, exposing the genitals is true nakedness. Adam and Eve may have made "jump suits" for their entire bodies for all we know. (We are not told how they learned to sew!) Since they had no prior knowledge of sexual exposure, we don't know the body parts about which they were sensitive. Furthermore, the account may have only been peripherally (if at all) about *physical* nakedness. The more important aspect most certain-ly has to do with *nakedness of one's personhood*, the basic nature of the human being without a cover! However, it is important to not get caught up in the minutia and lose the central message: the impor-tant theological premise here is that by the process of temptation came the birth of sin and thus the experiential knowledge of good and evil.

Prior to the encounter with the serpent there was no such con-cept as "good" and "evil." All things were of God, and only one state existed — that which was. The mental machinations resulting from temptation had not occurred. The results of psychological mind dabbling had not occurred. After the encounter, we have Adam and Eve experientially going through the full spectrum of the mind, from innocence to guilt. They showed us the mental gyrations that many centuries later would be called sublimation, displacement, rationalization, and denial. They showed us ourselves in depth. They revealed the essence of being human and the wish to be oth-erwise — the presence of guilt and the ambivalence surrounding it. There is no evidence that they (or we) did not enjoy the "eating of the fruit." It is just that they (and we) do not want to accept that to which it leads. The loss of innocence is not the cause of the pain.

The pain comes from dealing with the guilt. This is where theology enters the picture — the introduction of real guilt.

Guilt Shattered Innocence Forever

The introduction of "guilt" into the human conscience must have been traumatic: to be wrong for the first time and for that "wrongness" to be so pervasive and all consuming. The drama of this is really only understood within the context of what the guilt stood for and its consequences. There is no mention of forgiveness, reconciliation, restitution, or any other way out. Guilt was real and permanent. It is important to understand the basis and importance of guilt. The establishment of guilt was the initial step in the story of redemption of the human race. As Tillich reminds us, "The consciousness of guilt cannot be overcome by the simple assurance that man is forgiven. Man can believe in forgiveness only if justice is maintained and guilt is confirmed" (Tillich, 1951, p. 288). A concept of redemption was not available to Adam and Eve. However, knowledge of their guilt and the payment for indulging their temptation was more than available. Their minds were able to comprehend transgression and its consequences, but the promise of the Christ and, for that matter, the redemptive promise of the Old Testament was not part of their knowledge. It would come much later in theological history.

"Good" and "evil" are not simply the results of "human nature." To take such a simplistic view would be to argue that God should have provided for our fragile human nature in a better fashion. The account of the Garden of Eden is much deeper than this. It has to do with the "progression of salvation," i.e., the method by which the Creator provided for humankind to enter into the history of God's call, to recognize and indeed realize the essential nature of the human race in a history and future of salvation. Guilt, therefore, is an inextricable element in the plan of salvation. Our individual refusal to allow ourselves to fit into that plan is the ultimate sin, but the ultimate promise hedging against that sin is "Christ in you the hope of glory," as preached by St. Paul.

The unfolding of the historical plan for redemption of the human race does not become more efficacious as time proceeds, but by necessity it becomes more inclusive. "Seeking the kingdom" has been the search from the beginning. Jesus' words, "But seek first his kingdom and his righteousness, and all these things shall be yours as well" (Matthew 6:33, *RSV*) were not a new admonition. For those who know the Torah, this is just a new recital of an ancient message. It is understandable that people of Jesus' day did not recognize this old/new message, but it is amazing that so many Christians believe this to be new information.

The search for the Kingdom of God began in the Garden of Eden without a roadmap, written or verbal. It continues to be our search to this day; however, we have a roadmap — the Holy Scriptures. Jesus insisted that He had come to fulfill the law. What is called a "new commandment," namely, that we love God supremely and each other as ourselves, is but an affirmation and a summation of all that had been proclaimed since the beginning. Jesus said that He did not come to abolish the law and the prophets but to fulfill them. In other words, he accepted his place in history just as each of us must. The "Eleventh Commandment," requiring that we should love each other (Matthew 22:37–39, *NRSV*), is the sum total of the entire history of God's revelation. As a matter of fact, Jesus had no new admonitions. Although He was without sin, His task was to fit into the history of salvation in His most unique way. Although very different, each of us must also fit into that history in our own unique way, affirming the Christ who bridges the past and the future. In spite of the universal commandments of Jesus, we are permitted to maintain our own individuality.

PSYCHOLOGY DOES NOT OFFER
REDEMPTION — ONLY RELIEF

Prior to the time of the Ten Commandments, there was no revealed plan for the redemption of humankind. History to that point was one tragedy after another, including murder and mayhem. In retrospect, each of the great Old Testament episodes was an object lesson of the unfolding pathway, part of a history that would continue to unfold. Someone has said that, simply put, history is "His-story." When we understand the introduction of temptation, the submission to it, the resultant guilt, and our history of attempting to deal with that guilt, it is easy to understand "history."

Psychology has worked very hard for many decades to return us to innocence and displace and deny guilt. To deny guilt personally and corporately for the human race is to deny reality. Any concept of redemption is sterile without the recognition of guilt. It is no wonder that when psychology undertook to "save us all" that it started with guilt. Of all the things we do not wish to feel, guilt would probably be very high on the list. This is particularly true if we see no way of relieving ourselves of the guilt.

Psychology did not offer a mechanism to relieve our guilt. It offered ways to relieve our *feelings of guilt*. These are very different things. Feelings and reality are not always in agreement. In this case, they are not even in close approximation of agreement. However, when psychoanalysis came along with promises to assuage the human conscience — without restitution, reconciliation, or any other reality-based behavior, it is no wonder that we bought it lock, stock, and barrel! Those with deep enough pockets spent years, several hours per week, absorbing this frequently false but good *feeling* from psychoanalysts and psychotherapists.

We are again reminded of Robert Bork's words in *Slouching Toward Gomorrah*: "Many people were particularly attracted to what they took to be the message of the new science of psychology ..."

(1996, p. 281). Of all the brands of psychology that have sprung up, humanistic psychology may have been the most believable. It is also possibly the most dangerous to Christian belief. It uses a vocabulary that sounds very religious, even theological. Many of its leaders were clergypersons. It was easily integrated into liberal theology. Built on many Freudian assumptions and following the lead of psychoanalysis in promising help to the troubled soul, humanistic psychology gave birth to the greatest neuroses of all time: that the idea to feel obligation and guilt was abnormal! The era of humanistic psychology placed a negative on "should," "ought," and all other obligatory-type words, thus leaving a single alternative — that which one *wants* to do. The only legitimate good is what *you think* is good. Good then becomes that which you want to do, that which makes *you feel good*, and that which comes from *within yourself*. That which others think you "should" do is extraneous and not usually, if ever, in your best interest. Hedonism in geometric proportions! Narcissism in the ultimate! On behalf of the entire human race, individual narcissism led to misery for every creature to be born. William Golding writes so succinctly in *Lord of the Flies*: "Ralph wept for the end of innocence, the darkness of man's heart ..." (p. 187). "Ralph" represents the entire human race. *The Lord of the Flies* presents a different garden, a different Adam and Eve, and a different serpent, but the same story of struggling with good and evil. The story of the Garden of Eden has been presented over and over again in literature. Walt Disney's *Beauty and the Beast* is yet another rendition of the age-old struggle between good and evil.

Psychology has promised modern mankind the ability to both displace responsibility and enjoy the fruits for which it did not work — both promises which psychology cannot deliver, nor can anything else. Paul Vitz correctly states that "psychology has become more a sentiment than a science and is now part of the problem of modern life rather than part of its resolution" (1994, p. x). Much as the snake in the garden beguiled Eve to believe that she could be as all-wise as God, psychology beguiled humankind into accepting a program to ignore all that the garden account taught us. Through Freud and his followers, psychology reshaped the moral and ethical conscience of humankind by inventing the Ego, Super Ego, and Id. These imaginary psycho-anatomical parts have promoted a massive delusion which when fully accepted prevents the true history of salvation from being understood. They established the direction of human change as coming *from within the human* rather than *from a supreme source* — God.

The Freudian Anatomy of the Mind

Sigmund Freud invented the Id, Ego, and Super Ego and upon these constructs attempted to give psychological anatomy to the human mind. The mechanism to protect self (Ego) from all attacks, whether good (Super Ego) or bad (Id), became known as the "mechanisms of defense," indicating, of course, that the arrows shot from the Id (the base human) and the Super Ego (the conscience) are both negative and harmful to the Ego — the reality self. Many "mechanisms of defense" have been identified. However, the one most damaging to be considered here is "denial," doubtless the most egregious of all defense. Anna Freud (Sigmund's daughter, who was trained in psychoanalysis primarily by her father), in her classic book, *The Ego and the Mechanisms of Defense* (1967), defined "denial" as *one* of the mechanisms. Denial, in truth, characterizes all *three* of Freud's mental anatomical parts — the Id, the Super Ego, and the Ego. Freud did not intend for the mechanisms of defense to be used theologically — quite the opposite. Therein is the problem. It is not possible for one to fit into the Christian message while entertaining thinking based in denial. To attempt to assist humankind out of the basic human predicament without a concept of the supernatural is to assume for humankind a delusional high place in the universe and its salvation! When we consider what place of power psychology and theology will have in the ultimate history of the human race, this discussion takes on interesting parameters.

Although there are certainly followers of Freud who attempted to wed psychological knowledge with theological belief, there are several basic problems inherent in such an attempt. The greatest conflict and irreconcilable difference is the problem of denial: *with an omnipotent, omnipresent, omniscient God, denial is impossible. Without denial Freudian psychology is not possible.*

Freud Created His Own Trinity and Even the Church Accepted It

The Id, according to Freud, represents our most base person — the animal instinct within us — which must constantly be denied in order to live as a person in the human world. The Super Ego must be constantly denied, likewise, since we are incapable of meeting such insatiable righteous demands. The Ego is, of course, the most needy of all mindparts and must undergo constant denial lest we see the true human predicament and our inability to change it. This tripartite denial causes the psychologically minded individual to live in a delusional world, with a false peace and with brand new neuroses. Psychosis is the denial of reality. Neurosis is the inappropriate adaptation to reality. If we must interpret psychoses and neuroses by Freudian definitions into our religious world, we are by definition theologically psychotic, i.e., denying the love of God and living as if it does not exist. So there we have it — the Garden of Eden all over again: unsatiated and unsatiable humans, the struggle of the Super Ego over the Id, and the ultimate victory of the Ego by the process of denial, thus permitting vulnerable humankind to emerge and procreate generation after generation of struggling, denying psyches!

The fundamental struggle of the human is not to fight neuroses. The fight is in dealing with reality as well as denying that same reality which produces psychoses. Reality is the fulcrum on which all experience is balanced. Reality is the scale on which all perception is weighed. Being willing to pursue a personal journey into one's own salvation requires willingness to risk both one's history and the future in the service of faith. Psychological methods to deal with the "gymnastics" of the mind are not intended to solve essential quandaries of the soul. Because the struggle of the human is not one of neuroses, the mechanisms used to solve neuroses will not work. The problem is one of good and evil, not the *perception* of good and evil, nor is it even the changing definitions of good and evil. The problem is one of basic *agreement* with God or basic *disagreement* with God. However, since some congregations accept the *perception* of evil as defined by society, the resultant resolution is nothing more than neurotic peace — a feel-good fantasy. Behavioral expectations have changed, creeds have been altered, and new definitions of "sin" have emerged. Whether brought about by psychology or religion, the resolution of one's dreams and one's experiences does not equal resolution of one's basic problem — the problem of good and evil and how to fit into the universal plan of God.

Psychology came to what turned out to be a delusional rescue in a most unusual fashion. It occurred primarily through Sigmund Freud, an ethnic but not religious Jewish neurologist, who denied all theological belief. His correspondence with the Rev. Oscar Pfister offers interesting dialogue regarding Freud's lack of inner peace and self-assurance. Freud admittedly had not gained these benefits from his own theories. Since Freud viewed religion as an illusion, obviously to believe in such was to him and his followers neurotic. However, the views of Freud were only theories. Like all *theories*, theories relate to theories. They do not necessarily relate to reality. However, the church in its eagerness to find acceptance in the secular world of new professional thought incorporated the new Freudian trinity into the perception of theology.

Freud Had a Few Things Right and a Great Deal Wrong — Very Wrong

Freud and his followers led the march to abolish guilt, fear, and neuroticism. Unfortunately, Freud did not grasp that guilt is not a "feeling," but a fact. He did not understand that fear is not abnormal, but the result of human weakness and that neuroticism is only a manufactured word to describe the tension produced by the human struggle with good and evil. His assumption that our neuroses could be "resolved" is therefore also erroneous. One does not "resolve" the loss of innocence. It is necessary to accept that loss as real, but be quite unwilling to tolerate the escalating results from such. Lost innocence results in escalated acts of disobedience, and hence a deeper and deeper recognition of human despair. It frequently becomes the proverbial "catch-22:" the more we sin, the more comfortable it becomes, the more hopeless a righteous life seems, and therefore the more we despair and live accordingly.

Freud and many other theorists (like Hamilton, Hobbes, and Schopenhauer) built their theories by studying humankind at its worst. Freud based his theories on abnormal, maladjusted patients. Theories such as these speak only to the abnormal and therefore measure everything against an abnormal baseline. He assumed that normal behavior would be the opposite of abnormal, but since no human is totally normal or totally abnormal, there is no way to establish a valid baseline for either one. This kind of deception has been accepted largely in the name of science, in spite of the fact that true scientific knowledge can be proven and measured. It is our wish to know what is normal and what is abnormal that causes us to accept such illogic, not factual information. A. H. Maslow (1954), the noted pioneer psychologist, spoke harshly about the negative contributions of psychology: "I wish to discuss one such major mistake: psychologists, namely, their pessimistic, negative, and limited conception of the full height to which the human being can attain, their totally inadequate conception of his level of aspiration in life, and their setting of his psychological limits at too low a level. The science of psychology has been far more successful on the negative than the positive side; it has revealed to us much about man's shortcomings, his illnesses, his sins, but little about his potentialities, his virtues, his achievable aspirations, or his full psychological height" (pp. 353–354).

Much as the snake offered more than could be delivered, so has psychology promised and failed to deliver. Psychotherapy, in the form of psychoanalysis, was from its inception "purchased peace." At first only the wealthy could afford to lie on the analytic couch, sometimes as frequently as every day and at considerable financial cost, to have their neuroses massaged. There are stories of wealthy persons who even had their analysts accompany them on vacation so their analysis would not be interrupted. What made this service so indispensable? Why were those who could afford any luxury willing to pay exorbitant sums just to talk? And, if that were not enough, they talked to a doctor who rarely talked back! The promise was that their neurotic behaviors would be resolved. However, resolution did not necessarily mean change of behavior, but rather of insight, which was then presumed to result in modified behavior. The psychoanalyst, sitting behind the couch as the neutral interpreter, would assist the patient's Ego in coming to grips with the unfortunate Id and the demanding Super Ego, thus producing a "well-balanced" personality.

As we have discussed, insight does not necessarily change behavior. Change comes not from knowledge, but from the will. Hence, we are back to the real problem — temptation and what we do with it — the action of the will upon it. The real difference between human beings and the rest of the mammal world is, simply put, humans have the capacity to superimpose their will upon behavior with some degree of insight and understanding. We have no evidence that such is the case in the "lower" species. We know that animal behavior can be modified, but there is little if any evidence that it is accompanied by insight or understanding.

Neuroticism was defined graphically by St. Paul when he said, "I do not even acknowledge my own actions as mine, for what I do is not what I want to do, but what I detest. But if what I do is against my will, then clearly I agree with the law and hold it to be admirable. This means that it is no longer I who perform the action, but sin that dwells in me. For I know that nothing good dwells in me — my unspiritual self, I mean — for though the will to do good is there, the ability to effect it is not. The good which I want to do, I fail to do; but what I do is the wrong which is against my will, clearly it is no longer I who am the agent, but sin that has its dwelling in me" (Romans 7:15–20, *REB*).

What an incredible admission of the human predicament and the difficulty with reconciling the human will to the human wish! The struggle between two equally powerful forces, regardless of their source, produces a ripping tension. St. Paul's admission is the clearest description of what psychology has called a neurosis. Furthermore, he gave us the answer to a diametrically opposing and powerful force — the human will.

The human struggle is not neurotic, but real and essential to our ultimate salvation. The resolution is therefore not one manufactured out of mental imagery, but out of a solid belief in that which cannot and does not need to be proven — the grace of God. The power to make this determination is not a psychological mechanism, but rather a matter of conscious choice. Human will enters the picture. Being human is what it is all about. Having the ability to consider everything and to make choices, to decide, and to accept responsibility as well as accountability is the human legacy. St. Paul takes his place among all of us in the human race who find the dilemma overwhelming because it most surely produces psychological tension.

The human will is the ultimate form of personal reality. It is the essential bridge between the conscious and the unconscious. It is the only part of the human that we can personally control. Ultimately, whether in religious conversion or in healing psychotherapy, the will is the determining factor. Outward actions do not necessarily change the will. Knowledge does not necessarily change the will. The will is often undaunted even by an "aha" experience of insight. Even peer pressure and authority frequently do not change the will.

The story is told of the child who was *asked* by his teacher to sit down. The child said, "No," to which the teacher *told* him to sit down. Once again he said, "No," even more forcefully. The teacher then *commanded* the child to sit down. The child responded in the deepest philosophy known to the human being, the language of the will, and said, "Alright, I'll sit down, but I'll still be standing up inside!"

The human will determines the course of our thinking and our acting. Theology cannot have its message accepted in the presence of an oppositional will. Psychology cannot utilize its methods in the presence of an oppositional will. When a person becomes willing, both the message and the method can be accepted. Herein lies a major difference between theology and psychology. Psychology, in the absence of the mystery of the Holy Spirit, must employ mental manipulations, i.e., psychological methods of persuasion. Theology needs no such methods. It is founded upon the *premise* and *promise* that the Holy Spirit is the Spirit of God and that the message is the method.

However, the will is ultimately at the helm. The story is told of the farmer who was asked by his minister how he was doing. The farmer said, "Well, I feel like I have two dogs inside me, a black one and a white one, and they are constantly fighting." The parson asked, "Which one is winning today?" The farmer replied, "The one I say 'sic-em' to!" Both recognized the power of the will.

The new snake, which is psychology, has been equally as powerful as the original serpent in the garden, but it has also been equally ineffective in dealing with the human predicament. The new garden, which is the church, with the promised "Tree of Life" has offered a similar false serenity, tranquillity, and peace as the original serpent's garden. Both the snake as a prototype of psychology and the garden as representative of the church have equally failed in many ways.

Frederic Howe (1867–1940) is reported to have said, "… the most characteristic influence of my generation" was an "evangelistic psychology … that seeks a moralistic explanation of social problems and a religious solution to most of them" (Strauss and Howe, 1997, p. 154). This is certainly not a description of our times. Today it would best be said that the most characteristic influence is still evangelistic psychology, but that it seeks a *moralistic* and a *psychological* solution to most of them. The psychological solution (particularly humanistic psychology) rarely calls for action. As long as we are at peace with our inner person, there is no external measure of judgment. It becomes a belief factor, which on the surface sounds entirely compatible with religion.

Feeding into the psycho-babble theology is the Protestant church with its misinterpretations of the New Testament Epistles regarding the worthlessness of good works. This biblical "malpractice" has portrayed Christianity as an effortless ride. In the struggle to differentiate itself from the Roman Catholic Church, Protestantism has overemphasized grace to the exclusion of good works. James of the New Testament earnestly preached that a proper balance be given to faith and works. "Works" in Roman Catholic theology emphasized specific physical actions and specific "price tags," called penance, to be paid for various sins. Roman theology carried works to the ultimate and it seemed that the only way for the Protestant emphasis upon faith to be heard was to essentially negate works. It is, of course, not necessary to ignore faith to do good works. It is also not necessary to ignore good works to display faith.

It is encouraging to see that after centuries of division on the subject of faith and works, the Roman Catholic and Lutheran Churches have settled the matter and issued a joint declaration to the effect: "Together we confess: by grace alone, in faith in Christ's saving work and not because of any merit on our part, we are accepted by God and receive the Holy Spirit, who renews our heart while equipping us to do good works" (*Time*, July 6, 1998, p. 80).

The role of faith in Christian theology cannot be overemphasized. For by faith, and by faith alone in Christ, we are promised eternal life. Since faith is surely the basis of all spiritual life, what then is the problem? The problem is that any attempt to resolve the human predicament by human means becomes a return to works rather than faith. Psychology has failed to relieve our guilt because it relies on imaginary mental constructs and "doing things" — works. It has succeeded by producing massive denial. What psychologists frequently call "resolved neuroses" is nothing more than a revisitation of the mechanisms of defense. That is to say, we either rationalize, displace, or sublimate and then ultimately deny. Whatever the mind does with our innermost conflicts, Freudian, Humanistic, or any other kind of psychology, they do not "go away" by utilizing mental gymnastics.

Psychology originally placed its emphasis on individual psychoanalysis, sequestering the patient away from spouse and family. There was no communication with anyone and even the spouse or family was not allowed to participate in the "resolutions." The analyst did not talk to anyone in the family or vice versa. The relationship between the analyst and the patient was sacrosanct. There was little room for anything but the agreed upon "new neuroses" that developed in concert between analyst and the patient. Confidentiality was worshipped. Until recent years when legislation invaded the sanctuary of confidentiality, even personal harm or harm to others was shielded. Now professionals have what is called a "duty to warn," as well as other legal requirements that protect others from otherwise unknown and potentially dangerous actions by the patient.

In psychoanalytic tradition, the patient was judged to be ready for discharge from treatment when all the neuroses were "resolved." This was an individual, in-the-mind conclusion which found agreement between the patient and the therapist. It did not, except by patient report, take into account the reality functioning of the patient in the home, marriage, work, school, or other arenas of life. Rather than allowing for the "good works" of the patient and the patient's human network, the termination of analysis occurred when both the analyst and the patient felt comfortable — never mind those with whom the patient lived!

The Theories of Family Therapy Gave Psychology Insight

Much to its credit, it was family therapy that introduced the hard work of resolution by inviting into the therapy room those with whom peace needed to be made, thus requiring a faith-at-work environment — a producing faith, a working faith — to truly resolve (change) personal and family dysfunction. The "systems" approach to human existence has been most helpful in all of psychology and theology. We are not individuals who live alone. We are parts of communities, and communities are parts of larger communities. All are systems — systems of conflict, conflict resolution, jealousy, hatred, love, fear, and all parts, both constructive and destructive, of "systems." These systems do not die with generations, but compound themselves upon the previous ones and generate more for the succeeding ones. The "fall" of Adam and Eve began the long decent of the human race into guilt and shame that would spur every generation to find a way out. Of all the psychological developments, the family therapy movement has been the most helpful in putting the dynamics of human interrelationships into both context and perspective — as well as helping to find more answers than any other psychology.

Before the fall in the Garden of Eden, there was innocence and hence no conflict. Where there is no conflict, there is no need for resolution. In the absence of innocence, there is continual need for resolution. Resolution is a mental process. It is based entirely upon faith which produces constructive action. Action of any kind cannot precede faith. Faith is the operative word for this human necessity, and faith is not easy for the human. Jesus was clearly aware of the great difficulty with believing. He said, " If they do not hear Moses and the prophets, neither will they be convinced if some one should rise from the dead" (Luke 16:31, *RSV*).

Jesus established the basis for faith as simple belief. Actions do not produce faith. Actions may provide a basis for the human mind to build faith, but faith in its strictest form relies on nothing other than belief. From the Garden of Eden throughout history, the message of faith did not change — the Messenger did. Jesus was correct. A risen dead man would not convince everyone! As a matter of history, not long after, Jesus would again establish the truth of this profound matter by the personal example of His life and death! Even some of His disciples did not readily believe the risen dead man!

So, there are major differences between the snake (psychology) and the garden (the church). There are also similarities. The serpent and psychology both offer *knowledge*: "You will be like God, knowing good and evil" (Genesis 3:5). Although psychology used different language, as we have seen, humanistic psychology promised the same self-reliance and self-sufficiency. Both the church and psychology promise *hope*. Psychology offers hope for the appeasement of the agonies of the mind. The church offers appeasement for the agonies of the soul. Hope is the eternal dream of every living

human being: hope from the assailant of pain; hope from the agonies of terminal illness; hope for all that is sung in the great spiritu-
als of slave days, such as "Swing low sweet chariot, comin' for to
carry me home;" hope for all that comprise the words of so many
gospel songs being sung in every Protestant church, such as "What
a friend we have in Jesus, All our sins and griefs to bear" and "My
hope is built on nothing less than Jesus' blood and righteousness."

The problem is that hope is not a simple "here and now" thing.
The concept of hope rests in the future. Its very etymological origin presumes the future. There is no present tense to the word
"hope." Hope is a feeling. "So faith, hope, love abide, these three;
but the greatest of these is love" (I Corinthians 13:13, *RSV*). All
three concepts are ethereal and demand constant vigilance and dili-
gence. Love remains the greatest because faith and hope are seen
most clearly in the actions of love — which it turns out are the
application of both faith and hope. The horrors of the holocaust
remind us all too well that faith and hope alone are not enough.
Furthermore, when they are displaced by the absence of love, disaster can and has occurred. The Nazis most surely had faith (in
Adolph Hitler) and hope (for Germany), but they most certainly
lacked love!

It is no wonder that the human race has always been willing to
listen to almost any new philosophy or propaganda that fulfills the
deepest yearnings of the heart. In many ways, the serpent did not
have a tough job. Being an opportunist is all it took. Psychology
took the same road. It was just a more verbally elaborate one.

6

The "Being Real" Neurosis

*Everyone's "being real" neurosis of yesteryear
is society's psychosis today.*

THE CHURCH, ITS MINISTERS, and its parishioners have entered into an age unlike any other in our
history. Knowledge, particularly scientific knowledge,
including psychology, has doubled and redoubled over
and over again. The impact of that knowledge and its resultant
practice has profoundly changed the world in which the church
must function. In order to understand today's religion, one must
understand the role that psychology, medicine, and education play
in our society.

The age of modern psychological enlightenment in the 1960s
and 1970s produced a generation of unfettered, uninhibited self-
worshipers. Popular writers seemed to equate "authenticity" with a
kind of psychological nudity. A person stripped of defenses is not
real, but really sick. No one can function without defenses, i.e.,

boundaries and a framework for a concept of the self. To lose these boundaries leaves one at the total mercy of one's environment: without the ability to make decisions and to have concern for self or others, that person certainly does not have the tools for a productive life.

NOT EVERYTHING IS FOR PUBLIC CONSUMPTION

The many "how-to-do-it" books which emerged in the early 1960s, and continue to this day, have helped produce a pseudo-realness which undresses psyches that should have been left fully clothed and have given these persons permission for a kind of public psychological defecation which is harmful to themselves and everyone else. The "hippies" of the 1960s and 1970s were criticized for their expression of "authenticity." However, although it appeared to many to be a weird way to do things, in truth, their ways were not significantly different from the proliferation of lectures and books on how to strip the psyche in public and call it "spiritual growth."

"Group sessions" became very popular in local churches and elsewhere, led by psychologists, pastors, or even totally untrained "therapists," for the purpose of "being honest" with each other. Often these sessions actually turned out to be studies in comparative emotional pathology. After bathing in each other's psychological filth, the minutes of the meeting could aptly read "a good time was had by all."

This kind of pseudo-honesty attracted a considerable following which has continued well into this century. There is actually a school of psychotherapy known as "Integrity Therapy," wherein the therapist becomes one of the group and bares his/her own soul as well. It is difficult to know whether this is "bearing one another's burdens or "the blind leading the blind." Often this kind of "realness" is portrayed as being synonymous with "openness" or "honesty." Just how "open," "honest," or "real" can one be? Is it possible to live psychologically undressed in front of everyone all the time?

The Real Person

So, is there anything such as a "real" person? Of course there is. That person is a spontaneous person who is able to cope with self, others, and the environment. That person is a mature individual with mature propriety regarding the time and place for words and actions concerning him/herself and others. That person does not need to "talk everything out," but knows when to insist on verbalization and when to allow for the healing quality of silence. That person knows when to let others look inside, but doesn't persist in forcing others to peer down his/her psyche as if examining a sore throat.

It is necessary to add the dimension of maturity to "being real." The mature person has a very acute sense of propriety. There is an understanding that some things are done in private and other things are done in public. There is a realization that some things that are appropriate in one public setting are inappropriate in others. There are some things one can do on the street corner, but other things are best done only in privacy. There is great value in mutual sharing — mutual concern and group interaction about that which effects the group. Most of us grew up in a closed, repressed environment, and the term "openness" sounds like a breath of fresh air. Many persons hyperventilate on that kind of pseudo-openness. We sometimes fail to recognize that openness also requires vulnerability. And, once again, vulnerability that looks to psychology for resolution is often disappointed.

It reminds me of the proverbial "old feller" in many hometowns when we were children. He is the one who did not change much and was the same regardless of whom he met or where he was. His precisely aimed spurt of tobacco juice was inhibited only on the church steps. He looked very artificial in anything other than overalls and could hardly wait to get home from church to rid his unsophisticated neck of that irritating tie. He didn't lie to anyone. He didn't need to. Everyone knew him for what he was, but, by the same token, he didn't tell others what he thought of them either. It wasn't that he was incapable of being "honest" or "open," he simply had respect for himself and for others as well. The only unrealness he knew was getting all "scuzzied up" to go to a wedding or a funeral. When he died it seemed almost a transgression of his person to bury him in a white shirt and tie. That "old feller" is no doubt our best model for "being real."

A generation ago, the Puritancial system held to pretty rigid "do's" and "don'ts." Fortunately, these formidable structures have been modified. However, our children and their children's children may well be forced into similar modifications of the system that we now call "being real," since it imposes a different but nonetheless formidable set of "do's" and "don'ts." We now see a severe misuse of words such as "freedom," "honesty," "community," and we are building a system that this time is for postmodern Pharisees rather than Puritans.

In times past (and some still today), those who had funds to do so "rented" their own "therapist." Prior to that time, some folks obtained the services of a psychiatrist or psychologist. One is reminded of the Texan. When asked what he would do if he needed a psychiatrist, he said, "I'd buy one!" The term "therapist" was accepted and became fashionable in recent times, and a wide variety of persons, with an even wider variety of education, began to hang out their shingle: "therapist." Furthermore, the practice of clinical psychology, psychiatry, and social work were regulated by licensing laws, but the term "therapist" usually avoided any established educational criteria for practice. Clients who had the financial wherewithall signed up for the traditional 50-minute hour at least once per week (more for those who could afford it) and were confirmed in their "O.K.-ness." Those who did not have funds to hire their own confirming therapist found groups which served that purpose quite well, and a lot less expensively. Alcoholics Anonymous, Recovery, "growth groups," and a plethora of other group therapy organizations sprung up, both within and outside the church.

PSYCHOLOGICAL PRACTICE BECAME A NEW KIND OF CONFESSION

The psychology movement within the church during the 1960s and 1970s revived the time-tested practice of "confession," only they called it "growth groups." They revived "forgiveness," only they called it "acceptance." They promoted public confession in the "small group processes." Such public catharsis had not been seen in the church since the Welsh revivals at the turn of the 19th century.

In many ways this was a helpful age, for the church and for psychology. It brought to light the great hunger and intense personal need for methods to deal with guilt, loneliness, and hopelessness. Unfortunately, most of the methods and messages that were brought into the church were secular in origin and philosophy and were not in truth parts of the church. The language of these messages was psychological, not theological. It was very much like Alcoholics Anonymous using the church library for their meetings or the Boy Scouts using the gymnasium. These were not "sanctuary" functions and by-and-large they were not clergy-moderated meetings. They were not rooted in the creeds of the church. They were not based on Biblical theology. In actuality they were not part of the church, but simply a group which *used* the premises, and they were not financially contributory to the church.

A plethora of books, both religious and secular, appeared on the scene: books such as *I'm O.K., You're O.K.* by Harris and *Man the Manipulator* by Shostrom. Self-help books jammed popular bookstores and the *Psychology Today* magazine brought psychology into popular parlance. The evangelical segment of Protestantism had "psychological evangelists" such as Clyde Narramore, Ph.D., who made psychology sound like theology (and if not a new systematic theology, certainly the methods by which theology should be applied in daily life). Seminaries began to teach "pastoral counseling" and the American Association of Pastoral Counselors was founded. Missionary Boards of the major denominations and the Roman Catholic Church began to use psychological testing, counseling, and screening techniques before sending their ambassadors overseas.

The first signs of "mega-churches," such as The Crystal Cathedral of Robert Schuler, appeared with psychological counseling centers central to their ministry. Many of the larger mainline Protestant churches took on full-time Pastoral Counselors, started counseling centers in the church building, and actively attempted to integrate the Christian life and mental health.

Leaders Tries to Keep Theology Central

In the 1960s and 1970s when humanistic psychology was at its pinnacle, many organizations and denominations attempted to keep theology central, while using this new-found psychological toolbox. The Roman Catholic Church also used psychology widely for the purpose of screening applicants for overseas ministries. The Rev. Vincent J. Herr, S.J., at Loyola University in Chicago, was a pioneer from whom this author learned much. The Roman Catholic Church attempted to keep theology central even in the basic sciences. It was not easy for many theologians and theologically based institutions to give way to the Cartesian model that split the mind and body and largely ignored the soul. So much was this true that for this author, who registered to study neurological psychology at Loyola University, it was also a requirement to study "Thomistic Thought and Theology" as well. The Rev. John Vayhinger, Ph.D., at Garrett Theological Seminary (Methodist) in Evanston, Illinois; The Rev. Vernon Grounds, Ph.D., at Denver Theological Seminary in Denver, Colorado (Baptist); and certainly even psychiatrist Karl Menninger, M.D., at the Menninger Clinic in Topeka, Kansas, as well as numerous other leaders in the field, saw the necessity of keeping psychology as a *tool* and theology as the *message*. Other psychiatrist authors, such as E. Mansell Pattison, M.D., Truman G. Esau, M.D., and Smiley Blanton, M.D., share this same view, and their writings and practices reveal that fact. The Human Potential Movement, based in humanistic psychology, blossomed. Dozens of clergy jumped on that bandwagon. There were also many well-educated, theologically oriented psychologists who attempted to blend psychology and theology. Among them were Rollo May, Anton Boisen, Wayne Oates, Granger Westberg, Seward Hiltner, and dozens more. Many valuable insights were gained, and there were definite benefits from the cross-fertilization that occurred. Organizations were born such as the American Foundation of Religion and Psychiatry and the Religio-Psychiatric Clinic of the Marble Collegiate Church in New York City. Interest in spiritual aspects of mental health were promoted in many of the leading mental health clinics and organizations in the country. We owe these persons and organizations a great deal for what they achieved and for what they showed us cannot be achieved.

In Spite of Herculean Efforts, Psychotheology Got Out of Hand

These professionals did not, however, support the "flakey" and extremely faddish elements that came into existence as well. The popularity to "vent your spleen" continued as a pseudopsychological movement, however, and became a national fad. It seemed that propriety and even public decency had been thrown out. Much as the urban canine population sought the nearest fireplug, these folks went from church to church and from group to group "spilling their guts," with little if any insight into what "public vomiting" did either *to* them or *for* them — or for anyone else. It was a movement, much like any other social fad movement. There was a structure, albeit extremely varied, from group to group. There were rules, such as do not judge, and there was acceptance, such as whatever one does, so long as the participant claimed it to be "honest," it was "beautiful."

After these newly structured "testimony and confession" meetings, the participants often spoke of "feeling clean," "being forgiven," and feeling free of guilt and shame. It is important to recognize that the emphasis was based on *feeling*, not what was considerate, right, or even appropriate. Reconciliation, repentance, and other approaches to reversing one's life style did not usually accompany these wonderful, new feelings — humanistic psychology at work.

By a combined effort of churches and these groups, humanistic psychology blossomed. "Touchy-feely" psychology was the fad, hugs were in, there was great respect for "individual differences." We all knew not only what we felt, but what others felt as well. Nothing was taken at face value — rather than "what you said," it became "I *feel* that what you were saying was ..." or "I sense that what you really intended to say was ...." Although these were attempts to grant great individuality, in truth it became a way of telling others that they really did not know what they wanted to say and that we knew how they "*really*" felt, and that they *should* feel free to express it! This was a tremendously hubristic presumption under the guise of this new humanistic psychology movement! It became fashionable to abandon one's birth name and adopt a new name from your "inner person:" Eastern nation names such as "Natasha" with a myriad of spellings, to name only one that comes to mind. Clothing became extremely individualized. Beads and sandals became trademarks for "authenticity." Men with their shirts unbuttoned to their waist symbolized "openness" and the newfound freedom to many. The bra-less female spoke of that same freedom. It was time to "let it all hang out."

WHAT YOU CALL IT IS WHAT IT BECOMES

In order to properly understand how deeply psychology has transformed the church, one must look to the area of most intellectual change — education. The psychoeducational revolution brought about an ability to discriminate between individuals with normal and those with subnormal (and of course supernormal) intelligence. Not since the French government funded Alfred Binét to devise a method for separating out those of lesser brainpower had there been such a revolution in the educational system.

The IQ test became psychological gospel and its inerrancy determined whether a child was "gifted," "normal," or needed some other label. From the 1980s forward, the IQ test has become more and more in disfavor and less trusted to properly discriminate true intelligence or, for that matter, academic ability. The noted and respected author-neuropsychologist, Muriel Lezak, Ph.D., addressed the American Psychological Association in 1990 on the subject "IQ Rest in Peace," affirming to "the trade" that a resting place for the archaic determiner of children's futures should be found.

Psychological assessment continues to have an important and valid place in the appraisal of human potential. However, valid psychological tests are only performed by a well-trained, experienced, professional examiner. Tests in the hands of lesser-trained individuals are dangerous in nearly every instance. Yet, most I.Q. testing has been done by less than professionally trained examiners — persons with a master's degree or less. Therefore, many children have been misplaced and misdiagnosed and many lives have been ruined. Just as many have been hurt by being placed in gifted programs to benefit their parents' egos as have been damaged by being placed in classes which were inferior to their abilities. Examiners were influenced and unfairly pressured — from the upwardly mobile parent who could not face the fact of having a child with an IQ no greater than their own to the financial agenda of the public schools. Thomas Sowell, a senior fellow at Stanford University's Hoover Institution, wrote *Why Won't My Son Talk?* (1997), in which he encouraged parents of late-talking children to obtain additional *private*, professional evaluations. Although the public schools provide such, he reminded us that there are "built-in incentives" — such as government money — for the school to put children into special programs.

The psychological profession superimposed a diagnostic nomenclature that further eliminated individual differences and lumped everyone into a variety of diagnostic categories, ranging from neurotic to psychotic — or perhaps more generously what can be called "organic," i.e., physiological. Patients sometimes are just seen as going through a phase and are labeled "adjustment reaction." Such labels are rarely helpful in the long run.

The Human Condition Got Labels — Not Answers

As previously noted, *The Diagnostic and Statistical Manual* published by the "little APA" (the American *Psychiatric* Association, meaning it is smaller in membership than the American *Psychological* Association), was developed as a "medical model." It meant that all individual differences were deviant in some fashion. The interesting sociological phenomenon of all this is that educational, political, psychological, religious, and other professions let them get by with it — and such continues to be the case to this day.

The power of this diagnostic "success" has been awesome to say the least — much of society has relinquished its ability to determine differences, understand human behavior, and determine educational programs to the medical and psychological professions. *Psychiatry* represents the abnormal aspects of mental functioning. The profession of *psychology* represents the normal and developmental aspects of the human as well as the aberrant and ill. However, the American Psychological Association has not published a diagnostic manual. Only the American Psychiatric Association which represents the deviant and sick has done so. What is considered normal, abnormal, neurotic, psychotic, sick, well, and deviant has forever changed every clergyperson's role. The definitions of these conditions are indelibly engrained into the literature, language, and programs of all of our social and religious institutions.

School programs have come and gone, individual students have benefited and at times have been ruined, and teachers have wrestled with what labels to put on their students. Children who did not succeed have been called EMH (educable mentally handicapped), MBD (minimally brain damaged), or ADD (attention deficit disorder) with or without H (hyperactivity). Each generation found a new label for children with difficulties in learning. Many truly gifted children have been wrongly diagnosed because their brilliance was seen as disruptive or even hyperactive. Teachers, although unfairly maligned by these problems, have all too many times been placated by prescribing methylphenidate (Ritalin) to children who needed it only to quiet them down. No one doubts that Ritalin changes behavior. Many things change behavior, but changed behavior does not necessarily mean that it is better for the child. Sometimes these children are only quieted while Ritalin produces side effects which may not be so desirable. Instances have been reported when there were from a fourth to a half of the students in a single class on the drug — it is highly dubious that they all needed it. The American Psychological Association, in *The Monitor* (December 1997, p. 27), reported that Gerald P. Koocher, Ph.D. (of Harvard University), when researching his book, *Children's Rights and the Mental Health Professions* (Wiley, 1976), said he "actually saw children being sent home from school with a note from the principal saying they wouldn't be allowed back unless they had Ritalin prescriptions." He also said, "Today some schools give teachers checklists of behavior that could be symptoms of ADHD." It is absolutely amazing and incredibly dangerous that we now have school teachers and principals actually diagnosing and prescribing medication!

The truth is often not in the need for medication. Steven C. Fowler, Ph.D. (quoted in the same issue of *The Monitor*, p. 27), adjunct professor of toxicology and pharmacology at the University of Kansas, is quoted as saying, "Giving children drugs to treat behavioral problems implies that behavioral problems are a disease ... Abnormal behavior or less than desirable behavior may instead be a product of a child's history or environment ... What we need to do is to move from a disease model into a kind of behavioral problem-solving model." Dr. Rhonda Lee Fisher believes that the drug Ritalin frequently actually produces a placebo effect. A placebo is a substance that has no pharmacological effect, which is given to a patient who supposes it to be medicine and is frequently told by a physician that it is medicine. We all know parents who are convinced that a given medication will work so they become much less anxiety ridden and behold their children's behavior changes! Dr. Fisher asserts that the improvements in children who take medication are not necessarily from the drug, but from increased parental attention and other factors. Some of these children are also given drugs such as Prozac (a powerful antidepressant) because they are viewed as depressed. Children certainly can and do become depressed. However, whatever diagnosis is given, the most important thing is to figure out what is actually going on in the child and in the child's family. Depression is often masked family dysfunction, personal failure, and/or social pressure. To treat the condition as depression alone sometimes is ineffective at best and avoids the real problem at worst.

Labels have value, however, particularly if the person using the label realizes its fickleness. Labels allow a kind of professional short-hand, but the problem is that they also trap individuals into groups — groups in which similarities are presumably greater than differences. Often, the label ("diagnosis") is based on the most prominent feature observed, ignoring all others. Sometimes the most *prominent* symptom is not the most *important*, only the most obvious. We then have persons diagnosed on the obvious, not necessarily the most important. For instance, if hyperactivity is the most obvious observation, Ritalin comes to the rescue — but what is it rescuing?

Essentially, everyone has become diagnosable. Some escaped being diagnosed, not because they didn't have a diagnosis, but because they did not have the *money* to see a psychologist or psychiatrist, were *lucky* enough not to be sent (often against their will) to a diagnosing professional, or were *smart* enough to avoid seeing such a person! Even in many churches, by virtue of the clergy's training in Pastoral Counseling, some attempt to diagnose. There is an axiom in medicine which says: "a proper diagnosis leads to a proper treatment." The axiom is doubtless true. The untruth is in the assumption that a diagnosis is the *proper* one.

The greatest value in a diagnosis is money. As Woody Allen is credited with saying, "Whatever you are talking about, you are talking about money." Diagnosis means more federal and state money for special programs, special teachers, special treatment programs, Workman's Compensation, Social Security benefits, and a multitude of other funding sources. It is not financially profitable to have too many normal students. Furthermore, we have vacillated back and forth through the years as to whether "special" students need "special programs" or whether they do better when placed within the normal milieu in which they must learn to live.

EVERYONE WANTS TO BE "REAL," BUT NO ONE KNOWS WHAT THAT IS!

The "Being Real Neurosis" has led this psychologically driven age down many strange pathways. Whenever funds become available in our society, it is important that we meet the requirements for accessing that money. Therein lies the value of a diagnosis. The masses of "normal" children must rely on "normal funding" and tax levies that frequently fail to be passed by voters. "Special programs" are designed for the disadvantaged for one reason or another; therefore "special funding" is developed.

To be diagnosed is to be "exceptional" in some way, i.e., handicapped. Genius persons are frequently, by virtue of their eccentricities and unusually high intellectual abilities, socially inept and ill-fitted. So why are they not "specially funded" as well? In truth, they are frequently placed in "gifted programs," where they tend to only accelerate their social distance and hence their handicap, making them even less capable in "normal society."

To be handicapped in today's world is valuable. The step from "everyone a diagnosis" to "everyone a victim" is a very short step. The psychology of the 1950s through the 1970s which made us O.K. also gave us someone else to blame. It's not my fault! This ideology even extends to no-fault automobile insurance. We are more comfortable when no one is to blame, particularly if it could be us!

The age of taking no responsibility continues to take its toll. When it is no one's responsibility, it is no one's burden to change and hence fixing it is no one's job. From the "being real" ideology, we moved to the "victim" age. Moving from the highly individualized O.K. person to the 1990s victim was easy. The once "I'm O.K." person is now often the tax role's responsibility.

Problems Continue to Proliferate

Everyone's "being real neurosis" has become society's psychosis. Someone said that the neurotic builds sky castles, the psychotic lives in them, and the psychiatrist collects the rent. In this case, neurotics build the castles, society turns nonreality into reality, and the government (our tax dollars) goes broke paying the bills.

Today we have yet another aberration within the "being real" world. It is known as the "repressed memory" cult. Although any psychologist understands that there certainly are "repressed" memories, all trained mental health persons also know that the human mind is extremely vulnerable. Hypnotic thinking can lead a person into nuances of him/herself to be sure. However, that same thinking can lead one into the nuances of the thinking of their therapist as well, intentionally or unintentionally on the therapist's part. Certainly not all therapists practicing questionable techniques are Christian; however, some claim to be so. There are therapists who are "unlocking" past "repressed memories" of patients and giving them "insight" into child molestation, sexual improprieties, and other abusive relationships that are entirely fictional. Often these "newly found" answers to current problems are only substitutes for being able to deal with real problems. Sometimes these manufactured problems become a "real problem" and set the person on a future lifetime of alienation, hurt to others, and anger that is never resolved.

This is not to say that abusive relationships do not occur. They certainly have happened and continue to happen. In clinical practice, this author has encountered many such situations. As a matter of fact, I do not know of a single "multiple personality" that did not have sexual abuse as a significant part of the patient's history. Many psychologists and psychiatrists corroborate my findings. However, the discovery of sexual abuse as *part* of the history is a very different thing than to *presume the presence* of such and risk, providing the patient with a much needed, but perhaps dangerously wrong, answer to his/her problems. When sexual abuse is present, it surfaces clearly and concretely when probing for a "total" picture. If a therapist is intent on finding sexual abuse, and overreacts to minutia to create it, such can almost always be found. All too many persons have found a way to hide their own neurotic, even psychotic, inner conflicts by blaming someone else for something that is accepted as a truth, when it is only a neurotic (or psychotic) need of the patient and a fad (or unethical act) of the therapist. The "repressed memory" fad has reared its ugly head in churches as well as therapy rooms, with less than adequately trained persons attempting to "discover" and "treat" these unfortunate persons. The "discovered" results were more often than not iatrogenic. In instances where true repression has occurred (the author and a psychiatrist practice partner have treated such), expertly trained professionals are *always* required.

These persons have broken with reality, but because the "repressed memory" movement is accepted by many both in and out of the church, they feel very self-righteous. The self-righteousness is even further expressed by "going public" with "what their parents did to them." There are cases where families have been totally destroyed, reputations ruined, jobs lost, ministers defrocked, and legal suits initiated, which were built entirely upon the psychotic quicksand of these "unearthed memories." No greater "passing the buck" method has ever been invented as that which enables persons to place the blame on others — even their supposed loved ones — for their own indiscretions and psychological problems.

If psychosis is defined as a break with reality, which it is, we don't have to look very far to find many public/society psychoses. There is little in our world more pathological than the public exhibitionism and voyeurism that have become fashionable. Talk TV shows, tabloid stories, and local newspapers frequently profit from this newly found public psychosis. Previously unconscionable behavior now has incredible market value. The more bizarre and the more nonreality based the story is, the more it is worth. Athletes illustrate the most egregious behavior only to be given multimillion dollar contracts, and their behavior eventually leads to even greater draws at the box-office. The "Being Real Neurosis" has turned into societal psychosis and has become very real — and very costly.

It is to this psycho-educationally driven society that the church must minister. The church's mission is not to identify, diagnose, or treat neuroses. While taking the work and research of the psychological profession seriously, and using the knowledge for better understanding and methodology, it must not forsake its ordained purpose — the message it has "to tell to the nations."

7

What We Want and Need

Some wants we need, some needs we want —
wisdom is knowing the difference.

QUESTIONS REGARDING the meaning of life are as old as the human race itself. We are each brought face to face with that question many times during our lifetime. The unforgettable words of James Stockdale, Ross Perot's vice presidential running mate in the 1992 Presidential race, were "Who am I? Why am I here?" Stockdale was, of course, repeating the words of past philosophers.

NO ONE CAN SATISFY US REGARDING THE MEANING OF LIFE

Although not always in such a philosophical form, even very young children ask those same questions. Talk to a child who is contemplating suicide and see what that child says, or have a meaningful conversation with a youngster faced with the inevitable terminal end of leukemia. While holding such a youngster, 7 years of age, in my arms, with ashen face, transparent skin revealing every vein, and sad eyes that had fallen deep into hollow, dark optical orbits, the child asked me, "If this was going to happen, why did I get born?" Good question. No answer.

Talk with a young woman, 32-weeks gravid with her first-to-be-born, who has just learned that her child is hydrocephalic or severely deformed. Birth defects are mostly explainable genetically, embryologically, and medically. However the "why to me" and "why to the innocent" are impossible to explain. They are much more difficult to defend — for they seem to be such a waste of human life.

Then one looks at such giants as Stephen Hawking, brilliant doctor of the physical universe, who was not expected to live another few years, but has outlived all predictions and brought to the world some of the most stellar and innovative insight into the actual origins of this universe. Unfortunately, he is a person that some people might look upon with pity.

One remembers Helen Keller, Ray Charles, and a host of others who through blindness have taught us how to see. Many with no ability to hear the birds sing have taught us how to hear. Many with no feet have taught us how to walk. Those with no tongue have taught us how to talk. Is it possible that those who must overcome such great obstacles in life are here to teach those of us with few if any disabilities how to live?

Although the meaning of life is highly individualized, many questions about that subject are more or less universalized. Edward J. Carnell, an evangelical theologian of the late 1940s, described the great question of our universe as the "human predicament" and illustrated it by quoting the famous lines from *Ole Man River*: "tote that barge, lift that bale, git a little drunk and land in jail." In other words, work to earn a little pleasure, enjoy that small pleasure, and end up in big pain. The end of a great expectation: sweat to earn only a little gain and end up in pain that cannot be measured.

We Want Purpose

As much as we want to know the *purpose of life*, we want to know the *meaning of death*. The human predicament is entangled with unanswerable questions at both ends, and as if that were not enough of a quandary, life is embroiled with the same kind of questions all the way through. The longer one lives, the more questions one must face and the more theories of life and death emerge — the more theories, the more questions; the more questions, the more theories; the more theories, the fewer answers. Answers to the riddles of life do not come from questions and they do not come from theories.

Most religions have established the purpose of this life as preparation for the next life. Such dogma only presents further questions regarding the meaning and purpose of this life and adds to those questions the lack of evidence regarding the existence of a future life.

The hopelessness that many see in their future is often experienced in strange ways while they are still living — depression, grief, loneliness, and desolation — and should we live long enough, some will face that painful and long goodbye known as dementia, Alzheimer's type. Those who are spared this ignoble end risk years of misery in pain and sometimes their quantity of life has little if any quality. Increasingly, heroic abilities by the medical profession prolong existence. The real question is *what* are we prolonging. Much of it is hardly recognizable as "life."

Nowhere is *want* and *need* more graphic than in the struggle of the forces of life and death in the terminally ill. The incredible, mind-boggling wrestling match between want and need on the part of the patient, caregivers, and the family is apparent in a life-and-death technicolor kaliedoscope.

Quantity of years without quality is the worry of every senior citizen. With the "graying" of America, we will see more and more "vegetating" in America. However, many senior citizens are spared disfiguring and dementia-related infirmities and move through their final years with beauty and grace, truly inspiring us. These persons continue to give us hope. We can hardly criticize the medical and pharmaceutical professions as they to continue to search for the chemical Utopia. When we see the advancements that have been made in the quality of life and the quantity of pain-free life, we are grateful. However, when we see the quantity increased without quality, it takes us back to the meaning of life and we ask once again, when is life really over? Is it possible to prolong the vegetative physiology beyond the life of the inner person? A recent publication, *Who's Right, Whose Right?* (D.C. Press, 2001) edited by Robert Horn includes the struggling words of thirty professionals, including C. Everett Koop, M.D., and certainly offers many thoughts but no answers.

What we *want*, of course, may be drastically different from what we *need*. Some needs we want, and some wants we need. Many wants are unneeded, and many needs are unwanted. Sometimes we do not know what we want and rarely do we know what we need.

BOTH RELIGION AND PSYCHOLOGY CAPITALIZE ON OUR NEEDS

Both psychology and religion try to make us want our needs — or at least what they presume to think we need. Sometimes they want us to need that which supports their wants.

Dealing with the complications of life and the inevitability of death is no task for the amateur, nor is it a task for the expert, for there are no objectively definitive answers. Given a place in the peaceful Garden of Eden, we would all succumb to the promise of knowledge as did Adam and Eve.

The ultimate conflict of want and need, theologically, has been most graphically illustrated to us in recent years in the "right to life" and "right to die" movements. In both cases, what one *wants* is clearly to escape what seems to be merciless pain and suffering. It would appear from even a cursory study of the Christian Bible that suffering and pain are within the domain of what we *need*. How to reckon these two opposing positions is most difficult. Medical and psychological ethicists, a relatively new profession, now enter the picture. Their attempt to unscramble this problem often makes it even murkier because what was formerly a private and independent decision has now become a public decision, highly dependent upon many other elements, including the medical, psychological, religious, and even legal world.

Psychology and religion both attempt to help us make those determinations. The problem is that it is so much easier to determine our wants than our needs. Hence, we frequently leave some of the most essential decisions up to others. "Master, tell me what I must do to enter the kingdom of Heaven," said the rich young ruler. When Jesus told him to give away all of his wants (sell all he possessed and give it to the poor), he went away sad. We might hear a patient say, "Doctor, tell me what I need to solve my problem" or a parishioner say, "Father, tell me what I must do to receive forgiveness for my sin" or "Pastor, tell me, what I must do to be saved?" All are seeking to gain what they need through "father confessors" (or now with both male female clergy, we would probably more properly say "parental confessors").

The story of the rich young ruler would indicate that there is an important relationship between our wants and our needs. It appears that the rich young ruler needed to deal with his wants before he could deal with his needs. Since we can know our wants, but not always our needs, we often depend on some other source for this knowledge. However, the method does not seem to work by depending upon psychologists, physicians, priests, ministers, or rabbis. One is reminded of the film *Life With Father*, in which both the wife and the clergyman clearly *needed* for father to be baptized. Father did not *want* to be baptized and saw no *need* of it. The wife and the clergyman had made their *wants* his *need* and he did not *want* their *needs*, nor did he *need* their *wants*.

It is not often possible to rely on others to determine our needs. By the same token, it is terribly risky to depend upon ourselves. More often than not, when at the point we need to make such a determination, we are not in the emotional, physical, or spiritual frame of mind to do so. One of the best radio commercials that I have heard is for a funeral home. It reminds us to make our wishes known while we are still able to do so and to not leave some of the most important decisions of life up to others to make after we are dead. Good point. But that is not easy either — for these are not truly needs — but once again wishes. How we wish to have our body disposed of and what kind of headstone we wish to have are wants, not needs. At that point in our pilgrimage, we no longer determine either wishes or needs. We can be certain that our needs are being determined by an infinitely wiser Mind.

Want has an emotional base. Need is anchored in self-preservation, either present, future, or both. Want is an intellectual thing — we can imagine it, think about it, visualize it, and enjoy the thought. Need is more difficult to determine and is a more deeply emotional thing — sometimes we can only "feel" it. We cannot describe it or visualize it. As a matter of fact we are reminded in the New Testament that sometimes we pray with "groanings than cannot be uttered," meaning that our inner spirit cries out in a language only understood by the Eternal.

Want is a higher brain process that may be called "cortical," meaning that it occurs in the thought process part of the brain. Need is closer to the brainstem, the instinctual part of human beings, and is therefore "subcortical." Want is temporal, with roots in the here and now. Need is eternal, beginning before we were born and continuing throughout our entire present and future journey.

By making a sacrament out of psychology, it is easy to trust both religion and psychology for determining our needs. The more sacred we make the language and method of psychology, the more it appeals to our inner wish to be told what we need. Theologizing psychology and then using these terms from the pulpit make them sound almost biblical. Psychologizing religion makes theology sound so applicable and appealing that we are easily lulled into dependency by this strange vocabulary. The problem is that even should we do both — believe in psychologized theology or trust theologized psychology — we still have not fulfilled our wants, nor met or determined our needs.

The great questions of life, such as "why am I here?," pale in the face of "where am I going?" Questions such as "what do I want?" have little relevance when placed along beside "what happens when I die?" The question of human suffering, one of the greatest questions of all, is not the question of octogenarians who have 80+ years of experience dealing with suffering. Their "soul wish" is to know "what next?"

It can easily be argued that a majority of persons *want* a religion that works and a religious context within which to live and rear their children. It can also be just as easily argued from all we know from anthropology, sociology, psychology, and our own experiences that we *need* a religious community that is capable of helping us shape our faith to live better lives.

We Want to Believe

Our history and current practices declare our wish and intent to believe in God. Our coins continue to declare "In God We Trust," the United States still has a "chaplain" for the Senate, and the House and Senate legislative assemblies still open with prayer. Although sometimes perceived by those who offer it as a "generic" prayer, there is, of course no such thing. The clergyperson, whomever he/she may be, is of some denomination, is of some religious body, and has some particular kind of theology. "Generic" prayers are like faceless dolls. Such prayers have presence without identity, but the person offering it has both known presence and religious identity, most often known to the audience.

Much seems to be made about our President (and all presidents from the beginning of the United States) attending church (of course, we spend millions of dollars in tax dollars to provide Secret Service protection for him to do so). The magazine *George*, in December 1996, centered an interview around former President Clinton's belief in God, placing it in the same issue as an interview with the Rev. Dr. Billy Graham and a research poll pointing to American's belief in God. What an interesting contrast in the public visibility of one's faith and behavior. The obvious editorial intent was to purport that the most powerful President in the world, the most prominent preacher, and the American people all believe in God. A careful review of the three stories made it impossible to be certain if the intent was for Dr. Graham to support the religion of the President, or whether the President was supporting the evangelist, or since the American people also believe in God, whether one could tell a difference between the faith and lives of the two persons.

Politicians frequently utilize both our wants and our needs to buy votes. They appeal to the "historical" roots of our nation and a 'better life" for everyone. In spite of the horrendous argument today in the United States regarding the separation of church and state, no politician would attempt to run for office on an atheistic platform. Joseph Waumbaugh in his book, *Floaters*, states that: "The Australians believe Americans to have forsaken history and tradition." Certainly in my travels in Europe I have found many British and European folk, particularly clergy, who would agree. We *want* to think that we still value both history and tradition; however, our expressed *need* contradicts such and is often limited to public display for purposes of secondary gain. In the Presidential elections, much is made of the religious preferences of the candidates and there is of obvious interest that the voting public will see them as religious persons. There is nothing wrong with that. It is absolutely right, if done for the right reasons. At other times, our righteousness is exceeded only by our hypocrisy!

The argument about whether there should be prayer in public schools would be a non-issue if it were not for those who believe in God and, for whatever reasons, *need* and/or *want* religion to be a prominent feature in their children's lives. The very fact that there is so much national debate over religion speaks to the sizable audience of persons who believe that religion and life cannot be separated.

THE END RESULT OF RELIGION IS WHAT WE WANT

We see religion as a means to an end. We do not necessarily want to live religiously, particularly if some of that religion runs contrary to our *wants*. We definitely want the end benefits from what we believe religion offers for our *needs*. The end effect cannot be separated from the means, i.e., the redemptive power of God. The means cannot be separated from the end, i.e., the universe displays the glory of God. We see religion as a means to an end — usually a selfish end. True Christian theology is remarkable in that it is both the means and the end! It allows for a uniquely personal, yet universal application of the method, while at the same time providing for the most selfish benefits — heaven at last!

We believe that religion will produce less crime, fewer drugs, more honesty in government, and more stable families. Religion is seen as a means to an end, not an end in itself. Therein lies the problem. Things done for an end result rarely produce the end we anticipate. Religion is either worthy of being an end in and of itself or it is not worthy at all. When religion ceased to be of singular value, we sought other means, including the psychological, to achieve our desired ends.

Psychology, per se, is probably not worshipped by anyone. However, since it made promises that could harness the carnal person and bring us into harmony with each other, as well as change abnormal behavior, psychology was seen as worthy of great adoration. Furthermore, these goals in human behavior were Christian goals as well. Ministers, priests, and rabbis supplemented (and sometimes supplanted) theology with psychology in the earnest hope that the combination could do what they had to admit their theology by itself was not doing — change human behavior.

Religion as a word in the English language comes from the Latin, i.e., *re* + *ligare*, which means "re" (to go back, do again, repeat) plus "ligare" (to bind). The question emerges, "To what shall we bind it back?" To listen to many theologians, or better said, religionists, we can have a meaningful religion without identifying the source for our "tying back." When one eliminates gender, ethnicity, and finally succeeds in making the Scriptures ethnically, gender, and politically correct, it leaves many who would like to believe so confused that their nonpolitically concerned minds can't find what it is they are to believe.

They find it virtually impossible to find answers for their own woes or fragile daily life, while trying to be philosophically engaged in "correctness." Since being "correct" is such a new concept in our culture, it makes many persons wonder how religions worked for all the centuries before our new-found "correct" enlightenment.

Furthermore, if one makes God genderless, should not all Biblical personages (or should we say illustrations of humankind) be genderless as well? What would this mean for Jesus' teachings? Jesus taught in parables. By definition, parables are for communicating a message, not for the accuracy of the detail. Therefore, was it a "woman at the well" or was it a man, in which case the story is about wives not husbands. Maybe Jesus was talking about "just people." Possibly gender does not matter. It becomes ridiculously apparent that we could carry this analogy out until there is no story at all and hence no message. Understanding anything, whether it is the Bible, theology, or for that matter any subject, is impossible without concrete points of reference. Religion like all else becomes an amorphous, nonunderstandable mass of confusion without specific reference points. Although, the message can be applied to many different situations, our thinking must start from a concrete recognizable frame of reference.

We do not have the privilege, or ability, to selectively decide whom in the Bible we will neuter and in which ones we will allow gender. Furthermore, the more we turn the Scriptures into another version of *Aesop's Fables*, the less there will be to "tie back" anything. The ability to "tie it all back" is infinitely more important than making certain that our grammar and language are culturally correct. Ages change and that which is important to each age changes, but the need to have something solid to which to anchor our faith does not change. The words of the old Sunday School song, *My Anchor Holds Through the Storms of Life*, still ring true for those who believe. It is doubtful that making sure our language is gender, ethnically, or politically correct will anchor much of anything. As a matter of fact, it probably does much to untie what many folks had pretty well secured!

Can Churches Step Forward and Help Us Reattach?

How shall we get back to the job of "re-ligare," i.e., binding, re-attaching, retying, and reanchoring? We could return to an absolute literal interpretation of the Scriptures. We could invent another social or psychological premise, such as "Situational Theology," which ties "theo = God" and "logos = word" down to the situation at the moment and the context within which belief is required; or "Liberation Theology," which ties God to the improvement of life, particularly for the poor and oppressed; or "Feminist Theology," which ties God to an understanding of the Higher Power from the perspective and experience of women; or "Process Theology," which ties God to being in process; or "Ecological Theology," which ties God to a particular understanding of our earth and recent cosmological understandings. An almost endless list could be made of theologies that are identified as being specific to some aspect of thought or life. We could espouse Luther all over again and "reform" what we believe by designing a new list of theses to tack to the church door. None of these attempts will work. They have all been tried and if they had worked, we would have the evidence at hand. We do not have such evidence. Instead we continue to search for new theologies.

The search for a meaningful religion is today obvious in the Western world. A recent, quick glance at a newsstand while waiting in an airport was most revealing. There were several popular magazines that carried on the front cover topics of religion, including *Atlantic Monthly*, *George*, and even *Popular Mechanics*. Newspapers are replete with articles regarding religion. There have been several recent "best seller" books showing the American thirst for religion. Typical are Bork's *Slouching Toward Gomorrah*; Bennett's *Book of Values*; Gomes' *The Good Book*; Canfield's *Chicken Soup for the Soul*; and a host of others, far too many to mention here.

It is also clear that no amount of debate will stop the religious search and the expression of that search in our society. Pope John Paul II's 1998 visit to Cuba was a dramatic demonstration of the human's willingness to persevere for religion even in the face of one of the world's last strongholds of Communism. History is replete with martyrs for their faith. Lest we think of such sacrifice as occurring only in "ancient history," numerous persons in the latter half of the 20th century have been imprisoned, tortured, and put to death for their faith. Religion is one of the most powerful drives in the human being. Although not regularly recognized by biologists, physiologists, and most social scientists, religion represents an internal force that often exceeded even the preservation of one's self.

The primary importance of religion in the United States, in particular, cannot be overstated. The primacy of religious freedom was the foundation stone placed in the New World by the pilgrims. The Rev. Dr. Peter Gomes is correct when he reminds us that the Bible and Western culture, particularly American culture, are inextricably intertwined and we cannot separate the two regardless of how hard we try. "To fail to understand the religious dimension of the American culture is to be unable to read that culture or its nuances in any effective way" (1996, p. 55). It is a total waste of time to debate *whether* religion should be part of American education, politics, and public life. The question is only *how*. A culture in which religion is so ingrained as it is in the American way of life, American constitution, American education, and even in our unconscious and preconscious thought processes cannot survive if that part is removed. Such psychosurgical maneuvering would (and in truth has already begun to) produce nothing but mass confusion.

John F. Kennedy, Jr., in his "Editor's Letter" for *George* (December 1996), stated: "Historically many Americans have believed that the mission of these 'United States' is inextricably linked with God's will on earth. And though separation of church and state is a tenet of our national faith, perhaps it's not surprising that religion and politics are so entwined — for passion and conviction animate both the sermon and the stump speech."

Our process has been totally wrong. Our eagerness to produce a politically correct society has caused many to create empty spaces for which there is nothing to put in its place. *It is more damaging to believe in nothing than to admit to an imperfect faith.*

Mike Fillon, showed us the length to which scholars will go to find a basis for faith in an article dealing with the search for scientific proof (*Popular Mechanics*, December 1996). "Technology and a better understanding of natural processes may explain how these seemingly impossible events may have occurred" (p. 39), wrote Fillon when speaking of accounts such as Noah's Ark, Moses' parting of the Red Sea, Lot's wife turning into a pillar of salt, and Lazarus rising from the dead. He continued "What the Bible's authors interpreted as miracles may have been phenomena of nature" (p. 40). If we could find proof, by definition it would destroy faith. The "proof" cited in this article as evidence for incidents recorded in the Bible requires more faith (at least to most of us without such imaginative "scientific" minds) than to believe the happenings the way they are written. For instance, the account of the "burning bush" is suggested to have been the result of a natural gas seepage that was ignited by lightning, and Lazarus is reported to have simply come out of a coma. Since the account states that Lazarus came out of a tomb, the coma theory doesn't quite account for how a person so weak from a recent coma might do such. The point is clear: to believe the extended and circumlocutory attempts of science to explain the mysteries of the Bible requires as much faith as it does to believe the stories in the first place. Faith is "the evidence of things unseen." Faith, therefore, also includes the *absence* of things seen.

Furthermore, why the necessity to prove that the Red Sea parted or if Lot's wife turned into a pillar of salt? The reason is not only obvious, but poignant. Some need to prove the reality of such happenings in order to establish their belief in the other parts! But why do all that work so that we can believe the rest of it? Because the masses of Americans want to believe the Bible and we must be intellectually secure. Since the essence of religion is belief, and since the purpose of the Biblical narrative is the message not the verbal illustrations of the message, why then the concern? Many persons view themselves as too intellectual to believe the Bible's "far-fetched" stories. What they miss is that the "stories" have nothing to do with faith-truth, per se — these narratives are provided as a *basis* for faith. When so-called "scholars" seek beyond even common sense to find "the answers," usually it has nothing to do with either faith or truth, but with the pseudo-intellectual vindication of one's own doubt.

Therefore, if we can prove the intellectual and scientific integrity of the "miracles," we can believe the rest of the Scriptures without invoking a miracle within ourselves! That would be the ultimate destruction of all faith. When, and if, we succeed in destroying the "fact" of the "miracle," we will have destroyed the possibility of the human to reach beyond mundane human experience and find anything greater than ourselves!

Secular Literature Joined the Sacred in Seeking Theological Anchors

The *Atlantic Monthly* (December 1996, p. 68) devoted 14 pages to an article entitled "The Search For a No-Frills Jesus" by Charlotte Allen. It is the story of the quest for the "historical Jesus," the real words of the Teacher, the real world of His time, to thus strip away those words and elements which might not be rooted in actual history. "So scholars read those books over and over and try to find something new there, or try to bring another discipline — literary criticism or sociology or anthropology — to bear on what they read, or hope that archeologists will dig up new stones and new texts to explore." Robinson, one of the scholars quoted in the article, stated, "I think that Jesus was an important person ... It's sort of a pity that all that most of us know about Jesus is from the creeds, which we can't believe in" (p. 68).

Robinson continued, "When many educated Europeans and Americans lost their religious faith, at the beginning of the nineteenth century, they began subscribing to the notion, still current, that the main purpose of religion is its social utility as an enforcer of morality among the poor, inspiring them (for example) to quit drinking and pull up their socks ... However, ... saints and mystics did not need a reconstructed Book of Q or a consortium of scholars in order to find the words of Jesus that directed them to give their possessions to the poor and to abandon all concern for their own fortunes. They found those words in the place where they have always called attention to themselves — in their Bibles." The very fact of the intense interest in the *Q Document* (*Q* stands for *quelle*, i.e., *source*), testifies to the underlying need to find a basis for something to believe in.

Americans want to believe. According to *George* (December 1996), "60% believe the world was created in seven days, 78% believe in angels, 86% believe in God, 75% believe in life after death, 86% believe in heaven, and 77% believe in hell." In this poll, the Luntz Research group surveyed a cross-section of 800 Americans, small number of subjects perhaps, but the findings are doubtless similar to those which would be found in a sample of 80,000. A survey of the most respectable polls reveals these statistics to be essentially the same in year 2000. As they point out, Americans want and need to believe in something, preferably someone, even if it is only in a political candidate, a candidate who can even persuade them against their better judgment.

Americans not only want to believe what the Bible says about the here and now, but they also want to believe what it says about the future. Most persons when barely pushed admit to some apprehension if not outright fear regarding the future. No one likes "hellfire and brimstone" sermons (except possibly the one doing the preaching), but many persons are convinced of the truisms of those sermons regarding the future. Jonathan Edward's famous sermon, "Sinners in the Hands of an Angry God," was preached in 1741 and continues to be a hallmark of Calvinistic theology to this day. His rigidity regarding the practice of the Christian life resulted in his ouster from the pastorate, but he ended up as president of the now famous Princeton University.*

Many Christian believers, although not as outspoken as Edwards, continue to believe the basics of his sermon. Both hope and fear of the future continue to dare the Christian and non-Christian mind alike.

The tremendous interest in "near-death" and "out-of-body" experiences can be directly attributable to our uncertainty about the future and our desperate attempt to find out. Even persons who deny any possibility of the "near death" experience are captivated by experiences recounted by believers in such. The same is true of voodoo, witchcraft, seances, and all sorts of charismatic and extrasensory encounters. The human does not want to be strictly earthbound and refuses to accept that such could be the case. To further bolster our belief in a beautiful, happy afterlife, we never hear about persons who have had a near-death experience which occurred at the gates of a flaming, fiery hell! It is always tranquil, bright, beautiful, and peaceful.

The recent increase in the belief of reincarnation allows both the denial of death and the guarantee of an afterlife. Reincarnation

---

* Jonathan Edwards became president of the college (originally The College of New Jersey, established in 1739) in 1757. The position became vacant by the death of his son-in-law, Aaron Burr (the elder). In 1752 the college was permanently located in Princeton. Then on the occasion of the 150th anniversary of the college, the name was officially changed to Princeton University.

and the discovery of "past lives" also tend to support beauty and greatness at both ends of our earthly existence. Like near-death experiences which are almost always peaceful and beautiful, past lives always seem to be great. I have never met a person who was a criminal or a garbage collector in a past life!

It is obvious that humans, besieged by the problems of daily earthbound living, want and need peace and perfection at both ends of our life on earth.

Interest in the future is absolutely beyond any intellectual understanding. It is an emotional issue based primarily upon fear. Jeffrey Sheler, in *U.S. News and World Report* (December 15, 1997), stated, "Belief in apocalyptic prophecies is not just a phenomenon of the religious fringe. According to a recent *U.S. News* poll, 66 percent of Americans, including a third of those who say they never attend church, say they believe that Jesus Christ will return to Earth some day — an increase from the 61 percent who expressed belief in the Second Coming three years ago (p. 63)."

Our *want* and *need* for religion penetrates every facet of our lives — and of course — even politics. The "religious right" of this decade has proven itself to be more a body-politic than a religious movement. To allow religion to influence politics is unavoidable. When something is truly believed, it will impact everything. However, when religion takes on the identity of other social institutions, it ceases to be singularly religious any longer.

By the same token, it is confusing for the masses to see and hear so much attention paid to religion, referred to so frequently by government officials, even the President of the United States, and not believe that it is basically a political tool. Former President Bill Clinton is reported to have increased his use of "God Bless You" in public appearances, thereby increasing his acceptance among much of the religious public.

Want and need for religion have become less identified with organized religious denominations, but have become more evident in business, health, and the social world. In the late 1990s, there was a major revival of interest in religion, however, not necessarily in the organized church. Prayer and its relationship to healing even invaded the medical world. Prayer and its value in daily life (even the power of prayer on vegetation and houseplants!) has become popular. Faith and its relationship to pain and many other applications of religion to life have blossomed in areas far removed from organized religion.

Religion seems to be divided into an extreme "right" and an extreme "left." The religious right is difficult to deal with, just as is the religious left — for both are slaves to that which they think they believe. Why "think" they believe? Because to most of them, the march has become more important than the message. Just as some "marchers" will join any line before they read the placard they will carry, both the religious left and right believe more in the cause than in the message. How do we know that? Because throughout the lifetime of things "*cause celeb,*" the message changes many times, the leaders of such causes practice chameleon techniques for political or other gain, and with blind discipleship, the followers march on without missing a step, even if the beat of the drum changes cadence. The purpose of the march changes, but the marchers continue to march on without noticing the difference!

Most causes that invoke a religious basis do not in fact have a clearly theological premise, but rather a *want* for what they hope the power of religious persuasion can do. They want those who hear their mantra or observe their demonstration to find some deep need which would even remotely identify with their cause and convince them to jump on board. In many instances, the public use of religion is a wholly selfish act that has no basis in anything remotely theological, even though such groups proclaim with gusto various select Bible verses to support their cause. Both these person's *wants* and *needs* are usually exhibitionistic and opportunistic. When observed carefully, these would-be religionists are anything but that and studiously avoid any possibility of a personal application of the message they proclaim.

As Peter Gomes stated so well in his treatise, *The Good Book* (1996, p. 281), "Biblical religion is not an exercise in self-improvement and private therapy." We could rightly add, nor is it an exercise in changing others, governments, or for that matter societies. It is intended to bring about change in ourselves, which in turn, brings about changes in everything we do, touch, and think. When we start at the wrong place, we end up at the wrong place. Practice does not make perfect — unless we practice correctly. As a trumpet player and teacher, I can tell you that incorrect practice only produces very well-rehearsed errors!

If religion and psychology are to serve us well, both will need to return to the fundamental purposes that they serve and stop meddling in the other territories. Psychology must continue to work on dealing with human behavior, and religion must get on with helping us transcend our humanness.

8

Are There Answers and Can It Be Fixed?

It is not that we have no answers — we do not like the answers we have.

IN PROCESS OF WRITING THIS BOOK, I asked friends, acquaintances, strangers, and wanderers in airports, restaurants, and other public places what could be done that would cause them to be excited about the church? What could the church do to improve itself? Many of these people thought I was a bit strange for asking the questions, but they gave me very sincere, sometimes blunt, and sometimes staggeringly insightful answers. Although the list in this chapter is far from complete, perhaps in some cases is unfair, sometimes purposely argumentative, and at other times cynical, a wise merchant listens to the customer and takes even the most hostile response seriously.

As it turns out, answers to the dilemma of religion and psychology do not have to be *found*. We are already in possession of them. The Church, i.e., the body of Christ, is not broken — it never has been, it is not now, and it never will be. The earthly saints that operate its terrestrial organizations (the churches) await perfection in a life to come. In the meantime, for current leaders, discerning how to run the organizational church on earth is a formidable job. The answers have been there for many years, but we have abandoned them in the search of answers we wanted to hear. There is a pillow in our home that was given to my wife by a loving grandchild, which reads: "If mom says 'no,' ask grandma." This is largely the method we have used. If the answer we get is less than gratifying, we search until someone gives us an answer we like better. This has happened in psychology, and it has happened in religion. In psychology we have searched until we were assuaged with "it's not your fault," and we have searched in religion until there were no verities, only suggestions. In both psychology and religion, the answers we have been willing to accept have not helped release us from the feeling of human futility and failure.

The problem is *not* that we are left without answers. Clearly the problem is one of a willingness to hear the answers and to follow what we know is right. Sometimes, ordinary common sense tells us that what we are doing will not work. I am reminded of a minister friend of mine. He told of a parishioner who said she was going to do a certain thing because God had told her to do so. Whereupon the minister said, "God couldn't possibly have told you to do that because He's smarter than I am, and even I know that's crazy!" At other times, we only have to look at history to know that the method we are trying has been tried before and failed. There are other times when it is easier to "throw out the baby with the bath" and start all over. A critical analysis of both psychology and religion shows that there are ways to fix the current dilemma.

ALL IS NOT LOST — NOT BY A LONG SHOT

Psycho-Babble Leads to Psycho-Dabble

This book does not condemn the multitude of ministers and churches who have adopted the latest knowledge available and attempted to build or rebuild the church with psychology and the social sciences. Many of those persons and congregations gained what they could from that movement and have moved on. Most of them found that the "counseling connection" is best left to well-trained professionals. Some churches, in order to maintain that ministry, have doctoral-level, licensed professionals on their staff so that the spiritual ministries and the psychological ministries can work together, yet remain true to their discipline and intended function. Others, unfortunately, are "behind the wave" and are still being swept along by the undercurrent of less than well-trained persons, dabbling in ministries they know little about and accomplishing little — sometimes doing considerable harm. However, there are ministers who found that theological preaching does work. They found that people will still attend church to hear solid Gospel as applied to life and that these people want to study the Bible rather than to learn about Freud and his followers.

Churches that are serious about allowing psychology to become a helpmeet to theology must not allow partially or poorly trained persons to witness Christ through incorrect and incompetent psychological services. This kind of dabbling causes far more harm than good and in the end is a malpractice of theology and psychology alike. Doctoral-level trained persons with a deep Christian commitment and the knowledge of how to *implement* the Christian message rather than *supplant* or *confuse* the message should be team members. There are well-trained Pastoral Counselors and they have proven their worth over and over again. However, there are also those who are neither pastoral nor counselors!

If It Ain't Broke, Don't Fix It

There are many parts of both religion and psychology that are not broken and are working very well. It is important to not "throw the baby out with the bath water," but it is important to throw out the dirty bath water. This cannot be done until after the bath is done. It has taken many years for both psychology and religion to take this bath. No one can, or should be, faulted for attempting to take the best of two worlds and make a better one. The church (local congregations) has in the main fulfilled many of its claims for many years. Those periods of time that have been particularly effective have followed major upheavals in religious history, and the church has come to the rescue of its people. To be certain, there have been periods of time when the church was more effective than at other times, just like any other organization run by humans.

At the time of the birth of Christianity, the religious world was already in upheaval. If one takes the Jewish religion of the Old Testament seriously, the patriarchs, prophets, and priests were not exactly successful in curbing the human appetite and turning it toward God; however, the prophets endured and the message continued. By the time of the birth Christ, there were enough doubts about the value of their religion that many were ready to hear a new message — and a new message and a new Messenger came. One only has to read the Old Testament to recognize the chaos, mayhem, and destruction that was going on, just as it is today, often in the name of the Holy One. After all, it was an Old Testament Jew who brought the new message, and He was crucified for it!

Some might say that such a position as this detracts from the New Testament Christian message. It does not. It merely recognizes human weakness and the power of evil. The restlessness and doubts present at that time made people ready to accept something new. By nature, humans prefer to keep the old, even with its known faults, than to switch to something new. This is particularly true when we are asked to forsake family tradition, family values, and beliefs. Childhood beliefs do not fade easily. Therefore, the New Testament message had to be very plausible and attractive, and there had to be enough people who were searching for more than Old Testament Judaism offered. Otherwise no one would have been willing to believe in the "Star in the East."

Sometimes things appear to be broken when they are not. We frequently perceive something to be broken when in truth we simply don't know how to use it. I have a friend who sells new cars. He tells me that the number of folks who bring their brand new car back because something is "broken" is "interesting." He gets into the car with them, shows them how to "make it work," and they leave happily with the never-was-broken automobile now "fixed." Both psychology and religion have such parts.

The sheer survival of the church in the face of poor management, personnel deficiencies, and theological abuses proves its inherent worth and ability to survive the onslaughts of hell. The church has endured murder, mayhem, and much more, while ignoring every one of the *eleven* commandments — ten in the Mosaic Law and the New Commandment given to us by Jesus. The Church, Protestant and Roman Catholic alike, have both been flagrant in ignoring their unique "new commandment:" that we love God and one another. We have killed, pillaged, stolen, lied, and committed a list of "sins" longer than the Old Testament, Apocrypha, and New Testament combined, all in the name of God. The world continues to be replete with wars, all forms of slavery (legal and illegal), violent insults, and egregious behavior on humankind, all in the claim of God's Will.

Grab the Opportunity While It Is Here

There is much evidence of an awakening to the need for religion in America. Some polls even indicate a return to religion. There was certainly ample evidence in the 2000 election and in the events of terrorism we have witnessed regarding the interest, wish and need for religion. These "straws in the wind" would cause the corporate business world to seize the opportunity for marketing that would eclipse the Super Bowl. Traditionally the church has not marketed or advertised to any degree. It was just assumed that "if we build it, they will come." Maybe it is time for the church to seriously consider "advertising" — letting the world know that it is now "in vogue" to go to church.

Young couples with children seem to welcome the opportunity to put values in their children's lives. The huge interest and increase in home schooling is no doubt the result of an educational system bereft of the values parents want their children to learn. The church with a Sunday School is in a perfect place to augment what parents are in search of for their children. Many young parents I questioned were very outspoken about going to church because of what it offered their children. A frequent comment was, "I need it, but I want to be sure my kids get it." Even parents reluctant to admit they had any need for the church were eager for their children to be "brought up in the church." When I asked "why," they often didn't know or wouldn't say, but stated they thought it was important in the long run.

The church can capitalize on this "return to religion" movement. Parents are worried about the welfare of their children and are willing to place at least some degree of faith in the church, hoping it might help their children avoid drugs, curb sexual promiscuity, thwart violence, and help with a host of other parental worries. Additionally, these parents find they are spending their lives as workaholics, but that money does not satisfy all their needs or solve their problems. They have parents facing the "golden years," who are looking disease, ailing bodies, failing memories, and death in the face. Once again they hope the church will have something to help them. Also interesting is that "spirituality," an amorphous yet real thing, seems to be edging into medicine and psychology with less resistance. There is much less cynicism when doctors pray before performing surgery or psychotherapists encourage patients to seek spiritual guidance, referring to theology and even recognizing the value of the Bible for guidance in daily life.

In my informal surveys, one constant remark had to do with youth and the children they will have. It could be summarized something like this: "The church is getting old, graying like America. It is not enlisting our children so it won't have our grand-kids either." Without the youth and their children, there is no church of the future. The church will need to listen more closely to the younger generation — which in many instances it is doing — by having alternative times for worship, creative approaches, and approaches that we cannot write about today — because we don't know what they will be. The message can remain the same, while bringing in new methods. It is possible to differentiate between commercialism and evangelism. It is a fine line, but enlisting those we wish to reach will help in keeping that distinction. The younger generation will need to clearly understand the debt they are being left with and the potential obligations of the church that their elders more readily accepted and perhaps were more able to financial-ly support.

However, another common remark was, "Our kids just don't have the money to support the church. It's all they can do to buy their own home. The day of affluence seems to be dwindling, so how will our kids pay for all this?" Every mainline denomination minister with whom I spoke remarked that their denominations were basically "run by seniors" and that few young persons attend-ed the monthly, quarterly, or annual meetings. Seniors seem to be more in touch with the ramifications of a changed world order and economic and social impacts on the church than do most ministers and younger laity with whom I spoke. Their wisdom should not be spurned. This generation of seniors in the church might be the last

generation with both the interest and the finances to make meaningful changes.

Given the financial uncertainty of the next generations, church
leaders must now adopt budgets and programs that the younger
generations can (and will) support. Otherwise, by necessity, the
younger generations will abandon an organization that they cannot
in good conscience attend, feeling that they are "freeloaders." The
stone and stained glass of yesteryear, while having symbolic importance to earlier generations, may have little meaning for those who
cannot or will not pay for it tomorrow.

RELIGION AND PSYCHOLOGY CAN WORK TOGETHER

This book may appear to sound like the disciplines of religion and
psychology are archenemies and must be kept at bay. Not so.
However, careful attention must be paid to where each discipline
fits, when each is appropriate, and when, in truth, each can offer the
human condition help without further muddying the waters or
deceiving would-be believers. Of course, psychology has much to
offer and obviously theology does, too. Why the church got off
track is not as important as getting back to Biblically based preaching and teaching and a nurturing mission. There are many professions in both disciplines that are willing and able to assist in this reformation, but we must enlist them before more is lost in both
theology and psychology.

Admit That Psychology Isn't All Bad

Psychology has provided many benefits in the management of
human behavior. Like any other tool, however, when it is the only
tool we have, all problems are seen as fitting the purpose of that
tool. Someone rightly said, "If the only tool you have is a hammer,
then all problems must be nails." When psychology perceives every

problem as being of emotional origin, then, of course, psychology possesses the presumed instruments of choice.

Often this erroneous thinking actually comes from persons who have good intentions to bring together body, mind, and spirit into one. Much good has resulted from attempting to integrate and see the interconnection of our "parts." The holistic approach to thinking has helped us to see that the human is not a fragmented tripartite being, but one whole person consisting of at least three parts. Jan Christian Smuts, in his famous classic of 1928, *Holism and Evolution*, as well as many other contributors to philosophy, theology, and psychology since that time, illustrated the need to see the human in a more total sense, as a whole person. The Cartesian "mind/body" split does not work. We were not created as a tripartite entity, but even as the Divine Trinity, our unified trinity of mind, soul, and body that must of necessity always function interdependently.

The relationship of religion and psychology has been explored for centuries. Franz Delitzsch, in *Religion and Psychology* (1866), at that early date was exploring psychology and religion, including psychosomatic medicine, mind/body relationships, and issues of soul and spirit. Many scholars and writers preceded and have followed Delitzsch, including hundreds in the 20th century. The huge "pastoral psychology" movement and many Hospital Chaplain training programs focused on integrating the disciplines of religion and psychology. There were also other kinds of organizations and programs, such as the Menninger Clinic, the American Association for Clinical Pastoral Education, the W. Clement Stone Foundation, and many more, that contributed stellar work in an attempt to bring psychology and religion together.

All efforts to wed psychology and theology have not been in vain. The era of "psychologizing" theology may have actually saved an otherwise dying Church. At that particular time, the liberal theology afoot provided little basis for a personal faith. God was far away, if not perceived as dead by many, including some clergy. Humanizing the distant, already divorced from life, psychologized theology may have actually brought some life to otherwise meaningless creeds and rituals. The "God is Dead" (*Time*, April 8, 1966) movement, along with a new extreme right wing interpretation of Christianity, was splitting the Protestant church. The Roman Catholic Church was threatened because of massive defections and actual resignations, as well as nonattendance and noncompliance with church dogma. Attendance in the Roman Catholic Church fell to such an extent in some places that huge cathedrals closed and in some instances the church buildings were sold. There is no segment of Roman Catholic or Protestant Christendom that has not suffered in this century.

Some of the earliest persons to use psychology in an attempt to revitalize the church were spread across all religious lines. Bishop Fulton Sheen was an early "television evangelist" for the Roman Catholic Church, as was The Rev. Norman Vincent Peale for Protestants. There was a massive blend of Dale Carnegie's *How to Win Friends and Influence People*, with the Rev. Norman Vincent Peale's *The Power of Positive Thinking*, with Rabbi Joshua Liebman's *Peace of Mind*, and with the Sermon on the Mount. Some have said that this formula could allow a person to think positively, and thus win friends and influence people, while growing rich, and achieving peace of mind, all the while living in accord with the Sermon on the Mount! That would be quite an accomplishment.

Books flooded the bookstores pronouncing the marriage of psychological thinking and spiritual living. Suddenly, it was good religion to think psychologically. It was also strangely good mental health to think religiously. Yet there was certainly no integration of the disciplines in either the classroom or the pulpit. They were both fashionable fads yearning to become truths.

This movement produced considerable self-deception. As has been noted, an era ensued in which churches began "growth groups" and a "touchy-feely" community invaded many churches. To "tell all" became a new form of the old-fashioned "testimony meeting." Psychology had come to the rescue of dying customs. The time-honored, but dying tradition of the "testimony meeting" in many Protestant churches was resurrected as a new form of "touchy-feely self-transparency." It was now in good taste to tell family and personal secrets in public. To do so made one appear both spiritual and mentally healthy. However as clinicians and pastors discovered, often these public confessions were harmful to other family members, as well as to one's self, but it was the "honest" thing to do. Even if it hurt others, one could "feel clean." We need to ask whether this was psychological narcissism, religious hedonism, or both. Probably both and more.

In some churches, the meeting of local church groups became a new form of group therapy. Unfortunately, most groups were led by less than adequately trained therapists, often producing a greater pathology than was present to start with. Catharsis was often mistaken for conversion, and it was falsely assumed that to "get it out" was to "get it over with." The power was assumed to come from the act of confession. Peers often without credentials served as "father confessors" and spilling venomous information in small public groups was assumed to bring healing. Many Roman Catholics lost faith in their Church and no longer practiced confession in the church, but now often went to untrained leaders in Protestant Churches or to nonreligiously affiliated groups to publicly confess what they would not do with a priest in private! This movement proved to be as harmful (maybe more so) as it was helpful. Thankfully, this fad is now largely dead.

However, out of every age comes some good. There were many segments of the church that had grown weary of the new psychotheology. Unfortunately, most of that segment returned to a legalistic, literalistic form of "bibliolatry" which produces the very near-psychotic and unhealthy mental disturbances that psychotheology had attempted to eradicate. On the other hand, practicing psychologists and psychiatrists, as well as others in the social and medical sciences, had seen enough to be convinced of the mind/body connection and the value of rational spiritual thinking and its effect on both mental and physical health. Those accepting a rational approach to the mind/body relationship were a true minority and this now widely accepted body of knowledge is only in the very latter part of the 20th century being accepted with any degree of seriousness.

Christian thinking has always been in the minority worldwide, and still is today. Thinking holistically as Christians is very new. Holistic thinking among theologians and psychological professionals is even newer. There was an increase in holistic thinking occuring as we entered the 21st century. The latter part of the 20th century saw a rise of Eastern and mid-Eastern religious thought even in the Western world. Psychiatry as well as religion have thus been influenced, and Eastern thinking has confronted the Western concept of Christianity. In the early 1970s, psychiatrists and psychologists went to Eastern "ashrams" and other "Eastern" meditation centers to determine if Western psychiatry and Eastern philosophy could be integrated. Some professionals actually traveled to centers in the Orient for training. Many found valuable relationships between the two ways of thinking.

One reason Eastern thinking has been so appealing is its emphasis on the unification of the human person. Twentieth century preachers, in their attempt to find the dying God, and the God many said was already dead, failed to recognize the concept of the whole person. Ecclesiastical attempts to unify the person by introducing so much psychology did not work. There were some notable exceptions among scholars and theologians; however, by and large, the lay audience was listening to the preachers who had not studied psychology adequately. Major theologians were heard mainly in the universities and seminaries without contact with the lay public. The translation of proper psychology and proper theology did not find an intimate and fruitful wedding at the level of the church-going parishioner.

Recognize That Psychology and Religion Can Both Win

There are plenty of positive gains for both organized religion and psychology when they are used to augment and supplement, rather than to confuse and supplant each other. Understanding human behavior, marital and family dynamics, motivation, perception, and knowing the principles of how we learn are extremely beneficial areas of information for the pastor. Although many mental health professionals would deny such, understanding the human's need for God and accepting that our very epicenter is spiritual could be of great assistance in all forms of healing. Often an attempt to merge and combine things results in a loss to both. Without doubt, such was true in the marriage of psychology and local church-based religion. Scholars in both camps were able to philosophize about the integration with great eloquence, but that is not where the lay world lives. In pulpits all across the land, theology became pop psychology with a bit of religion thrown in.

Likewise, scholars both in psychology and religion discussed with fervor and some accuracy the relationship of psychology to religion, but again, as with the lay church-goer, the patient in the psychotherapist's office "just didn't get it." *The public simply could not accept going to church to be psychoanalyzed, nor could it accept going to the analyst to get religion.* Many organizations cropped up in an attempt to bring the two disciplines together, e.g., the Christian Association for Psychological Studies, the American Association of Pastoral Counselors, the Association for Clinical Pastoral Education, the American Psychological Association Division (Division 36) on

Religion and Psychology, numerous seminaries that developed doctoral programs in Pastoral Counseling, and many other programs and associations.

Psychology has not been integrated into the whole person in most instances in religious circles (or elsewhere for that matter), and certainly it has not been integrated into either Protestant or Roman Catholic Theology. The movement toward pastoral counseling attempted, and in some ways succeeded, in bringing into existence a body of literature that intellectually wed the two disciplines. Many pastoral counselors, in order to become even moderately successful in combining the two disciplines, left the parish ministry in order to teach or practice what they saw as a major breakthrough. Many left the ministry all together and hung out shingles as counselors of various sorts. Those who remained in the ordained ministry and the pastoral counseling field were already (or became) academicians. Their scholarly pursuits caused them to think they had made significant progress in wedding the two systems, but not discounting their accomplishments, it still did not work for most folks. The distance between the thinking of scholars in university "ivory towers" and the thinking of the person in the pew has always been great. In this instance, the distance was even greater due to the chasm between the seminary and the minister. It was moved a step farther from the pew. The layperson in truth doesn't care much about journal articles, memorial lectures, etc. They certainly don't want to learn a new fad language to understand their old and well-tested faith. They are looking for answers, not hypotheses or debates, and few if any are interested in playing chess with one's belief system.

Be Sure That Religion Wins

Maybe I should say that "churches" can still win. However, when discussing Roman Catholic and Protestant faith, it is clear that "religion" and "churches" are very much one and the same thing for most people. It is evident that there are sectors in Western society in which religion is "winning" in individual churches. Some individual community congregations are growing in spite of the fact that the parent denominations of those congregations across-the-board are losing members, even in large numbers. These denominations include but are not limited to the Presbyterian Church USA, Methodist Church, United Church of Christ, Disciples of Christ, Episcopal, and Roman Catholic. Religion as a pure theological process is not "winning" in most sectors of the mainline and Roman Catholic churches. In some instances, obedience in word may be witnessed. Nowhere is this more flagrant than in Roman Catholic congregations. The church message has been so repressive, that in order for religion to win, there will need to be another reformation! As these denominations continue to suffer membership loss, there are notable exceptions to this generalization. Some local congregations are being forced to build larger buildings because of increased attendance. Some are finding new places for themselves in the community while others offer enough to entice followers to drive long distances to services. Some are actually increasing their membership from the "unchurched," however, most are transfers from other congregations.

For all congregations wishing to broaden their ministry, it is important to see what is causing an increase in some groups and a decrease in others. To be sure, not all congregations see themselves as needing to "broaden their ministry." Some believe it is their job to feed their sheep and they have not attempted to enlist others. Surely, this is a minority report. The majority of congregations believe that they should be "evangelizing" and "bringing in the sheaves," in spite of the fact that they may not be doing so. As has been discussed elsewhere in this book, the deeper problem is that the tools for evangelism and mission have largely been lost, but they are not dead. The tools and skills available for evangelism and revival are still readily available.

A real difficulty is that local congregations will have to take the risk alone. There is little evidence that denominational leaders are capable of saving their own denomination, let alone local congregations. First of all, denominations are made up of individual congregations, and secondly, large institutions are always mired in the *status quo*, whether they choose to be or not. They simply do not have the mechanisms in place to revamp the organizational machinery quickly enough to make a difference. Organizational change is by and large a slow process. Local congregations, on the other hand, can "catch the Spirit" (to borrow a motto from a major denomination).

It would be worthwhile for mainline denominations to study the few religious groups that are increasing in membership to see why such is true. The Mormon Church is one of the most rapidly growing denominations. Is it because of the doctrine? Is it because of ecclesiastical structure? Is it because of the massive "evangelism" programs? Is it because of the rigidity of belief? Or is it because of a thousand other things? The answer is probably found in a combination of factors. Very few people start attending any church, Mormon or otherwise, *because* of what that church teaches. Few, if any, even know what is taught or what is believed until long after they have joined the group. Although most ministers and priests would like to believe otherwise, it is not their preaching or their doctrine. In truth, often preachers don't know and usually those joining don't know why they are joining. Relationships are probably a primary reason why people are attracted to just about anything! It may be that their relationships brought them to a good place and good beliefs. (However, we all know that unfortunate relationships take "good" people to "bad" places.)

Both psychology and religion can still win this conflict and each can contribute much more to our world. A powerful illustration of how our world reacts psychologically and religiously was witnessed in the sudden death and burial of Diana, Princess of Wales. The grandeur, enormity, and diversity in her funeral service once again demonstrated that true religion crosses denominational, ethnic, color, class, and all other artificial societal lines. Regardless of religious preference and world views regarding Lady Diana, throngs crowded the streets, read every newspaper and magazine, and were glued to the television. Although she was much criticized for her behavior, she was loved for her goodness and mercy. The message of New Testament love and forgiveness came through, without condemnation and without an assignment of guilt. There was no "pop psychology" message. The Church of England message, "There is therefore no condemnation," as preached centuries earlier by the Apostle Paul to the Romans, sounded loud and clear. There was a blending of Elton John's modern music (on the piano in Westminster Abbey!) with the chilling and demanding tones of that gigantic pipe organ and the traditional hymns of the church, coupled with the spine-tingling sounds of the Scottish bagpipe! The people inside Westminster Abbey represented every creed on earth, Christian and otherwise, and the streets were lined in a fashion that reminded one of the triumphal march of Jesus into Jerusalem, except the throngs were throwing flowers for Diana instead of palm branches for a living person, Jesus.

This amazing occurrence has many lessons for us all, among them:

1. People often go to a church service for what is going on in that particular service. It somehow has special meaning to them individually.

2. Although religious leaders might not admit it, the denomination or kind of religion, and the church in which the service is being held, is not important.

3. People go to church to hear the age-old truths that stand against the stark despair of their everyday life, so why disappoint them?

4. People go to church to identify with other sinners in a community where they feel safe. Safety comes in two forms: the hope and promises of God and the company of like-minded worshippers.

5. People go to church to hear a message that they cannot find in newspapers and pop magazines: everyone knows that the Scriptures are forever; they have endured the test of time individually and communally.

6. People go to church for music that appeals to their values, whether it is traditional "classic religious," gospel, or country. Many older persons (who are responsible for so much of the financial support!) identify with the majestic hymns of the church and the Sunday School songs that take them back to their religious roots.

7. People go to church to be with others who share common joys and sorrows. We are all equal on our knees!

8. People go to church for reasons that we do not fully know and should not try to find out. If we should find out, we might be surprised! Each person has a unique reason for worship in our quest for eternal life.

Allow Psychology to Win, Too

The true value of psychology and religion is the same in many ways. However, the only way either one will win is if the other is incorporated deeply within the parishioner or patient *without external persuasion*. The healing therapist is one who transcends him/herself and brings to the session the wholeness of a healing journey known only through experience. Psychology can no more win by adopting the language of religion than religion can win by adopting the language of psychology. Psychology is not the *entity* that must win.

Psychologists, psychiatrists, social workers, and mental healers of every sort are individuals who must find their way through the morass of pseudoscientific, paramedical, and socially invalid language. They must learn lessons from a personal spiritual journey. When this is done, psychology will be able to then translate the wholeness of the mind into modalities for human treatment. All good therapists know that therapists cannot be made. They can only be shown the road and encouraged to travel it.

Psychology must be willing to give up the concept of "diagnosis" and return to the person with the "problem." Diagnoses are a most arrogant approach to "fix" the person with a "problem" — perhaps even an attempt to superimpose our lack of understanding on those unable to defend themselves. The concept of "diagnosis" tends to lead to a chemical (medication) answer. The concept of "problem" tends to lead to finding a solution. Although medications may well be part of the solution, starting with the concept of "diagnosis" often blocks all avenues to find other answers. Starting with the "solution" approach allows far more exploration and freedom to find more than a temporary answer. Obviously, there are conditions for which life-long medication is in order. However, many patients have been kept on chemical answers for far too long simply because no one has considered other alternatives. Since all known medications have unwanted side-effects, some of them nearly as serious as the condition for which they are being taken, it behooves persons in the helping professions to search for every possible method to relieve human suffering, mental and physical, with as little chemical assistance as possible.

Psychology must become more interested in the person's health than their illness. It must become more intrigued with how one grows than how one "gets well." The therapist in true transcendent fashion will be a silent witness to every belief, a role model without attempting to do so, and a catalyst between the forces of *well-ness* and *dis-ease* without knowing precisely what makes the healing happen. Both psychology and religion are sciences of the human condition. They both are plagued by the human predicament. Neither of them can make any promises greater than the individual's faith and willingness to explore the unknown.

Psychology must give up Freud's notion that religion is a neurosis. Freud made many valuable contributions to understanding the human being. However, it was his own unresolved conflict that made it impossible for him to accept religion as a powerful positive attribute. Psychology will need to accept the fact that since the beginning of time, humans sought spiritual enlightenment and that psychological insight is not the same as spiritual enlightenment.

Insight helps us to know what is wrong — spiritual enlightenment helps us to know what to do about it. Insight is precisely what it implies — illumination into something. In our discussion, it is light into one's self. Spiritual enlightenment differs in that a spiritual dimension is added to the insight. Insight alone allows one to see — spiritual enlightenment provides answers as to what to do about it. This is where religion enters the picture. Insight is a term used by the psychotherapeutic world to denote new understanding. The secular therapeutic world speaks of insight, not spiritual enlightenment. This is because insight is seen as a mechanism to bridge the unconscious to the conscious.

However, herein lies a basic fallacy of the psychological world. The unconscious is the closest thing to the soul in our language. It represents our innermost unknown motives and desires. The unconscious is called by that name primarily because Freud could not reckon with the spiritual part of humankind. He could not admit the soul into his theories. Had he been able to integrate his psychological innovations with the spiritual, we would have a very different practice of psychiatry than we have today.

However, the real bridge between the soul and day-to-day reality is spiritual enlightenment which is more than psychological insight. Psychological insight is the "aha" experience when "it all comes together." Spiritual enlightenment is the experience whereby past experiences, present realities, and future applications all come together within the context of faith and within the framework of a spiritual journey. Spiritual enlightenment may include areas in which there is no "aha" and answers to very large parts are still missing, but enlightenment allows faith to dominate where fear would otherwise block action. Insight produces knowledge brought up from within the inner person (the unconscious). Spiritual enlightenment couples that new knowledge with a demand for action, thus truly bridging the unknown to the known, the unconscious to the conscious, and the soul to its Maker, in the real world.

Religion is the link between the conscious and the unconscious mind, or, to use other non-Freudian words, it is the link between the known and the unknown. Psychoanalysis attempted to bridge that gap by exploring the unconscious through free association and dreams. Religion does not attempt to explore it. Religion through faith accepts the unknown and by the same token utilizes faith to improve and accept the known. The neuroses of psychoanalysis cannot exist within the framework of faith. It must be pointed out that even after one "discovered" in analysis the reasons for a given psychological problem, only faith in believing that reason and faith to change it can make a difference. Little did Freud and psychoanalysts realize the commonality of psychoanalysis and religion. Psychology and religion are peculiarly alike in many ways. They both require attention to relationships, interrelationships, truth, tolerance, and understanding and an intense desire to find the essence of the wholeness in life.

Psychology will need to utilize the deeper truths about human need and recognize that there is real guilt. Real guilt is only made worse by psychological acceptance of that which everyone, including the patient, knows should not be accepted but changed. Psychology must allow personal ownership of the vicissitudes of life.

Displacement, i.e., blaming others for your problems, has been decried by psychology since the beginning, yet the practice of blaming others has never been more rampant than it is today. The "victim age" has doubtless been greatly assisted by psychology and psychiatry. The legal profession coupled with the "victim interpretation" of psychology has rendered much of our society helpless. Personal responsibility is the essence of both psychological and spiritual health. Psychotherapists must start insisting that their patients assume responsibility for their own actions and stop the "blame game." Until this happens, neither psychology nor theology has any answers. It is only a new version of "the devil made me do it." The identity of the devil has changed, and at times the devil is mother, father, neighbor, employer, or anyone other than one's self. There is nothing new about the "victim age," except that we now have insurance, a legal system, and too often psychotherapists that reward the victim. Adam and Eve were the original "victims." Their problem was that God was quite unwilling to see them as such and sent them on their way with consequences, accountability, and a life based on both faith and faithful works!

Psychology must return to the basic values of life. It, like religion, prides itself on accepting all persons, all problems, and all situations, and again, like religion, often with little to offer. Psychology has deluded itself into thinking that acceptance is what people want. Sometimes this is true; however, psychiatry, unlike other branches of medicine, too often gives patients what they want rather than what their diagnoses require. It would be like giving a sedative to a patient who needed a cathartic or doing an appendectomy on a person who really needed an amputation. It is time that psychology assumes a professional stance and practices acceptance and rejection — not of the person — but of those behaviors which have proven to be "dis-ease" producing.

Psychology can emphasize the spiritual nature of patients and can rely upon spiritual resources. It is not necessary to "play priest" in order to appreciate the values of religious thinking and the benefits of prayer, meditation, Scripture reading, and the Sacraments of the church. Psychologists and psychiatrists do not need to be defensive about their faith or the faith they feel would be beneficial to their patients. They can even admit that psychotherapy is a handmaiden to proper spiritual growth. They can appreciate that psychotherapeutic and psychopharmacological methods help people reach higher goals in life, which ultimately can only be achieved by a personal spiritual journey. We need psychology and psychiatry — we just don't need them to *replace* religion or a solid spiritual faith.

Psychotherapists would be well reminded of the famous words of Carl Jung in a writing of 1932: "Among all my patients in the second half of my life, there has not been one whose problem in the last resort was not that of finding a religious outlook on life. It is safe to say that every one of them fell ill because he had lost that which the living religions of every age have given their followers and none of them has been really healed who did not regain his religious outlook" (Jung, cited in Glynn, 1997, p. 69).

THE POWER OF THE DOLLAR IS DANGEROUS

We have heard about the "power of the almighty dollar" since we were children. Why we call it "almighty" is clear to anyone who even casually observes the power of money over persons, institutions, and governments. The church is no exception to this power.

Stop Using the Church's Money to Pay for Its Own Disinheritance

Many universities, medical schools, and numerous other institutions began as denominationally related and funded organizations. Millions of dollars were spent to establish "homes of mercy," orphanages, homes for "unwed mothers," "old folk's homes," and other organizations that had names we no longer consider to be in good taste. However, the intent was sincere. The purpose was to use money contributed by church members for the purpose of demonstrating God's mercy and kindness. Christianity financed much of the medical world; then with the development of modern science, medical institutions felt no need to recognize the spiritual elements of human existence and discarded religion. Huge religious funding drives in America's churches were successful, and denominations poured millions of dollars into medical institutions that would soon totally ignore the spiritual reasons for which the money had been given. These hospitals and medical establishments would soon barely tolerate their own chaplains. Many Roman Catholic hospitals which were established and operated by caring nuns succumbed to big business. Actually, huge insurance companies disguised as healthcare organizations assumed control and the religious order was left with virtually nothing to do with the actual management and policy making — religion left out. Some hospitals with traditional religious roots are now struggling to bring spirituality back into healthcare.

Fortunately, this era is beginning to fade and some medical institutions are once again recognizing the value of spiritual thinking and the power of prayer. Many physicians, psychologists, and other healthcare providers now once again produce credible research and utilize the power of prayer and the healing of spirituality in their institutions and treatment regimens. The American Psychological Association annual convention in San Francisco (1998) held a very well-attended session on spirituality and health. Each year the topic of spirituality is one that draws huge interest.

Reconsider Whether the Church Should Be in the Real-Estate Business

On one single street in a Midwest town, there are thirteen churches within approximately four miles. There are even churches of the same denomination within less than one mile! There are eight church congregations within a two-mile distance. Four are Baptist, one is Anglican, one is Christian (Disciples of Christ), one is Methodist, and one is Roman Catholic. Within two blocks of that street, there are an additional four churches: one Lutheran, one Mormon (LDS), one Independent (nondenominational), and one Seventh-Day Adventist. Another building served as a church for the congregation of a major denomination that did not "make it." It is now being used as a denominational headquarters. Many of these churches are growing and doing very well. Almost all meet at the same hour, on the same day (Sunday), their parking lots are full, and earth-moving equipment can be seen as some construct additional buildings!

I once thought about calculating the combined cost of land, buildings, salaries, overhead, and other financial considerations and dividing it by the number of hours the buildings were used, but decided it would be mathematical futility. It boggles one's mind to attempt to think if there is effective stewardship in this situation. A formula, however, would be constructed something like this:

$$\frac{L + B + S + O + M + CI + D}{HU} = CE = ESR$$

Where L = land; B = buildings; S = salaries; O = overhead; M = miscellaneous; CI = Capital Improvements; and D = depreciation. There are doubtless other factors that should be included in such a cost analysis. However, all of these factors, and any others that should be included, would be divided by HU (= Hours Used) to arrive at the CE (= Cost Efficiency), or maybe we should say the ESR (= Effective Stewardship Ratio).

Granted, some congregations have little in common and therefore must have their own buildings, but is there really so little in common that four congregations of the same denomination cannot share costly building space? Has anyone asked what could be accomplished if schedules could be arranged to accommodate the congregations in the same building, using the funds required for building duplication in other ways? They all have services at essentially the same time, but is that essential to their faith? Does their doctrine make it *impossible* for them to meet at different times even on the same day? The Mormon (LDS) Church, although not accepted by many as a viable system of Christian belief, nonetheless provides an interesting use of time, space, and money. Mormon churches do not have paid pastors for church congregations, they use the same building for more than one congregation, and they frequently have multiple uses by more than one congregation occurring in the same building at the same time.

There are many arguments about why this model *cannot* work for mainline Protestant congregations, but could congregations and ministers be challenged to find arguments about why it *could* work? There is ample evidence in the New Testament that there was no encouragement or even mention of different denominations. As a matter of fact, Jesus said, "I will build my church" (singular) and He prayed "that they all may be one," indicating that He pleaded for unity and singularity of purpose and mission. Yet, by the same token, there is ample evidence that local congregations had many different approaches to the faith and even different methods of worship. Has the Protestant Church created a "congregational Tower of Babel" unnecessarily? It is hard to imagine what could be done if even a modicum of unity were achieved, between congregations who say they believe the same thing and belong to the same denomination.

For centuries the Roman Catholic Church has owned more real estate, all tax-free, than can be imagined. Protestant denominations have been known to maintain apartment buildings, shopping centers, and other commercial enterprises, all in the name of the church, for tax exempt purposes. Whole city blocks and acres of land have been kept off the tax roles. The IRS tax code is now a bit tougher, making sure that enterprises are within the specific mission of the organization claiming tax exemption. Church organizations have come under the scrutiny of the IRS and actually had to repay funds for what was judged to be for-profit activity under a not-for-profit charter. When we look at activities of religious organizations, it would appear that they have a long way to go. Should the government offer, and the churches accept, federal funding for social services, it promises to be an area of considerable confusion.

Get Rid of Financial and Political Dishonesty

It is not possible to recount in the pages of a small book the misuses and abuses of religion for financial gain, both inside and outside the organized church. Values translate too easily into dollars and dollars translate into power. The tax-exempt status of the church, most as 501(c) 3 (not-for-profit) organizations, has permitted it to use tax-exempt funds many times for clearly for-profit purposes. Preaching "separation of church and state" from one side of the mouth while enjoying the fruits of clearly for-profit enterprises out of the other side will need to have some pecuniary surgery! There have been ministers who essentially "told" their parishioners how to vote and what political agendas to support, while at the same time preaching the separation of church and state. This is a fine line — a very fine one — between preaching righteousness and at the same time influencing for personal gain those who trust their minister's judgment. In addition to state and national politics, there is the thorny issue of the private political agendas for which congregations are used to support. However, this is not an argument to cease preaching against, taking action against, or eschewing any form of social, political, community, and personal evil.

Churches that fail or refuse to see the Gospel as politically powerful have their heads in the sand. Carter so well elucidates this point in his book, *God's Name in Vain* (2000, p. 171): "... religion is, at its best, subversive of the society in which it exits. Religion's subversive power flows from its tendency to focus the attention and, ultimately, the values of its adherents on a set of understandings often quite different from the understandings of the dominant forces in the culture. The larger culture, … will always try to impose a set of meanings on all of its subcultures; … religion is almost always the one best able to resist. That resistance, in turn, is the source of diversity, of dialogue, and, ultimately, of change." Self-serving and petty issues must give way to the larger purposes and message of the Gospel if the church is to prove that it is indeed "almost always the one best able to resist."

Salute Caesar But Keep Your Eyes Open!

USA Today reported (January 31, 2001) a possibility that others have pondered: "Charles Colson, who went to prison for his role in Watergate, runs Prison Fellowship Ministries, a Christian group. He worked with Bush when Bush was governor of Texas and predicted Bush 'will make this succeed' at the federal level. Colson acknowledged, however, that his ministry withdrew from a similar state-funded program in Michigan because state law required jobs be open to non-Christians." There are *always* prices to be paid for support. It was no other than C. S. Lewis who alerted us to the seriousness of falling victim to methods designed to gain desired ends. The end often does not justify the means: it becomes the means and the means become the end. The inevitable confusion is a proverbial "can of worms" that cannot be untangled. Stephen L. Carter, in his provocative book, *God's Name In Vain* (2000, p. 57), reminds us of Cal Thomas' words: "If people who claim to follow Jesus and his kingdom get too cozy with government, it won't be the government that gets injured. It will be the church that is compromised."

It is hard to know what might have happened if the government had decided to subsidize the Salvation Army in its early days. In this past decade, we have witnessed what has happened to the practice of medicine, particularly Medicare, when it is subsidized — and ultimately controlled — by external government money and interest. According to the *Orlando Sentinel* (January 31, 2001), the Salvation Army and Catholic Charities have been receiving "more than one billion dollars annually to provide social services." A careful study of how these organizations maintain autonomy (if they do) would be helpful as potential models.

Keeping a clear line between monies taxed from everyone to render services to those chosen by specific faith-based groups will not be without complication, corruption, greed, and waste. However, with human need as it is, who can fault anyone for trying to alleviate some of the human suffering around us?

However, the fight of the Gospel is not against hunger, homelessness, and health. It is against the powers of the Evil One as *manifested* in those human needs. There will always be hunger, homelessness, and health needs as long as there are people. The temporal needs are important, but to what end? If the message of Christian theology is to be believed, it is only that we should find our way into the arms of a loving God and celebrate Him forever. While no one would argue that helping those in need is often an invitation to a loving God, we must make sure that the method is not considered the end and lose sight of the mission.

The issue then is *why* does the church care about the temporal needs of others? If in the future, as is currently being proposed, the church is offered government money for social services, can the church remember *why* it offers such services?

And Keep an Eye on the Road Signs, Too

Government involvement might mean government intrusion. Is there a connection between the gift, the giver, and the receiver? Is there ever not? At what point does the "piper" seek to get paid? Can any organization accept money without being responsible to the donor — and in being accountable is there a temptation to bend one's convictions and purposes for the benefits? The argument is one that we can already hear. It goes something like this: finally the government sees the benefit of the church and is willing to help us do our work (after all, all dollars are green — even theirs!). We see the "Caution" signs and the "Stop" signs in time to take action, but what about the "Merge," "Left Lane Ends," and most of all, the "Dead End" signs?

The very structure of the church demands budgets and business management of the same nature and extent as any other industry. Religion can thus become a commodity, not an organization in the service of faith. As a commodity, religion can be budgeted, bartered, and sold. The service of faith is quite a different thing. *Servicing* the faith *requires* faith. Faith does not lend itself to predictability. Maybe this is why (to our knowledge), in the New Testament, there were no buildings or congregations with salaried employees and huge budgets to support. The more capitalistic we become, the more the church will be forced to adopt commercial management methods. Commercial management methods do not wed well with the service of faith. There is no easy answer to this dilemma, except that faith, whether it be in practice or in the service of faith, is never easy by its own definition of living and working within the bounds of belief rather than knowledge. Money has always been a problem. Judas carried the purse for the disciples and found that out! Hopefully, belief and knowledge can find a common ground and balance each other out without selling out to materialism.

WALK THE TALK

The popular phrase "walk the talk" takes on new meaning when applied to the church — the one institution in our culture that claims to do so. Many churches, pastors, and members sincerely attempt to walk the talk. However, sufficient stumbling, weaving in and out of the truth, and hypocrisy have been so obvious as to disturb those who only marginally (or not at all) believe. Jesus reminded us that The Way is narrow and straight and not everyone finds it. Looking through a microscope at our daily walk and through a telescope at the larger picture — at the same time — is difficult, but we must do it.

Abide By Consistent Rules

If psychology and religion are both to win, each must attend to its basic *raison d'etre* in order to do so. The rules for winning will not be difficult to understand, but they will doubtless require courage to follow. It is not a level playing field. The rules in both disciplines constantly change. Church members and patients really don't care about what changes go on in academic or higher ecclesiastical circles. They just want to know "where's the beef," to quote a famous TV commercial. However, we can be sure the rules of both organized religion and psychology will be based on the "bottom line," personalities, and empire building. Sometimes the talk, whether religious or psycho-babble, is purely filabustering! The lay public has become accustomed to the menu and their appetites will not change easily regardless of soft-sell or hard-sell tactics.

Psychology will have a much easier time winning than the church, although both may be only Pyrrhic victories. Psychology, at least the human services branch, has entered the age of managed care and as such its business base is cold and calculated. Since the government and for-profit insurance companies pay for these services, the financial outcome is important. Psychotherapy, i.e., "processing" one's life experiences, is a luxury most persons cannot afford on their own, and one which most insurance companies will not cover. Therefore, psychologists no longer establish comprehensive treatment plans specific for their patients and they are not permitted enough time for adequate treatment. Crisis management, a superficial fix, or a Band-Aid™ is about all any but the wealthy receive today. A few short sessions must now correct the behavior — forget the underlying causes. It takes entirely too much time to talk about religion, therefore, even patients and doctors who want to discuss religion, values, or spirituality do not. Philosophical discussions about the relationship of spirituality to mental health are just too cost-ineffective and will have to find their place in the classroom.

On the other hand, religion still has as much time as ever. Churches, although accountable to a bottom line, are not driven by "for pay sessions" with their members. If ministers and priests will leave psychotherapy to the professionals, they can do much more about the spiritual lives of their parishioners. They can, and should, carefully use what they know about human behavior and apply its *methods* without changing the church's *message*. This will be difficult for most since many have been trained in the new pop psychology kind of homiletics. Pop psychology is easier to practice than sound academic, professional psychology or theology.

Many ministers have not been trained in an analytical, expository, hermeneutic style of preaching for the most part. Furthermore, such preaching requires a great deal of study and sermon preparation time. It is a "Catch-22" because as long as they attempt to meet their parishioner's "psychological" needs, they will not have time to prepare theologically based sermons. If they attempt to preach theologically based sermons, some in their congregations are apt to gravitate to other congregations. One would think that since many worshippers want the "old truths," they would be happy, but the problem is that because of years of confused psychotheology, all but the most astute are incredibly confused about what constitutes "good theology." Sooner than later, by the loss of members and the loss of income (probably in reverse order), mainline denominations will come to recognize the futility of their current "socially relevant" discussions.

There is no need to "modernize" theology. True theology is always modern. Theology has the unique ability to speak to all ages without modern idiom. Theology does not change with older versions of the scriptures, nor does it change with the discovery of newer manuscripts. The human dilemma, the nature of transgression, the fact of sin, the nature of forgiveness, and the quest for eternal answers remain the same. The great disciple Dieterich Bonhoeffer, who was executed by Hitler's orders only six days before the Allies liberated Berlin, reminded us in his timeless book, *The Cost of Discipleship*, that where nothing is demanded and where everything is approved, we give birth to "cheap grace." "Cheap grace is the deadly enemy of our Church. We are fighting today for costly grace. Cheap grace means grace sold on the market like cheapjacks' wares. The sacraments, the forgiveness of sin, and the consolations of religion are thrown away at cut prices" (1937, p. 45). True love is not always accompanied by "warm fuzzies." There really is such a thing as "tough love." Rather than attempting to reconcile Freud and Jesus, the Church ought to be about the balancing act of tender love and tough love.

Redefine Success

Ministers will need to return to a sense of "calling" which is more powerful than economic, organizational, or even psychological success. The concept of the huge church and fast growing congregation is truly delusional. There are isolated instances of churches that are fast growing. In today's world, they tend to be the "independent" sort, more "fundamentalist," and more "charismatic" and many times legalistically interpret the Bible. Even those churches that refer to themselves as "evangelical" and "conservative" are not growing as fast. In some areas of the country, they are losing members to the more charismatic groups. There are some congregations that are attracting truly new believers; however, in most instances, few, if any, new believers are added. Dying churches and growing churches are simply exchanging members. Few new fish are added; they simply switch aquariums. This is not a *religious* revival. It is not a *religious* movement. It is a *sociological* phenomenon. It is not unlike customers who shop, comparing one discount store to another and buying at the one they like best. If you ask those customers why they buy at a certain discount store, they will say that sometimes the prices are better, sometimes the service is better, sometimes the warranty is better, but sometimes its just "because." The same is true with church shopping.

Keep the Minister's Job Description Clear

It is very difficult, perhaps impossible, for clergy to meet their own personal needs while attempting to feed the flock. There is only a modicum of understanding by most ministers of the concept of "dual relationships" and "conflict of interest." These concepts are understood by psychologists and psychiatrists because mixing relationships and not being clear about the purpose of the interest in the relationship get in the way of therapeutic intervention. Too many clergy mix relationships without much understanding. Clergy tend to be so involved with their own parishes that they do not find friends in the larger community, among other clergy, in civic clubs, and in non-church related organizations. This is a serious mistake. It has cost many clergy their credibility, objectivity, and in too many cases their jobs.

Make a Home for Everyone

The church must become a place for everyone: every sinner who recognizes his/her sin; every sinner who does not admit to sin; every saint who continues to sin; and all the saints who think they do not sin. I say "become" a place for everyone, rather than "be," because most local congregations (although they claim to be) are in truth not such places now. Dr. David Steere, a well-respected pastoral counselor, points out so well in his book, *Spiritual Presence in Psychotherapy* (1997), that many do feel at home in today's church.

The church has continually changed its methods and its message in an attempt to bring people back into the fold, but in many instances it has not worked. The reason is that the church has changed its message to fit problems and lifestyles, rather than helping us to solve our problems and change our lifestyles to fit the Christian message. Whether we talk about abortion, divorce, or any other sociotheological concern, most churches have not faced these problems head-on. Instead they say that they "accept the sinner" and "reject the sin." In truth, many of them simply "ignore the sin." This may make some clergy feel "accepting," but it is like parents who turn their heads when their child does something "bad." Both the child and the parents know the truth and neither respects the other. Soon the relationship is damaged because both know that there is no basic integrity left. Steere points out that "spiritual homelessness" is found in absenteeism from church services: "Spiritual homelessness is more than a product of the decline in mainline church life. It ranks swell daily under the growing impact of multicultural discontent. Of course, we must include baby boomers among its numbers: 96% of them attended religious services as children; since then, 42% have dropped out and no longer attend any place of worship; 33% never left and 25% quit attending services, but have recently begun to return."

The local church is like a home. It is not a place where people do no wrong. It is not even a place where they always admit it when they do wrong. However, home is not a place where wrong is ignored and it is not a place where you are rejected when you disagree. The underlying value base of the home does not change simply because you wish to argue with it. The message of the home is based upon spoken and unspoken ideologies, values, beliefs, and superstitions deeply imbedded in ethnic, religious, and perhaps even genetic foundations. The church is the same.

One reason the church has had so much trouble attempting to become a home for everyone is because it has tried to continually change its language to fit a new Tower of Babel. It has tried to speak the languages of the unchurched and of social benefits, social causes, psychological health, and other psycho-babble. Home is a place where you know what language to expect. You know what you will be told, whether you like it or not, and it will be the old, familiar language, "yes" or "no" and rarely "maybe." In a weak attempt to maintain a stern voice, the church has turned to a "absolute maybe."

The church can offer a home to all persons. However, in order to do so, it must return to a vocabulary people know, i.e., one of sin and salvation, and give up foreign pseudotheological languages in favor of its own native tongue of "yes" and "no."

This does not mean that everything is "black" and "white." It means that the church offers a solid starting point for thinking persons to evaluate their own spirituality. Churches and parents who always say, "I don't know" and "maybe" are like ships without rudders. Children (and church members) can only think for themselves if they have a base against which to measure their beliefs and practices. Otherwise, it like trying to play basketball without a backboard: there is no basket and the ball never returns. You can only hit the basket if you know where it is, know how far you must throw the ball, and have a chance for the ball to return to you. In terms of theology, we have been taught that we have "all come short." None of us sincerely doubts that truth. However, we must know how far to go to keep from "coming short." Using illustrations from basketball, baseball, or life, a good home provides a backboard, home base, and a yardstick and calls the play with unequivocal decision! The church is "home base" for theology. Many persons would attempt to score a homerun if the church would provide better coaches, consistent rules, and a fair referee.

Keep the Message Regardless of Popularity

The need to be liked might have to take second place to the message. Throughout history, the prophets and truly great theologians were not usually popular and were often rejected, even persecuted. The Great Theologian, about Whom the New Testament is written, found that even the gospel of love, when flavored with "tough" love, resulted in crucifixion. Studies consistently reveal that ministers like to be liked. Several years ago (1971), two psychologists (J. Vayhinger and R. Cox) studied the personality traits of seminarians. They found that ministerial candidates tended to be strong in the "maternal" personality characteristics, i.e., kindness, caring, and warmth. They also tended to be dependent and enjoyed others being dependent upon them. They tended to be reluctant to cause conflict or to enter into conflict.

However, ministers who succeed in being leaders also need to have traits characterized as "paternal," toughness, decision maker, unafraid of legitimate conflict, and strength. It is unfortunate that psychology characterizes "maternal" and "paternal" this way (this author vigorously disagrees with it). However, since such were the wordings on psychological tests, the vocabulary is used here for consistency. The gender of the clergy person makes no difference: strong characteristics must be more evidence of the Gospel than the self.

Keep the Faith and Vision

Faith is well defined in all religions and is essentially the same in all of them. The Christian Bible defines faith as "the evidence of things hoped for and the substance of things unseen" (Hebrews 11:1). The church preaches the necessity of faith. Its actions are often more in accord with the empirical world of science than the spiritual world of religion and faith. The empirical promises of science are tempting because they appear to be more predictable than anything offered by the spiritual world and predictability is more alluring for budgets, salaries, and building mortgages. Predictability of financial stability is imperative because an essential ingredient of today's church is money, but faith does not lend itself to predictability.

The only antidote for a shaky faith is an unshakable vision. When the end is more important than the journey, the tribulations along the way are more tolerable. The baseball player who slips and twists his ankle on first base sometimes does not realize it until he has successfully run around second and third bases to home plate. Why is this? It is because his vision is so great it causes his brain to subdue the pain with endorphins, his own naturally produced narcotics. When the vision is weak, there is need for only a mediocre faith. Unfortunately, most of us are of little faith, but hope that it will be sufficient for the really great mission.

Many times the problem of insufficient faith is actually a lack of vision. Most of us do not start with faith: we start with what we need and, more often with what we want. Faith is an afterthought and usually requires perspiration to drive the inspiration. The vision is all some people seem to be capable of having. They dwell in the world of the imaginary and wonder why it never happens. If our vision is something we want or need sufficiently, we search for ways to make it happen. Without a vision of the end, there can be no joy in the journey.

The answer is in keeping *both* the faith and the vision. Many groups have rigidly held to the faith, but in the midst of that struggle lost their vision. Others have become visionaries, striking out with great and bold plans, but without a foundation of faith in anything beyond themselves and their immediate journey. The Scriptures say, "where there is no vision, the people perish" (Proverbs 29:18). On one hand, it is important to have a faith that is abiding because the journey on a visionary road can become bleak. However, on the other hand, a future goal, a focus, or a mountain-top experience carries one's faith far. *To have something greater than one's self, one's family, and one's own imagination is the transcendent experience of the combination of faith and vision.* Although its eyes have often wandered far, more than any other social institution the church has maintained a common vision. William F. Buckley, Jr. may be excessively laudatory, but he proclaims, "... the church is unique in that it is governed by a vision that has not changed in two thousand years. It tells us, in just about as many words, that we are not accidental biological accretions, we are creatures of a divine plan; that the God who made us undertook to demonstrate his devotion to us as individual human beings by submitting to the pain and humiliation of the Cross. Nothing in that vision has ever changed, nothing at all, and this is for all Christians a mind-shaking, for some a mind-altering certitude, with which Christians live, in our earnest if pitiable efforts to clear the way for a love that cannot be requited" (1997).

Keep an Eye on What Is Sacred

The church by its very definition is involved in all of life. Everything it touches is sacred — and the church touches everything. There is no way to separate that which is *sacred* and that which is *secular* when it comes to the church. The message of the church is to life — all of it: to the pretty and the ugly; to the kind and the unkind; to every polarity of every subject. This is the heart of the problem — the church must speak out and take action against wrong, all kinds of wrong, whether in politics, education, gender, race, or anything else that one might encounter on earth. The conflict is not *whether* the church should speak — it is *how, when,* and where it speaks. If we think that because we are in a country that ostensibly separates church and state that we are saved from this conflict, how wrong we are! The Old Testament and New Testament both are inextricably intertwined with the politics of the day. What do we think the crucifixion of Jesus was all about if it were not about politics? The fine line is how to be "*in* the world without being *of* the world." The question has to do with the direction of influence. As has been argued many times in this book, the real problem is that influence has come from the political and external worlds *into* the church rather than the other way around. We have ample examples in recent years of those who could not tell which way the influence was going and ended up in the wrong camp.

REMEMBER THE GREAT COMMISSION AND THE GREAT COMMANDMENT

The Great Commission, "go ye," and the Great Commandment, "love ye," often become mutually exclusive in the mission of local congregations. We forget the power of the commandment in our wish to love all in spite of all. We forget the love for each other in the zeal to get on with the job of converting the heathen "before it is too late." Both demands are upon us, but reaching the end as the "first-est with the most-est" must not blind us to those we trample or ignore along the way.

Continue to Be a Good Samaritan

As social programs fail, as they always do, the church will become more and more the logical provider of assistance to those in need. This is not bad. In fact, it is clearly Biblical and in accord with the mission of Christianity from the beginning. Some may infer from the earlier discussions in this book that the church is in error when being involved in social programming — wrong! Nothing delivers a more powerful message than a consistent, positive, day-to-day, real-life example of what we believe.

Keep up the good works — good works for the right reasons! There is no doubt whatsoever that the church should be involved in feeding the poor, housing the homeless, healing the sick, and clothing the naked. No one denies that Jesus exhorted us that "inasmuch as you have done it to the least of these, you have done it unto me." Good works in His stead are absolutely right. The secret in this is "in His stead," i.e., for the right reasons — a cup of cold water *in His name* — keeping in mind the "why" of the action as a reason for the action.

There was a story printed in the *Orlando Sentinel* (February 10, 2001) about a couple who were hippies in the 1970s and decided to travel from Florida to Missouri. Their Volkswagen broke down in the Ozarks and they could find no one to repair it. They became stranded near a farmer's home. The farmer took them in and gave them food and a place to stay while he fixed their car for free. Now some thirty years later, the couple is still together and she says, "That evening 'Mr. R' took my husband to a softball game, taking advantage, as he had done during the day, of talking about God's love. 'Mrs. R' took me to a ladies' Bible study, where I heard first-hand accounts of God's love and mercy. My heart was touched by these women, who were so gracious to me. The world saw a rebellious hippie. They saw a lost sheep. By midmorning the next day, our car was fixed, and we were on our way. We didn't stay in Missouri, but the experience changed our lives. The 'R's' generosity, hospitality and kindness had banished the rebellion and bitterness that we carried around with us. Replacing that rebellion and bitterness were an overwhelming sense of gratitude and newfound faith."

There are countless stories of good works reaping benefits such as these. At issue is whether Samaritan services are rendered as a social agency without Christian purpose or whether the services are "in His stead." Services rendered simply as social services without a Christ message are likened to the story of the one given a fish that feeds one for a day rather than teaching one to fish so that one may be fed for a lifetime.

The issue is not *whether* to be involved — the issue is *why*. What is the purpose, the reason, and the ultimate gain for the church to offer assistance to the poor, homeless, and hungry? Are these acts of kindness an end in themselves or are they holding the unfortunate hostage so that they may be proselytized? Neither should be the case. There are organizations, including many churches, that for centuries have been lighthouses to the lost, food kitchens for the hungry, and tents for the homeless. The Good Samaritan is only one of many New Testament messages about caring for one's neighbor in misfortune. No Christian should have the slightest question about the church doing good — in any form.

What then is the question? The question centers around motive. As government inevitably becomes more and more involved in American's lives, including the life of the church, there will be benefits — including money — to do that which the government wishes and needs. In spite of its foibles, the church is still the most powerful single social institution in the Western world. With all its mistakes, it is still the most effective body of persons to bring about change. It is still recognized by all, even unbelievers, as a formidable body. The concept of an "army" by the Salvation Army has through the years been a clear model for providing a powerful body of soldiers to move into battle — marching to the message of *Onward Christian Soldiers*. They saw and continue to see the task as a formidable fight against the Evil One in any manifestation, whether that be hunger, home, or health. They forged ahead "marching as to war," literally declaring war against hunger, sickness, and homelessness.

Train the Laity

In all ages, the church has been catapulted forward when lay members were educated. The most classic of all is when the Bible was unchained. At that time, the Bible was called the "Chained Bible" because it was literally chained to the pulpit and only ordained clergy were permitted to interpret it to the common folks. When the Bible was unchained and all could read and interpret for themselves, their "educated" clergy began a rapid and unceasing torrent of interpretations continuing to this day. They were concerned that the lay person would interpret the Scriptures differently than what they had been preaching. Indeed that is exactly what happened and continues today. The concept of a trained discipleship is not even new to the New Testament. The Rabbinate of the Old Testament (and today) rightly prided itself in teaching — teaching whom? — the laity. Jesus began his earthly ministry by teaching his disciples — lay persons.

Until recent years theologians, like physicians, have treated their knowledge as secret and unknowable by the "untrained." There is no intent in this writing to destroy those who are legitimately trained clergy, but there is an absolute intent to point out that eternal truth is available to other than the ordained.

It is time for the church to "unchain" the laity and let them be free to deal with their beliefs as they will. There is tremendous risk in such a process. The church might flounder even more than it does now. It may become virtually unrecognizable from what it now is. It might even close its doors in many places. The "church" according to most theological disciplines is "the people." The old saying we used to demonstrate to children with our folded hands is so true: "Here's the church, here's the steeple, open the doors, and there's the people." That is the church — its people. Most churches and few denominations act as this is really true. In actuality, the way we worship, what we say we believe, and how we operate our churches are according to the dictates of denominational leaders rather than the laity. In recent years, there are many instances when laity has taken on much more responsibility for leadership, however, it is still within the context of the clergy and denominational guidelines.

Is it time for another reformation? Is it time to recognize the "Jewish-ness" of the Christian faith and the "Christian-ness" of the Jewish faith? Could there be a "Reverse Reformation," this time uniting instead of splitting the Church? Is it time to recognize the "Catholic-ness" of Protestantism and the "Protestant-ness" of Roman Catholicism? Although this will likely not occur, asking the question seriously might do wonders in helping all sides to define not only what they *do believe*, but also what they *say* they believe.

Do we really believe one segment of society has the "truth?" While congregations as a whole seem to say that when questioned individually, few really believe that they know the "whole" truth. Some say that the church brainwashes its members. While this might be true in some extremist sects, brainwashing requires a much more concentrated attempt at coercion than most local churches have in place. However, every religious group I know, Protestant, Roman Catholic, or otherwise, uses all of its energy to convince its followers that it is right! In this sense the Church is no different than any other business that vies to keep its old customers and proselytize as many new ones as possible.

If we are going to educate the laity, the church must take risks with information. It must trust mature minds to think for them-selves. It must be willing to chance losing some and gaining others. It must be willing to practice the faith it claims to possess. It must be willing to believe that the Church will survive in spite of it all (and it will!).

Rediscover Discernment

The church has always spoken of "being led by the Spirit." Yet, nowhere is there more wrangling and search for "order" than in most churches, particularly those that are "mainline." Has is ever occurred to church leaders how incongruous it is to claim to be led by Spirit while debating over parliamentary procedure, ala *Robert's*

Rules of Order? There are still some groups that honor the art of spiritual discernment. However, most cannot put aside individual interests and personal empires long enough to hear anything other than a loud, denominational voice or to meet the onslaughts of the self-serving empire builders.

Parishioners often have better ears than the clergy and can tell the difference between action wrought out of discernment and action which is simply clergy and organization serving. Discernment, for the most part, is a lost art in our hurried, mechanistic way of living. Discernment takes time, introspection, selflessness, and honest seeking of the will of the group — and of the Spirit. It is difficult to talk and listen at the same time. Someone said that "every time a dog barks it loses a bite." There is something to be said for silent assemblies — and also for the ones that talk — but wouldn't it be nice to have a bit more of each in each place?

Maintain the Community

The nature of religion binds humankind together in communities of faith. Probably as important as what is preached is the nature of the community of faith where it is preached. Communities of faith have given strength to endure the most difficult times in history. Communities of the faithful remain loyal to each other even when they are outnumbered by their enemies. Communities of the faithful become faith in action and action in faith. They become the servants of faith and the faith of servants. Today, there is a real danger in losing the community of faith within the developing mega-church. Mainline denominations also risk losing more members as they strive to further commercialize faith and exploit theology. The relationship within the community is still more important than the differences in belief. We almost always have more in common than not — that which unites us is nearly always greater than that which separates us. *Belief is still more important than the answer belief brings*. There has never been a more potent solidifying agent for people than a community of like-minded believers. In truth, although we would like for others to believe exactly as we do, it really doesn't matter so long as we believe the same thing. A church, a club, a community organization, or a group is powerful when unified. The religious community from the tribes wandering in the wilderness to our postmodern synagogue and church offer the glue to unify minds, wed hearts, and bind lives together more uniquely than any other organization on earth.

A well-known Protestant hymn, *Blest Be the Tie That Binds*, tells it all:

> *We share each other's woes,*
> *Each other's burdens bear;*
> *And often for each other flows*
> *The sympathizing tear.*
>
> *From sorrow, toil and pain,*
> *And sin we shall be free;*
> *And perfect love and joy shall reign*
> *Through all eternity.*

> ***John Fawcett***
> *The Presbyterian Hymnal*
> *The Presbyterian Church, U.S.A.*

Without doubt, as a *community*, with all its *warts* and *zits*, there is no better support system, bonded group of persons, or other group of persons to promote redemptive theology than *the church*.

Weigh Carefully the Difference Between Culture and Acculturation

Adaptation to culture is the work of acculturation. It cannot be avoided altogether. However, the Church claims to have the message to effect culture positively. If so, we can't have it both ways. In other words, the Church cannot be constantly adapting to the changing cultural pattern and at one and the same time be attempting to change the very thing to which it is adapting. Its *methods* can and must adapt. Its *message* must not adapt. Staying abreast of human need is one thing. Agreeing to meet the needs lay people see, when those needs are not recognized by the Church, presents a serious problem. As much as most of us would like it, the Christian life was never promised to be happy, comfortable, or guilt free. To the extent that the Church attempts to create such, it is the work of acculturation, i.e., adapting to culture, not the work of the Church which is intended to change culture.

Educate and Train Clergy for Their Jobs

Seminaries desperately need to reevaluate the ministry. What are the actual duties of today's minister? What are the daily expectations from the church and its members? What are the tools needed to do the job? Are there some subjects taught in seminary that will never be used? Does the seminary need to look at the curriculum in the same way other professions have done and eliminate, add, combine, delete, change, and literally "go back to the drawing board?" Are seminary professors able to teach the next generation that which they will need when many professors are the product of an age that neither taught it or experienced it? If we have skipped a generation in teaching and practicing what we believe the church needs to be about, is it possible that seminaries will need to leap-frog back to an earlier generation to recapture their momentum and then leap-frog forward to deal with the future?

Seminaries and training institutions will need to determine what tasks are popularly undertaken, but perhaps are beyond the role of the clergy. They will need to educate clergy to not attempt all things, but when and how to utilize consultation, referral, and team ministry. Ministers need training in "setting boundaries," i.e., understanding their role and not confusing it with becoming a

friend, a lover, or a surrogate relative. They need help in understanding the meaning of the "dual relationship," i.e., attempting to
counsel parishioners while asking them to contribute to the church.
They need assistance in understanding "conflict of interest," i.e.,
attempting to be a pastor while relying upon the parishioners for a
salary. They need help in understanding the nature of "objectivity,"
i.e., how to help solve the problem without becoming part of it.
They need help in distinguishing between spiritual guidance, for
which they are trained, and psychotherapy, for which they are not
trained. They need encouragement to enter into life-long education
in order to meet the increasing demands of our fast-paced age. The
encouraging part is that many clergy are asking for these kinds of
skills and training.

Return to the Roots for Guaranteed Success

The way for both of these disciplines to win is for us to return to
their basic roots. Religion must get back to premodern and pre-
situational theology. However, since the Gospel is for all times and
in all places, it must move into postmodern culture without allowing that culture to replace its vital message. Churches and pastors
must return to the Old Testament and New Testament scholars, the
great church fathers, both before and after the reformation, and the
"voices in the wilderness" since then. Knowing what we now do, it
will be like the proverbial midget standing on the giant's shoulders —
in terms of what we will see.

Psychology, likewise, must find its roots. Those roots are not in
Freud. They are in the attempt to discover how the physiology and
chemistry of the brain works and how to understand human behavior within those terms. Centuries before Freud, great scholars
attempted to understand the mind/body connection. Spiritual
truths rather than religion were the topics of discussion. Religion
has always been how human beings exercise their beliefs.

Spirituality has always been private and only understandable to the individual experience.

Persons seeking guidance, counseling, and psychotherapy should not shy away from well-trained, qualified therapists, but it is important to understand the difference between what might be called "counseling" or "psychotherapy." Counseling centers on problem solving with strategic planning. Psychotherapy attempts to identify causes of the problem and correct those causes, believing that in doing so, the understanding that comes from that particular solution will spill over into other areas of life and prevent "dis-ease."

The therapist who is at peace with his/her own spiritual person will evidence such whether by intention or otherwise. Invariably, therapists with deep spiritual personal experience are spoken of by patients: "There is something different about that doctor." On the other hand, those who make a point of advertising their "personal faith" are often seen as self-aggrandizing. Psychiatrists and psychologists would do well to find their own spiritual journey as discussed so well in M. Scott Peck's *The Road Less Traveled* (1978). Finding that journey and following it could mean the salvation both of themselves and their patients.

Psychology will need to continue to identify what has gone wrong in interpersonal relationships that results in human suffering. It should not lose sight of the physiological and genetic aspects of human behavior. It needs to continue to incorporate those aspects into assessment and treatment. Religion must accept its role as a salvation enterprise and that even if life continues to be upsetting, faith has a more enduring answer. Religion does not solve neuroses. It may actually create some due to that fact that true faith is certainly at odds with much of society.

Sacrifice Personal Agendas

Church members must find a balance between believing everything and believing only what they are told. Careful observation of pulpit theatrics, both in churches and on TV, reveals only slight variations on many TV commercials. There is indeed little, if any, difference from infomercials. Both rely on mass psychology, the production of want rather than need, and frequently accomplish a sort of mesmerism, actually a form of hypnosis which was taught by Milton Erickson, M.D. Most ministers would certainly deny such, because they do not recognize their own techniques or the resemblance to hypnosis. Ericksonian hypnosis, the story-telling sort, is very subtle. It does not require a pendulum or a swinging watch for the audience to sway with. It requires only a careful arrangement of words punctuated by pregnant pauses and inflections of tone. Many preachers practice hypnosis without knowing it.

Television preachers, churches lusting to be the largest megachurch, struggling churches that feel they must get big to succeed, and ministers who practice more as "shrinks" than as pastors all have to stop trying to be the biggest "show in town." True religion is not about size: neither the size of the congregation, the size of the bank account, or the size of the radio or television audience speak to the presence or absence of true religion. Unfortunately, the agendas of too many clergy have to do with *personal* "success" — climbing up the professional ladder, acclaim, and other ego- and status-driven needs. However, it is not difficult to understand the needs and wants of ministers who more often than not are underpaid, overworked, and undereducated for the demands placed upon them, especially when given the status of religious leader.

In spite of all of this, ministers will be called upon to sacrifice personal agendas in favor of the greater good if the Church is to be saved. Congregations have been known to meet on an annual basis and establish their annual agenda — point by point — with target dates for accomplishment. Such exercises might be most helpful to the congregation and minister alike, thus avoiding many personal agendas and giving voice to the congregation being asked to participate.

ALLOW THEOLOGY TO AGAIN BE THE QUEEN OF THE SCIENCES

Renew the Power of the Pulpit

The proclamation of the Word always has been and still must be central to every Christian congregation. The New Testament Church has always asserted that the preaching of the word, i.e., the Bible, is the basis for all else that occurs within its ministry. The church possibly more than any other organization is built upon the verbalization of the word of its mission. The Word becomes the proclamation of God — the Word that "became flesh and dwelt among us," literally meaning that God's message is the Word, i.e., the Word is Christ and Christ is the message. Programs are important and must not be minimized — they are demonstrations of the Word. Pastors are important — they are models of the Word. The sermon is important — it is the proclamation of the Word. Followers are important — they are evangelists of the Word. The sermon is the verbalized Word; the symbols are the individualized connections of the Word to the soul; and the rituals provide for souls to be connected in the Word.

Keep the Language of Theology

Social science jargon is not what people go to church to hear. If they want social studies they go to institutions with expert professors in those fields. People go to church to hear experts in theological language — those who speak of sin, salvation, grace, hope, faith, redemption, conversion, salvation, and a myriad of other time-honored words that we recognize and personally identify with. They do not want to be caught up in a "politically correct" discussion of brotherhood, gender, sexual orientation, affirmative action, catharsis, neuroses, and other fad issues. There is, of course, more than a little argument about how much the church needs to force its members to become involved in these social issues. The fact is, however, that the church is in no position to force anything. Most mainline churches are begging for their own members to just attend, let alone become involved in fad issues, political arguments, and intellectual esotericism.

Parishioners may not be able to name the books of the Bible, quote long (or even short) passages, make their words come out in verbally beautiful prayers, and reach into the depths of theological interpretation of the Scriptures, but they expect their ministers to be able to do so. The parishioners may not be able to do so, but they can certainly tell if their pastors do!

Preach Hope Not Happiness

A mere scanning of Buddhism and Christianity reveals an immediate and dramatic difference. The Dahlai Lama is very clear in his writing on Buddhism that the reward of the religious (Buddhism) life is *happiness*. A book jointly written by him and psychiatrist Howard C. Cutler (1998) can be summed up by quoting its dedication page: "Dedicated to the Reader: May you find happiness." The Christian message is not happiness — it is *hope*. When and if happiness occurs is the byproduct of the Christian life which promises hope. He who searches for happiness doubtless finds only the search and never happiness. Christian theology can be seen in quotes from Saint Paul when he was writing to the new Christians in Rome. When discussing redemption, he says, "For in this hope we are saved. Now hope that is seen is not hope. For who hopes for what he sees? But if we hope for what we do not see, we wait for it with patience" (Romans 8:24–25, *RSV Holy Bible*). Again to the Romans he said, "Rejoice in your hope, be patient in tribulation, be constant in prayer"(Romans 12:12, *RSV Holy Bible*). The promise of hope always outweighs the search for happiness in Christian theology. As a matter of fact, happiness in the New Testament is the result of enduring — sometimes enduring persecution and tribulation. We are exhorted, "Behold, we call those happy who were steadfast. You have heard of the steadfastness of Job, and you have seen the purpose of the Lord, how the Lord is compassionate and merciful" (James 5:11, *RSV Holy Bible*). The story of Job hardly inspires one to imitate his life to produce happiness! Ministers who believe that they can convince a congregation that he/she or the Church can produce happiness are self-deluded. Those who preach hope will find welcome in any honest human heart.

Transcend "Bibliolatry"

Both the Roman Catholic Church and the Protestant Church are bogged down in Bibliolatry. They argue incessantly as to what is the "correct" translation of the Scriptures. This is the same kind of intellectual duel that Jewish scholars were famous for in ancient times and they continue today. The very fact that our Scriptures are "translations" refutes any possible idea of word-for-word infallibility. There is probably no greater divisiveness and congregation-splitting mechanism in the Protestant church than the varying opinions about the "inspiration" of the Scriptures. Various denominations and subgroups of denominations argue over the "verbal and plenary inspiration" of the Scriptures, yet all the average church member knows is that they are asked to buy a study Bible that was translated only a few years ago. Furthermore, many are unaware of the difference between the "inspiration" of the footnotes in their study Bible and the part that is printed in red and the other part that is printed in black. To most churchgoers, "inspired scripture" is whatever their preacher says it is.

The Roman Catholic Church has no less disagreement, but it has effectively solved the problem by officially taking interpretation out of the hands of the clergy and lay person. The Roman Catholic Church retains the sole ability to interpret within the Papal College. Priests and believers alike who do not agree are not tolerated to voice dissenting opinions and hence there is less public strife on this issue. This may not be a compliment!

The pronouncement from Pope Leo XII's *Providentissimus Deus* (November 18, 1893, cited in Buckley, 1997, p. 76) still stands as follows: "... it is absolutely wrong and forbidden ... to admit that the sacred writer has erred ... For all books which the Church receives as sacred and canonical are written wholly and entirely, with all their parts, at the dictation of the Holy Ghost ...." It should be noted, however, that as recently as 1993, the Pontifical Commission admitted that tensions regarding interpretation do exist; however, such interpretation is finally adjudicated and taught only with church sanction (see *Dei Verbum*, 10-Vatican II).

Whereas some segments of Protestant believers are enmeshed in Bibliolatry (worship of the Bible as a book), the Roman Catholic Church admits to "ecclesiolatry" (worship of the church and church leaders). In the Roman Catholic Church, the final dictum is pronounced by the Vatican and largely followed, at least in the pulpit. In the Protestant Church, congregations are free to interpret as they wish, preach as they wish, and, of course, to splinter as they wish.

The "literalism" of some groups is impossible to rectify with current developments. Even the churches that hold to the "verbal and plenary" interpretation of the Scriptures now publish a new translation every few years. Many have had to modify their statements to claim that the "verbal and plenary" inspiration applies only to the "original scriptures." The "original scriptures" are harder to be certain of now in the face of recent archeological discoveries.

Those who hold that every "jot and tittle" is truth and that "all truth" is in the current translations must now face the discovery of documents in archeological digs which are equal or possibly more accurate than those they accept. *The only way to counteract both of these extremes is to recognize the inherent message of the Gospel, regardless of how or by whom it is told.*

The problem is no doubt confounded by the many "truths" that are held within the "truth." While interpretation is not deplored, but rather believed always necessary to some degree, attempting to reveal in private, denominational, or even scholarly hermeneutics usually results in privatization, schismatic, and divisive maneuvers. Truth is ageless, nonpersonified, and can only be interpreted within the context of the whole. When truth is broken down to a series of "truths," they invariably carry the imprimatur of some individual, denomination, or self-appointed heavenly messenger. The same criticism could be offered for those who claim the "truth" against the "truth" of others. A case in point is the unnecessary battle waged by some of the "fathers" of psychology against religions, Sigmund Freud being a prime example.

Transcend Psychology

Let Freud and his followers "R.I.P." It is incredibly uncanny that a self-admitted atheist has affected Christianity to the extent that Sigmund Freud and his followers have. The same may be true for Jung, a somewhat disobedient follower of Freud. Of all psychoanalysts, Carl Jung is acclaimed by many in the psychological field as being the most "compatible" with religion. He was clearly a person of great values and spiritual depth. His emphasis upon symbolism and the spiritual bases for that symbolism makes his theories more acceptable to Christians than most traditional psychoanalysts. In truth, Jung's symbolism has little to do with theology. It has more to do with mysticism and mythology.

However, it is not necessary to take the opposite point of view that Freud, Jung, and their followers are all wrong: they may simply have nothing to do with theology. Then again, they may have nothing to do with theology *and* they may also be wrong! In any event, the simple story of God's love does not require psychological sophistication and it certainly is not enhanced by their concepts.

Deal with Pseudo-Pantheism

It was clear from many responses I received that persons who did not want to commit themselves to attend regular worship services often claimed they worshiped God on the lake, on the tennis court, out in nature, and in other recreational or "R&R" activities. While no one can deny the spiritual value of "communing with nature," more often than not, these were not "reasons" for not attending church, but excuses. Few, if any, really held to Pantheism as a personal religion. They held to pseudo-Pantheism without knowing they did. I, of course, did not try to explain that to them. (Occasionally I asked if they believed in Pantheism. They did not know what it is or how it was spelled.) These persons seem simply to subscribe to a popular notion about spirituality in some sort of vague way, and the "nature" argument lets them ascribe some credence to their absenteeism at church.

Preach to Life

Preaching theology to life is different than preaching life to theology. Constantly attempting to bring relevancy to theology is useless. Theology is relevant by virtue of its very essence. *When we attempt to rearrange theology to fit life rather than insisting that life must fit theology, we are attempting to make perfect that which is already perfect (the Gospel) by using an imperfect tool (life).*

Theology is a science — "the Queen of Sciences" some have said — but it is the science of faith. Life does not explain theology. Theology explains life. The truths of theology can be extrapolated and *used* over and over again, while the complications of life must be *explained* over and over again. Clergy who think they are being relevant by connecting many small life anecdotes with a verse of scripture are missing the point of both life and theology. Life does not explain the Scriptures, but it certainly explains our need for them. Theology connects the scriptures with the deep, ageless truths that apply to all life in all times. It is this foundation of theology that we must address in order to not have to learn every lesson over again in our lives and then repeat everything again in every generation.

Find Room for the Old/New Message

A friend of mine preached a sermon with a takeoff on the Kellogg's commercial about Corn Flakes™, in which Kellogg's urged customers to "taste it again for the first time." The sermon made an impression on me, suggesting the possibility of looking at the Scriptures "again for the first time." This might seem like a redundancy of terms or an oxymoron, but it is not. The old message is new every day because we each must make new and revitalizing applications of it everyday. The same is true for the church as a whole.

In its current configuration, the church might not have room for the old/new message. The message is as old as the Old Testament, yet as new as today. Unwillingness of a congregation to find room for that old yet new message was reported in the ministry of Jesus Himself. When Jesus attempted to preach to the Jews in their synagogues, He was thrown out. So he went into the streets and to the fields to preach His message. Denominations are deeply involved in the building of personal and corporate empires. Finances, politics, personal and corporate agendas, and much more are interpreted as being socially, theologically, and even Biblically relevant to the Church. There is adequate evidence that many church-goers are tired of this rationalization. Small independent congregations are cropping up all over. Major denominations are gasping for breath, while mega-churches continue as theological shopping malls. Yet, by the same token, can it be that they like Jesus have literally taken the message into the highways and byways and invited the outside in, while other congregations "preach to the choir" or insist that their insiders take the message outside? How each congregation finds room for the old/new message will doubtless be unique. For the church-at-large, it may take a major overhaul to bring about the reformation needed.

But Preserve the Mystery

Religion — any kind, anywhere, anytime — has been inextricably tied to mystery. By definition, the nature of faith requires the unknown — the mystery. The modern church, like all else in modern times, tries to find answers it can understand, with the hope that they will be quick and easy. Of course, they are not. We all know, in spite of our incessant search, that there are no quick and easy answers to the difficult questions of life: Who am I? What am I doing here? Where am I going? A myriad of other questions constitute the essence of life and the quintessence of faith. Without these questions there could be no faith and without the faith there would be no questions.

In this century, perhaps more than any other time in history, we feel that we are truly conquering the universe. Technology far outruns our understanding of what to do with the discoveries. In the wake of this enormous deluge of information and "know how," it becomes even more difficult to accept that there are many things that we *cannot* know and probably more things that we *should not* know. The church is one place in our society where it is *good* not to know everything and *even better* not to know everything, but to trust in God.

To be a Christian in the face of today's technological and scientific sophistication requires a vigorous exercise of both faith and reason. There is never enough faith to satisfy doubting. There is never enough reason to satiate questioning. Mystery, that indefinable, unexplainable, aphrodisiac of curiosity, is the only true solace. If the church were to do away with mystery, it would need to explain the unexplainable, answer the unanswerable, and define the indefinable. *Faith in the mystery and the mystery of faith are the essential cornerstones of the church and of all personal spiritual life to the Christian.*

Theology Must Meet Life in These Times

In spite of the fact that faith is absolutely essential, paradoxically, theology must be believable at some level. There is something within the hearts of human beings that wants to believe the unbelievable, yet at some level know it is true! Theologians have attempted to make religion "relevant" and their attempts have not worked. Why is that? It is because relevancy is not universal. It is not even commonly understood. That which is relevant to one is irrelevant to another. *Our individual "relevancy" has to do with our unique, individual problems, challenges, and experiences in our own daily life.* Although in our more intellectual and academic moments, we are concerned about trees, the spotted owl, and the color of the sky, most of the time we are in truth concerned about the struggles of our marriage, our challenging teenagers, or an aging parent.

The attempt to make theology relevant has resulted in rapidly changing fads of "systems" of belief. They should be called "systems of belief" rather than "beliefs" because they are systematized methods of artificially meeting the whims and wishes of parishioners on their modern and rapidly changing turf. These systems are usually designed to achieve ulterior motives, and hence they are not pure. They are intended, whether admitted or not, to reign-in straying church members, mollify those who wish to appear "religious," and protect the office of the ministry and priesthood.

While the oracles of the faith, the great creeds of the Church Fathers, and the Confessions are important to the scholars of the Church, the ordinary member could care less most of the time. They neither study them enough to understand the subtleties, nor do they worry about the need to absentmindedly repeat them as part of a liturgy. The ordinary church member wants to know if theology, i.e., logic of God, can help them through the turmoil of their own temptations, their family's storms, and the unrealistic expectations of their employers.

There are signs of agreement that may help those seeking a common message. The July 6, 1998 issue of *Time* (p. 80) reported that the Lutherans and Catholics have reached an agreement regarding the theological doctrine of "justification." "Last week — 457 years, several disastrous religious wars and dozens of denominational splits later ...." It would be helpful if one could believe that the argument has actually been over the doctrine itself. We all know that such is not the case. There are personalities, denomination, and religion-bound turf to be protected, centuries of literature to be upheld, and thousands of factors that we can only guess about.

The important thing is that there may be another opportunity to heal the wounds of the Church. One wonders if the Reformation would have ever occurred if the present Pope had been in place in the day of Martin Luther. There are certainly major differences between the Roman Catholic Church and the Protestant Church; however, they are only different, not necessarily any greater than those which exist between many Protestant denominations.

Theologians must find themselves "where the rubber meets the road." If ministers are unable or unwilling to do so, the laity will do it for them. That is occurring now. Most of the time it is done with silent assent by members inside the church and open rebellion outside. More and more the rebellion is moving inside. A practical, believable, workable, applicable theology does not destroy the myth, the faith factor, or the mystery. It does, however, unfetter theology from the hands of the holy caretakers, who have demonstrated more than sufficient doubt as to their capability either to be holy or to be adequate caretakers!

BE NOT ASHAMED OF RIGHTEOUS MARKETING

Discover Why Some Churches Lose Members and Others Gain Members

Verbal testimonials, research polls, and written literature attest to the massive exodus from traditional mainline churches and an increase in membership in the more charismatic, independent, fundamentalist, evangelistic ones. Church leaders cite many reasons for both aspects of this phenomenon. Those losing members are prone to claim that:

1. Fundamentalist congregations are perceived as having "all the right answers."

2. Fundamentalist groups offer simple answers to complex questions.

3. The fundamentalist mentality is a nonthinking one and appeals to those who wish to be "spoon-fed" and not have to think for themselves.

4. Charismatic congregations appeal to hysterical and theatrical personalities.

While these answers and hundreds more are given for the mass exodus from the mainline congregations, to rely upon them as being true begs the question. They may be "answers," but not true "reasons." Those who defend the mainline position assert their "deep spirituality," claiming others as being "superficial." They hold their belief to be intellectually defensible and the belief of "those others" as only emotionally based. None would deny that the ultimate goal of all Christian groups is to proclaim our need for God's goodness and salvation. *The simplicity of the Gospel is the heart of Christianity.*

Both "liberal" and "fundamentalist," particularly the extremist and more militant groups, camouflage the Gospel by their own self-serving trappings. It is easy for groups that are losing members to talk "sour grapes" in an attempt to rationalize things. They become defensive for the same reason(s) that anyone becomes defensive about anything — they don't have good answers! This reaction, is exactly that, a *reaction*. It does not bring back their wandering members. Members who transfer from the theologically liberal congregations to the more fundamentalist may have contributed only a paltry sum to their "liberal" church, yet upon transfer to the more fundamentalist congregation, they will "dig-deep." They may have groused about the financial straits of their church, the poor preaching, the length of the service, and a dozen other things, but somehow the fervency and dynamics of their new-found fundamentalist faith drives them to "spiritual" depths they have never experienced before. In their new congregation they give "until it hurts," endure longer sermons, sit through longer services, and are called upon to volunteer time and render services like they have never experienced before, and proclaim that they love it all!

If this happened in the business world, there would be a major investigation. Market surveys, special promotional programs, and top consultants would be brought in from around the world in an attempt to discover what is going on and why so many customers are being lost. But such investigations are not going on in churches. Even denominations not known to adhere to a predestination type of theology seem to be content to accept that "God will work in His way in His time." This *laissez-faire* attitude permits all sides to win because, after all, whatever happens is what God wants. I have often called this approach the "Catch-22 Can't Lose" philosophy. It goes something like this: A person is speeding through a busy intersection and barely missed a screaming fire truck coming from the other direction. He says, "God was with me! If I had been going any slower, I'd hit that truck head on!" On the other hand, if this same person were going slower, and did indeed smash into the fire truck, he would say, "Thank God for that accident. It was His will to teach me a lesson!" With these kinds of rationalizations, there is no way to lose! Each scenario is simply a different version of "God's will." A similar kind of nonsensical psychology is used by local congregations. The groups receiving new members are being "blessed" and congregations losing members simply bask in the belief that their "righteousness" is what is causing sinners to avoid them. Since they are doing God's will, everyone will eventually see it their way!

Listen to the Customers

The people who attend church are the customers — the laity. They are the ones who more often see both the forest and the trees. They are not bogged down in their own careers in the church; they are not dependent upon the church for their paycheck; they can leave the church or stay in it; they have the luxury of criticizing the church without worry of getting defrocked; they are the ones who keep "the store" open even when there is not a "manager" (pastor); and they are the ones who determine who the minister will be and when the minister will be fired (or transferred). In some denominations, a bishop or district superintendent decides on parish appointments, but in truth if enough of the congregation do not approve, they can leave the congregation and the minister who has been sent has no congregation! The customer wins in every business and the church is no exception.

Although there is no intent to paint the parish minister or priest as being insensitive, the fact is that it is very hard to see the trees when you are in the woods. By virtue of the clergy person's conscious or unconscious bondage to his/her parish assignment, it is not possible to see clearly. Few ministers want to be transferred to a smaller parish and rarely are ministers transferred (or "called") to a larger, more prestigious congregation by "taking on" their superiors in the denomination. Although fraught by a multitude of other problems, ministers in the more independent denominations wherein each congregation finds and "calls" their own minister, may have less difficulty with being held hostage by the denomination, but probably not by a local congregation.

Don't Measure Growth by Numbers

The box office at a theater counts numbers. Carnivals count numbers. Athletic events count numbers. A line waiting to get into the theater is not the same as a line waiting to get into a church — should we ever see such in today's world! However, we cannot claim that simply in the presence of crowds there is evangelism or Christian growth. Sometimes small groups are more productive in the long run than huge crowds. When evangelism is productive and the Christian message is received, the crowds will come. But it is a serious mistake to assume that because the crowds come there is concomitant spiritual growth. While sometimes multitudes were present, Jesus most often ministered one-on-one.

GET READY FOR THE NEXT GREAT DISCOVERY!

The next great discovery will be in the realm of the Spirit. The ramifications of this discovery for the church will be beyond our current imagination. The research is beginning to appear in solid, peer-reviewed, respected journals. Now that science has shown us how to clone other living things, and has unraveled the human genome, many persons will once again proclaim the supremacy of science and revert to the belief that science will "find our way out" of the human predicament. They truly believe that in the end science will answer the eternal questions of "who am I," "where did I come from," and "where am I going?" Those in awe of the wonders of science — and aren't we all — hold bated breath for the next great discovery, particularly one that will open the window of our souls. The sciences are not, per se, wrong or bad. They are different. Scientific findings can be quantified, even qualified, counted, classified in a nosology, and given formulae that causes even those who do not understand them to accept them as gospel.

To some extent, religion as differentiated from spirituality can also be numbered and counted. The "religious" person attends religious services, prays, reads holy writ, gives offerings, and has other visible, demonstrable kinds of behavior. Behavior can be observed by all, counted by the assembly, and judged by the authorities. "Spirituality" is the demonstration of the Spirit. It is an action of its originator, the soul, i.e., Spirit. The actions that we see, and which are in concert with our beliefs and/or prejudices, are judged as "religious," "spiritual," or "irreligious" and "nonspiritual." These quantitative and qualitative analyses rest easy with us because we personally determine our own measurements and interpretation of the results.

We greatly confuse actions of the Spirit because we do not differentiate *spirit* from *Spirit* (lower case "s" and capital "S"). We witness spirit in competitive sports, salesmanship, leadership, and other activities that call for animated, assertive behavior. Demonstrations of Spirit are more difficult for us to witness. When speaking of Spirit, it is easier to use the article "the" in front of Spirit, but that is like saying, "the" God, rather than the sole unity of the One God. Demonstrations of Spirit are sometimes seen as "spirit," but it was not "spirit" that created the heavens and the earth, it was Spirit. The word Spirit is synonymous with God. Recent versions of the Genesis account of creation use the term God rather than Spirit, in keeping with a more accurate translation.

As humans, we do not like be confronted with things we cannot understand. Looking at things we can call religious or spiritual is easier than dealing with amorphous things like "Spirit." The amorphous nature of Spirit may be time limited. There are "hard scientists" who disavowed the existence of any "supreme being" a few years ago, but now admit to the possibility. Others have completely changed their minds and are now firm believers, even Theists, many Christian Theists at that. Those who regarded theology as a philosophy to account for things that could not be proven are now acknowledging theology as the science of Spirit that needs exploration. Rather than denying its value, they are now researching it, which proves they think it must exist or, else they could not research it!

Dr. Ursula Anderson, a leading expert in pediatrics, mental health, preventive medicine, public health, and the philosophy of religion, herself a strong Spirit, describes a growing body of literature which is most convincing. If the church were to take seriously the findings of many of these studies, its preaching and teaching could bring about a revival of a solid theological sort that would literally shake the world. Anderson says in one instance, referring to the "biology of the soul," that "while biology shapes our impulses and aptitudes, it does not act alone. It functions within the context of personal experience and the energies within the person's environment — physical, emotional, and spiritual. This is really great and good news and explains why even though genes susceptible to various negative conditions are inherited, i.e., are biological givens, they may never cause disease if the early bonding experience and environment of the individual militates against this occurring by the dominant presence of positive and nurturing energies. This concept is already beginning a whole new approach to the prevention of cancer in women known to carry susceptible genes for breast and ovarian cancer" (*Immunology of the Soul*, 2001, p. 180). Anderson continues to cite other most convincing research about what happens when energy of Spirit is applied to the ills of humankind. She speaks of *inoculating, vaccinating,* and other invasive medical methods when dealing with soul illness. This kind of thinking could be revolutionary for the church's educational programs. We know the power of teaching and example. If teachers in Sunday Schools and church educational programs were trained to personally experience this life-saving concept and then teach it by these kinds of theologically invasive methods, the church would change!

The church can and needs to practice *invasive theology.* Can any one doubt what would happen in the world if the church itself were convinced that its message were truly life changing — even in health issues — and began applying Biblical theology properly? *The church itself does not recognize the power of that which it has to preach and teach.*

This is where psychology enters the picture of *invasive theology.* The world of psychology springs from a study of the soul. Although many scholars in the field would deny the spiritual, even the Spirit nature of psychology, the word itself is derived from a mythical representation of the soul. The terms mind, soul, psyche, and personality are often used synonymously, which is in error. The mind, i.e., cognitive abilities, the psyche, i.e., the internal personification of the self, and the personality, i.e., the externalized representation of the inner self, are all distinct and distinctly different. A fourth definition of "psyche," given by the *Webster's Encyclopedic Unabridged Dictionary of the English Language* (1996, p. 1160), helps us the most in recognizing that psyche is actually a word of "Neoplatonism, the second emanation of the One, regarded as a universal consciousness and as the animating principle of the world ...." The psyche has not yet been studied. The *manifestations* of the psyche have been studied and researched extensively — the psyche as Spirit, i.e., the emanation of the One, the manifestation of God — is something else.

When humanistic psychology, and in particular cognitive psychology, came into vogue, many thought they were well on the road toward understanding the workings of the psyche. Simply because we cannot affirm the Spirit with our five senses does mean its nonexistence. Only a few years ago the multiplicity of airwaves was denied because they could not be affirmed with scientific findings. We now have technological gadgets that work, are used every day, and are accepted readily as absolute, when in fact, some of them still cannot be fully explained by *proven* scientific knowledge. The scientific world operates on assumptions and when the result of an assumption works, it is considered *prima facie* proof. The world practices *invasive science*, meaning that if it works, it will be introduced into real life. Why is the church not doing more with empirical theology, i.e., that which is derived from experiments? Does the church not have centuries of empirical results from an invasive theology? Of course it does. Why then does it wait in the wings while an atheistic science refutes and threatens their very existence? It is because the church has bought science and psychology rather than faith and Spirit.

The next great discovery may very well not come from those who research science, psychology, genes, and the physical properties of the universe, but from those who study consciousness. The number of conferences being held around the world on the subject of consciousness is amazing, with presenters of renown, both in the physical and psychological sciences. In many instances these conferences are actually presenting massive evidence for the reality of the Soul and the presenters themselves are giving real life testimonies to the life-changing ability of what I call "invasive theology."

Many of them are equating *consciousness* to the *soul*. This is a serious mistake, but being the bright minds that these persons are, they will soon discover their error. Consciousness is a human attribute, an ability, not a thing. The "thing" is the soul which from time to time our consciousness "sees," but as "through a glass darkly" by our consciousness. Cognition is not the same as consciousness.

Cognitive psychologists rely upon the dictum that proper thinking will result in proper action. We all know that this is simply not true. We all do things (actions) that are contrary to our best thinking (cognition). The fact that we *think*, and can therefore affect our actions by our thinking, will become considerably less important than the fact that we are Spirit and therefore our thinking and our actions result from a higher power within us. Many persons create a great difference between being religious and being spiritual. To be sure there is a difference. That difference has been described in this book, however, the reasons given for that difference are not those given by the ordinary person. Huston Smith in his book, *Why Religion Matters* (2001, p. 255), relates the story of a Barbara Walter's interview in which she asked her interviewee if she felt that in a given act she had sinned. The interviewee "hesitated, shifted in her chair, and then answered, 'I'm not very religious. I'm more spiritual." Smith continues to rightly point out that religion means to "to rebind." As this book has also pointed out, we must have something to rebind to, i.e., something solid enough to tie onto through the storms of life. Smith then makes a profound and accurate statement: "Being no more than a human attribute, spirituality is not institutionalized, and this exempts it from the problems that inevitably attend institutions — notably (in religious institutions) the in-group/out-group tensions they tend to breed."

The fields of psychology and religion may actually come together in the future in a most unexpected fashion. Being professionals who cannot deny research results, atheistic and otherwise nonbelieving psychologists might be confronted with studies on the consciousness, soul, and Spirit that are irrefutable. Their literature and practice may well change far more than it did with the introduction of Freudian psychoanalysis. The awakening for social scientists could be more earth-shaking than anything that has happened in the field to date. The same is true for theologians, who have made every effort to make their theology relevant, but alas finally find that the true relevancy is in the basic truth of theology, i.e., Theology, not in its pseudoscientific interpretations. A religious revival could erupt founded in Christian theology and experienced by Spirit!

NOT A SURPRISING FINDING

Much of this book came from unknown persons. In my quest for what people were thinking, literally thousands of friends, strangers, and weary travelers were queried. Although many of their responses to my questions about the church were sometimes surprising, the general interest that the questions aroused was not. It was not at all uncommon for a waitress, garage mechanic, or a waiting airline customer to go back to their friends or other persons and start asking them the same question. On many occasions, others whom I had not personally encountered came over to me to discuss the question I had given to their fellow worker and to offer their opinions. On one instance in a busy restaurant, there were five servers who all came to the table where I was eating with friends and wanted to talk about the church and their personal experiences. One waitress cried as she left the discussion, saying: "My husband is bitter about it all and won't go to church with me." The intensity of the discussions amazed me. There were very few people, fewer than I can count on one hand, that did not want to talk about their feelings regarding the church and religion. More often than not, other circumstances ended the discussion such as a server needing to pick up an order or a passenger leaving to board a plane. Frequently, discussions sprung up in an airport waiting area sparked by the continued interest of someone I had questioned.

The generalized interest in religion did not surprise me. The interest in the church did not surprise me. The intensity of feelings about religion and the church did not surprise me. The surprise was that in the face of such interest that so many of them said that they rarely, if ever, attended church. Maybe attention to some of their responses could make a difference.

Psychology and religion, after all, are both sincere in attempting to help us to live a better life. Psychology must keep its emphasis upon life, for it has no after-death promises. Religion, while trying to help us have a better life, subrogates this life to eternity in which we are promised more than is attainable on earth. Both psychology and religion have tremendous value, but for different reasons. *The confusion results from not understanding the basic premises of each — keeping clear about what is psychology and what is religion.* Each discipline has value and each discipline can complement the other. They need not compete because they are not mutually exclusive. In the end, spiritual hope is the only cure. True religion is about the unfolding of the totally incomprehensible love and grace of God in the presence of human frailty.

Benediction

Rise Up, O Men of God!

Rise up, O men of God!
Have done with lesser things;
Give heart and soul and mind and strength
To serve the King of kings.

Rise up, O men of God!
His kingdom tarries long;
Bring in the day of brotherhood
And end the night of wrong.

Rise up O men of God!
The Church for you doth wait,
Her strength unequal to her task;
Rise up and make her great!

William P. Merrill
The Presbyterian Hymnal, MCMLV,
The Presbyterian Church, U.S.A.

Author's note: This should be read, "Rise up, O people of God." Some versions use "church," some use "saints." I prefer people; "church" is too ambiguous, "saints" is too presumptuous …

Denouement

THE WORD "DENOUEMENT" portrays my best intentions with regard to this book. *Webster's Encyclopedic Unabridged Dictionary* (1996) has several definitions of the word denouement. The first is: "The final resolution of the intricacies of a plot, such as of a drama or novel." The church will continue to attempt answers to resolve our many questions. Psychology will do likewise to the extent that such is expedient and financially rewarding. Another definition of the word denouement is also most fitting: "The outcome or resolution of a doubtful series of occurrences." The value of the resolutions that the church or psychology will offer is dubious indeed. The final answer to the drama of birth, life, and death will be that incredibly sacred resolution that each of us will find within our own faith. I attend church regularly. I have done so all of my life. After reading this book, one could unabashedly ask, "Why?" The Church is kind of like family — even in the worst of times — it is still home. The Church, although fraught with all that is in this book — and much more — still offers the greatest hope for personal, societal, and world change. All other systems are so inundated with bureaucracy and governmental interference that there is certainly no room for hope. The Church, by virtue of its independent status from governmental and political interference, could still rise up to meet human need and societal salvation.

However, it is important to differentiate between "The Church" and churches. "The Church" is the body of Christ on earth that espouses the message of Christ and eschews the Evil One. "Churches" are local groups of believers who meet together in the name of Christ and only at times are truly faithful representatives of

"The Church." It may well take another reformation to bring about a better conformity of "The Church" and "the churches." It will take strong, independent leadership and a willingness to lead another reformation — a new Martin Luther perhaps. Luther did not know for certain whether he would have any followers when he tacked the theses to the church door — but he read the times well and knew the discontent of believers. So it is today. There is little room to doubt the discontent of the believers — who will lead the reformation?

References

Albom, Mitch (1997). *Tuesdays With Morrie*. New York: Doubleday.

Alcoholics Anonymous (1952). *Twelve Steps and Twelve Traditions*. New York: Alcoholics Anonymous Publishing.

Allen, Charlotte (December 1996). The search for a no-frills Jesus. *The Atlantic Monthly*, pp. 51–68

Anderson, Ursula (2001). *Immunology of the Soul*. Sanford, FL: Health Access Press.

Anon. (August 1996). The next church. *The Atlantic Monthly*, 16 p.

Anon. (December 23, 1997). As worshipers dwindle, a pastor does double duty. *Wall Street Journal*.

Anon. (February 13, 2001). Debt smothers young Americans. *USA Today*, p. A1–2.

APA. *The Diagnostic and Statistical Manual* (II, 1968; IV, 1994). Washington, D.C.: American Psychiatric Association.

Armstrong, Karen (1993). *A History of God*. New York: Ballantine.

Becker, Ernest (1973). *The Denial of Death*. New York: The Free Press.

Bennett, William J. (1994). *Book of Virtues*. New York: Simon & Schuster.

Blanton, Smiley (1959). *Now or Never.* Englewood Cliffs, NJ: Prentice-Hall.

Bork, Robert (1996). *Slouching Toward Gomorrah.* New York: Regan Books.

Buckley, William F., Jr. (1997). *Nearer, My God.* New York: Doubleday.

Canfield, Jack (1996). *Chicken Soup for the Soul.* Santa Barbara: Chicken Soup for the Soul Enterprises.

Carnegie, Dale (1940). *How to Win Friends and Influence People.* New York: Pocket Books.

Carter, Stephen L. (2000). *God's Name in Vain.* New York: Basic Books.

Clay, Rebecca A. (December 1997). Are children being overmedicated? *APA Monitor*, 29(12), pp. 1, 27.

Cox, Harvey (1966). *The Secular City.* New York: Macmillan.

Cox, Richard H. (Winter 1966). The pastoral counselor — who is he? *Journal of Pastoral Care*, p.12.

Cox, R. and Vayhinger, J. (1971). A study of psychologists holding theological degrees. *Psychology Bulletin*, 4(2), June 1971, pp. 10–13.

Dahlai Lama and Cutler, Howard C. (1998). *The Art of Happiness, a Handbook for Living.* New York: Riverhead Books.

Delitzsch, Franz (1866). *Religion and Psychology.* Edinburgh: T. and T. Clark.

Erikson, Erik (1964). *Insight and Responsibility.* New York: W.W. Norton.

Fillon, Mike (December 1996). Science solves the ancient mysteries of the Bible. *Popular Mechanics*, pp. 39–43.

Freud, Anna (1967). *The Ego and the Mechanisms of Defense, Revised Edition* (reprint). New York: International View Press.

Glynn, Patrick (1997). *God the Evidence.* Rocklin, CA.: Forum.

Golding, William (1954). *Lord of the Flies.* New York: Capricorn Books.

Gomes, Peter (1996). *The Good Book.* New York: William Morrow.

Harris, Thomas (1974). *I'm O.K., You're O.K.* New York: Macmillan.

Holifield, E. Brooks (1983). *A History of Pastoral Care in America: From Salvation to Self-Realization.* Nashville, TN: Abingdon Press.

Hostie, R. (1957). *Religion and the Psychology of Jung* (trans. G. R. Lamb). New York: Sheed & Ward; as quoted in Vitz, Paul (1994), *Psychology as Religion, Second Edition.* Grand Rapids, MI: Eerdmans.

Jung, Carl (1933). *Modern Man in Search of a Soul.* New York: Harcourt Brace.

Kennedy, John F., Jr. (December 1996). Editor's Letter. *George.*

Koch, S. (1992). The nature and limits of psychological knowledge: lessons of a century of science, in A Century of Psychology as a Science. Washington, D.C.: *American Psychological Association*, pp. 75–97 (original work, 1985).

Koocher, Gerald P. (1976). *Children's Rights and the Mental Health Professions.* New York: John Wiley & Sons.

Kubler-Ross, Elisabeth (1990). *The Power of Healing.* Englewood Cliffs, NJ: Prentice-Hall.

Langer, S. K. (1963). *Philosophy in a New Key.* Cambridge: Harvard University Press.

Leary, David E. (2001). *American Psychologist,* 56(5), May 2001.

Maslow, Abraham H. (1954). *Motivation and Personality.* New York: Harper.

Mayer, J. P., Ed. (1969). *Democracy in America.* New York: Harper.

Menninger, Karl (1973). *Whatever Became of Sin?* New York: Hawthorne Books.

Novak, Michael (1997). Business as a Calling; as quoted by Jim Pinkerton, We're All Protestants Now, *USA Today,* April 9, 1997, p. 11A.

Peale, Norman V. (1987). *The Power of Positive Thinking.* New York: Prentice-Hall.

Peck, M. Scott (1978). *The Road Less Traveled.* New York: Simon & Schuster.

Reeves, Thomas (1998). *The Empty Church: Does Organized Religion Matter Anymore?* New York: Simon & Schuster.

Reiff, Philip (1966). *The Triumph of the Therapeutic.* New York: Harper & Row.

Royce, Josiah. *The Modern Psychotherapeutic Movement in America*; as quoted in Holifield, E. Brooks (1983). *A History of Pastoral Care in America: From Salvation to Self-Realization.* Nashville, TN: Abingdon Press.

Sheler, Jeffery L. (December 15, 1997). Dark prophecies. *U.S. News & World Report,* p. 63–71.

Shostrom, Everett L. (1967). *Man the Manipulator.* Nashville, TN: Abingdon.

Smith, Huston (2001). *Why Religion Matters*. San Francisco: Harper Collins.

Sowell, Thomas (1997). *Why Won't My Son Talk?* New York: Basic Books.

Steere, David (1997). *Spiritual Presence in Psychotherapy*. New York: Brunner/Mazel.

Strauss, William and Howe, Neil (1997). *The Fourth Turning*. New York: Broadway Books.

Tillich, Paul (1951). *Systematic Theology*. Chicago: University of Chicago Press.

Tillich, Paul (1957). *Dynamics of Faith*. New York: Harper.

Tournier, Paul (1962). *The Meaning of Gifts*. New York: Harper.

Trueheart, Charles (August 1996). Welcome to the next church. *The Atlantic Monthly*, pp. 37–58.

Vitz, Paul (1994). *Psychology as Religion, Second Edition*. Grand Rapids, MI.: Eerdmans.

Waumbaugh, Joseph (1996). *Floaters*. New York: Bantam.

Weber, Max (1964). *The Protestant Ethic and the Spirit of Capitalism*; as quoted by Jim Pinkerton, We're All Protestants Now, *USA Today*, April 9, 1997, p. 11A.

Webster's Encyclopedic Unabridged Dictionary of the English Language, New Revised Edition (1996). New York: Gramercy Books.

Westberg, Granger (1961). *Minister and Doctor Meet*. New York: Harper.

Wilson, Edward O. (1998). *Consilience*. New York: Vintage.

Index

mission   ii, iii, 15, 16, 20, 24, 28, 46,
47, 51, 52, 53, 54, 55, 68, 80, 81,
83, 85, 86, 203, 217, 232, 239, 250,
251, 253, 262, 264, 275

missionary   14, 17, 24, 51, 52, 54, 55,
70, 144, 192

Missionary Orientation program   52

model prayer   102

money   6, 13, 14, 16, 17, 24, 25, 33,
40, 51, 55, 58, 59, 61, 62, 63, 65,
72, 85, 92, 93, 97, 100, 132, 134,
135, 136, 137, 159, 196, 199, 200,
230, 231, 247, 248, 250, 253, 254,
262, 266

mores   28, 34

Mormon Church   240, 250

mortuary science   105

Moslems   68

music   17, 88, 89, 90, 91, 92, 98, 241,
242

musicians   91, 92

mystery   xxv, xxvii, 104, 181, 282,
283, 285

mysticism   xviii, 35, 36, 280

N

nakedness   169, 170

National Council of Churches   52, 78

natural   xviii, 19, 169, 218

need   i, xi, xvii, xix, xxx, 5, 6, 8, 14,
17, 23, 24, 25, 26, 27, 28, 29, 32,
34, 37, 46, 49, 50, 51, 52, 53, 54,
61, 63, 65, 70, 71, 76, 80, 81, 85,
89, 90, 94, 96, 97, 98, 100, 103,
104, 105, 106, 107, 108, 115, 125,
126, 129, 131, 132, 133, 134, 135,
137, 139, 143, 146, 149, 150, 151,
157, 160, 168, 180, 181, 184, 185,
189, 190, 191, 195, 198, 199, 202,
205, 207, 208, 209, 210, 211, 212,

213, 215, 219, 220, 222, 223, 224,
230, 231, 233, 235, 237, 239, 244,
245, 247, 248, 251, 253, 256, 257,
258, 261, 262, 264, 266, 271, 273,
274, 276, 281, 283, 284, 286, 290,
291, 295, 299

neuroses   144, 174, 176, 177, 178,
179, 183, 184, 203, 245, 273, 276

neuroticism   18, 178, 180

new beginning   129

new image   xi, 117, 125, 126, 127,
128, 129, 131, 132, 135, 136, 137,
138, 139

New Testament   4, 14, 51, 56, 60, 81,
106, 142, 182, 210, 228, 229, 241,
250, 254, 261, 263, 266, 267, 272,
275, 277

nonattendees   57

norms   i, xv, 34, 73, 118, 122, 123,
125, 126, 128, 153

not-for-profit   12, 62, 94, 96, 251

O

O.K. psychology   32

Oates   xxvi, 193

Old Testament   56, 131, 149, 165,
171, 173, 228, 229, 263, 267, 272,
281

original scriptures   279

original sin   163, 165

out-of-body experiences   221

P

pagans   87, 89

pain   27, 46, 105, 123, 131, 164, 169,
170, 171, 186, 207, 208, 209, 223,
262, 263, 270

pantheism   280